DESEGREGATING CARY

North Carolina

DESEGREGATING CARY

North Carolina

By

Peggy Van Scoyoc

A Passing Time Press book

Desegregating Cary
North Carolina

Published by Passing Time Press
Cary, North Carolina
pegvans@aol.com
http://caryhistory.webs.com

First published in 2009

Printed in the United States of America

CONTENTS

1. INTRODUCTIONS.. 3
   Introducing The Town 3
   Introducing The African-American Community........................... 4
   Introducing The White Community.. 12

PART I
LIVING UNDER SEGREGATION

2. CARY BEFORE DESEGREGATION 27
   Cary And The Civil War.. 27
   The Twentieth Century 31
   A Brief History Of Education And Civil Rights
   In North Carolina 34
   Black Colleges And Universities 39
   White Public Primary Grade Schools....................................... 40
   Black Public Primary Grade Schools.. 42

3. AFRICAN-AMERICAN LIFE ON THE FARM BEFORE
   DESEGREGATION 47
   Getting Off The Farm.. 57

4. OTHER AFRICAN-AMERICAN OCCUPATIONS IN CARY
   BEFORE DESEGREGATION 65

5. THE SEGREGRATED COMMUNITY 77
   The African-American Experience.. 78
   The White Experience.. 91

6. SEGREGATED AFRICAN-AMERICAN SCHOOLS 99
   Berry O'Kelly High School.. 100
   Cary Schools.. 102

PART II
DESEGREGRATING THE COMMUNITY

7. DESEGREGRATING THE COMMUNITY BEGINS.............115

8. THE PLAN TO DESEGREGRATE THE SCHOOLS 121
    Interim Solutions – One-Grade Schools 134

9. CARY HIGH SCHOOL THE FIRST DAYS AS A
    DESEGREGATED SCHOOL...139
    How Black Students Were Treated At School...........................140
    Getting Through It..144
    Extra-Curricular Activities...145
    Sports..146
    Why They Endured It...149

10. THE TEACHERS AT CARY HIGH SCHOOL...........................151

11. DESEGREGRATING OTHER SCHOOLS.................................163

12. THE SECOND YEAR AND BEYOND 171
    After High School – What They Did Next....................................173

13. LESSONS LEARNED 179
    Trailblazers..187

14. BEYOND THE SIXTIES..195
    Busing..195
    Far From Over 200
    Cary – Then And Now..202

ACKNOWLEDGEMENTS..213

CHAPTER 1

THOSE WHO DESEGREGATED CARY HIGH SCHOOL:

Lucille Evans

Brenda Hill

Gwen Matthews

Esther Mayo

Phyliss McIver

Frances White

Henry Adams

Paul Cooper Sr.

INTRODUCTIONS

This book is a compilation of oral history interviews that were conducted with people who lived in or near Cary, North Carolina in the mid-twentieth century. Forty-three people have told their stories to members of the Friends of the Page-Walker History Center as part of Cary's oral history project. This book does not contain exact transcriptions of those interviews. The transcripts have been lightly edited for clarity and readability.

Recording oral history is an endeavor to preserve life experiences of average citizens, told in their own words as they recall them, sometimes decades after the events occurred. Over time memories can fade, and facts and time sequences can become confused, so the stated events may not be strictly accurate. However, the overall narrative can have tremendous value and meaning to the community. The narrators tell us not only what happened, but also how they personally experienced those events. Many of the people interviewed took great personal risks to talk about their experiences and to express their emotional responses to those events. Their memories reveal attitudes and ways of thinking from the perspective of an earlier local culture, which are the foundations on which today's culture was built. Much about the ways of life described in these stories no longer exists. But learning about an earlier culture, and about what people thought and felt at that time can help us understand why we think and feel the way we do today.

The following stories reveal vivid images from American history. These tales are deplorable and haunting, and they are also heartening, courageous and enlightening.

INTRODUCING THE TOWN:

In 1854, the North Carolina Railroad (NCRR) laid tracks from Raleigh to Hillsborough that ran through what is now downtown Cary. The village of Cary was founded by Francis (Frank) Page who arrived about the same time as the rails. Frank was a lumberman who moved to this area because there were lots of trees. After building a home where Cary Town Hall now stands, he built a sawmill and used the closest train station in Morrisville to ship out his lumber. He built a store and a post office near his home and served as the first postmaster. In 1868, the Chatham Railroad laid tracks through Cary and built a depot near the Page home. So Frank built a railroad hotel facing the tracks, which he later sold to Mr. Walker. Today the restored Page-Walker Hotel is Cary's cultural arts and history center.

In 1870, Frank also donated land and lumber to build a private boarding school at the head of Academy Street in downtown Cary. Originally named Cary Academy, the school had a good reputation throughout the state and attracted students from all over the South. Thus, the school and education became the heart of Cary.

By 1880, there were 316 people living in Cary. Town limits encompassed just one square mile. The main intersection was at Academy and Chatham Streets, and Cary was primarily a rural crossroads for an agricultural community. The surrounding area was primarily made up of small tobacco and cotton farms.

By 1960, Cary's population had grown to 3,356 which was only 2% of Wake County's population. Agriculture was still the primary source of income. The town limits had been expanded to encompass six square miles, but the school was still in the heart of the town. By 1970, Cary had grown to 7,339 people. In 2008, Cary's population had swelled to an astounding 135,000, and is now 15% of Wake County's population. The significant portion of the population growth began when Cary became the bedroom community for Research Triangle Park, which was established nearby in the early 1970s. When IBM built one of its largest plants in the world in the Park, many other companies soon joined them, creating thousands of jobs in the area. From 1960, Cary's population has doubled every decade, and continues to be one of the fastest growing towns in America. By 2008, Cary had a total of 55 square miles within its town limits.

INTRODUCING THE AFRICAN-AMERICAN COMMUNITY:

George Bailey: I was interviewed on March 19, and again on March 25, 2009. I went to school in Cary at Kingswood Elementary School until I was twelve years old. My mother had a problem with the principal of the segregated school that we were going to, and she chose to pull all of us out of that system. We had two homes in Cary, but education was so important to her that we moved from Cary to Raleigh and bought another house. So I never was raised per se in Cary because we moved away.

When I was about twelve, my father put me to work as a plumber. That's how I got into the business. By the time I was fifteen, I had four people working for me, and some of these guys were forty years old. I was in charge of putting in all the fixtures and so forth for apartment complexes.

I went to Ligon High School in Raleigh. When I finished college at Agricultural and Technology (A&T) State University in Greensboro, I went off to the Peace Corps. When I came home from the Peace Corps, I started a company and was back in business. My brother Herbert was my partner in developing Evans Estates.

I'd been the black sheep of my family. I have done things that no one would think I would enjoy, or that were not the stereotype of what black folk were doing. I don't know of any black mountain-climbers, for example. I have climbed many mountains. I am a world traveler. I have been to thirty-five countries and lived in four countries in Africa. I went through two coup d'états and one invasion in Africa.

Education is very important to my wife and me. I have three daughters. One graduated from UNC-G in biology, one graduated from Carolina in industrial relations, and one graduated from State in bio-medical engineering.

Herbert Bailey: I was interviewed on March 31, 2009. My family has always lived on the original farm located on Evans Road. I was born on August 20, 1945, and I have been in Cary on the family's original farm land most of my life. I attended Kingswood Elementary School, and then I attended Berry O'Kelly High School in Raleigh.

Upon graduating from A&T State University in Greensboro, North Carolina, I began my short-lived teaching career up north. Teaching was not the career path for me so I came back home. Soon afterwards and desperately in need of work, I did a utility job for my dad in downtown Raleigh. At the end of that job, my father said, "Would you like to be in business?"

I said, "Yes," and I've been doing business in Cary ever since. Because of this start, my chosen life's work has evolved into utility/pipeline contracting, following in the family footsteps, and I have been in business for almost forty years.

I have been married to my wife, Anita for 37 years. Our three children attended Northwoods Elementary School, West Cary Middle School on Evans Road, and to Cary High. My children's experiences in school have been quite different from mine.

After high school, my oldest daughter, Kim, started college at NC State University, and then transferred and completed her degree at North Carolina Central University in Durham, majoring in teaching. My second child, son Joe, went to NC State University and finished his degree in zoology. He then came to work for me. After about six months, he decided he wanted to go back to school to get a degree in business. We still work together, and he's doing an excellent job. My baby girl, Brittany, also went to NC State, but did not finish. Instead, she joined the army, and she's been gone ever since. I think she's due to get out this year.

Clyde Evans Jr.: I was interviewed on March 28, 2000. George and Herbert Bailey are my nephews and Linda Evans is my daughter. I was born in 1918, and went to school at the Cary Colored School, which was a two-room school. Then I went to Berry O'Kelly High School. I worked with my grandfather, Charlie Evans, from the time I was ten or twelve years old.

During World War II, I spent six years in Portsmouth at the shipyard. I was in civil service, and worked in a mechanical establishment with the navy, repairing big guns and ships. We saw that all the ships had what they needed. I went to Fort Bragg and was examined at the end of the war. I was A1, ready to go, but they dropped the A-bomb before I was sent to the Pacific.

My father, Clyde Evans Sr., gave me a piece of land when I got married, and I built this house by myself. He gave all his children a lot of two acres of land down Evans Road. I have eight children.

Linda Evans: I was interviewed on May 22, 2003, and I am the daughter of Clyde Evans Jr. I was born in Cary, actually born in the other side of this house on Evans Road. I went to East Cary Elementary, now called Kingswood. When I was eleven years old, we moved to Raleigh to be near my grandparents because my parents were getting a divorce. My two older sisters graduated from Berry O'Kelly. I was in the seventh grade when I went to a mixed school for the first time, to Hugh Morrison Middle School in Raleigh. I graduated from St. Augustine College in 2002. I have two grown boys, and I am a single parent.

Jeanette Evans: I was interviewed on April 9, 2009. My mother, Lucy Turner, was born in Cary, and my father, Connie Reaves, was born in Moore County near Sanford, North Carolina. My father moved to Cary as a young man, where he met my mother and they got married. He was working on the railroad, doing whatever was needed to put in the railroad tracks. They had ten children in all.

I married Herbert Evans. He was born in Apex. When he was about a year old, they moved to Cary. His father was Loveless Evans, and his mother was Maude. My husband is a plumber. He has Alzheimer's now and is in a nursing home. I have two children living. I had a son who died in a car wreck in 1977. I have two grandchildren and three great-grandchildren.

I managed the Dorcas Thrift Shop in Cary for fifteen years. I was there from day one, and I help out at the Carying Place, an organization that assists people at risk of becoming homeless. I love to help folks. I get it from my mother who was a church missionary. When I was small, everywhere she'd go I was right behind her on her coattail, doing what I could to help someone. She helped all around the neighborhood. If anything was going on in the neighborhood or church, a visitor was there to help. We don't have them now like we used to.

Phyllis Cain: I was interviewed on August 26, 2009. I was born in this house, on the border between Cary and Raleigh, off of Chapel Hill Road. My mom was born in Apex, and my father was born in this area, and worked for the Seaboard Railroad. My mom originally was a housekeeper in people's homes, and later she worked at Lufkin Rule Company in Apex. After she retired, she worked at a center with elderly people. My father's name was Clancy D. Cain, and my mother's name is Gussie Horton Cain. I have one sister and I'm seven years older than she is. She went to Cary High School.

My freshman and sophomore year, I attended Berry O'Kelly High School. But it closed in 1965 and they built West Cary High School. It was a segregated high school for two years. I graduated from West Cary in 1967, in their last segregated high school graduating class.

Lucille Evans Cotton: I was interviewed on March 13, 2000. I am the fourth of five children born to James and Gertrude Evans, and I'm the baby girl. I was one of the first six African- American girls to attend Cary High School in 1963, along with Gwen Matthews.

SJ (Samuel James) and Leonia Farrar - SJ: We were interviewed on May 28, 2003. Our daughter is Carolyn Rogers. We came from the Chatham and Wake County area, right off a tobacco farm. We grew tobacco, sweet potatoes, corn – all of that hard stuff, right out of the ground. My father was a sharecropper and our parents never had much education. My father was a local preacher too, but was not allowed to do anything but sing and hold prayer services. He couldn't even write his name. That's our background, very, very poor. My parents had eight children. My father died when I was nine years old and my mother continued to work on the farm with all of us. We were just field hands. I went to a one-room school in Farrington, Bell's School, on the Wake and Chatham County line.

In 1957, I left the farm and started work in Raleigh at Southern Building Supply as a truck driver. I bought some land from the Evans family on Evans Road, built a house and moved the family to Cary. I went from truck driver to a cabinet installer/helper at Southern Building Supply. In 1972, I went into business for myself as a cabinetmaker. I also started in the ministry in 1957, the same year we moved to Cary. Eventually, I was appointed superintendent of 23 churches in my district.

(**Leonia**): My family didn't have quite as hard a time growing up. Daddy had nineteen children, and I'm the seventh child. Daddy was a sharecropper too. I went to the Apex School. We married and I'm the mother of eight. After my last child started school, I went to beauty school and was a beautician for many years. Most of our children are educated.

Carolyn Farrar Rogers: I was interviewed on May 22, 2003. My parents are SJ and Leonia Farrar. My dad's folks came from the Chatham County, Pittsboro area. We lived in Green Level, which is west of Highway 55. As sharecroppers, we worked the "man's" land. We would get up early in the morning before daybreak and go out to the fields. Then when it was time to harvest the tobacco to take it to the market to sell, Daddy gave half of his profits to the owner of the land.

My dad decided he would get us off the farm, so he gave up sharecropping and moved us to Cary. Daddy started working at Southern Builders driving trucks, and he also worked as a chef at a place in Cary called Proeschers Restaurant, which was right across the street from the then Taylor Biscuit Company. While working at Southern Builders, Daddy learned how to build cabinets. Later he became a cabinetmaker and opened his own shop, Farrar's Cabinet Works. The first shop was in the backyard of our house. After closing the first shop, Farrar's Cabinet Works relocated to Chatham Street in Cary. Daddy taught my brothers to build cabinets, bookcases and bathroom vanities. Now all three brothers are cabinetmakers and eventually Daddy turned the business over to them. So we've come a long way, coming from nothing going to something, because of my daddy's drive and motivation. If there was something that he wanted to do, by golly, he was going to do it. I inherited that drive.

We came to Cary in 1959, when I had just finished my sixth grade year at Apex Consolidated High School, as it was called at the time. When we moved to Cary, I started school in the seventh grade at what was called East Cary Elementary. Now it is called Kingswood. From East Cary Elementary, I went to Berry O'Kelly High School, still living on Evans Road. Then I went away to Barber-Scotia College in Concord, North Carolina, where I majored in English and minored in French.

After working in South Carolina for awhile, in the fall of 1969 I came home and got a job at, by then desegregated Cary Elementary School. I was one of the first black teachers at Cary Elementary, and when I started, I was one of three black teachers on staff. Prior to that, I lived in an all-black neighborhood, attended an all-black elementary school, went to an all-black high school, went to an all-black college, and taught at an all-black elementary school.

Leroy and Betty Farrar – Leroy: We were interviewed on July 22, 2003. SJ Farrar is my brother, and Carolyn Farrar Rogers is my niece. I was born in 1926. My parents were sharecroppers in Green Level. My father died when I was fourteen.

Betty and I got married in 1948. We returned to the farm as sharecroppers for maybe five years, then we left the farm and moved to Cary. We bought land on Evans Road and built a house and we have been here ever since. We have six children.

When we left the farm and moved to Cary, I went to work with Reynolds Aluminum Supply Company in Raleigh. I drove a tractor and trailers for them for 23 years. I retired from Reynolds, but I still work there part-time.

I also sing gospel, all over the country. I do solos and then sing with two groups in my church. We have a lot of ministers in our family and all of us sing.

(Betty): I was born in Chatham County. We were sharecroppers in Olive Chapel and later we moved to 64 Highway. I had been there about a year or two, when we got married there.

Sallie Jones: I was interviewed on April 23, 2009. I was born right here, near the corner of North Academy Street. My mother was born in Cary also, and my father was born in Morrisville. My father's father came to Cary sometime around the 1870s from somewhere in Warren County.

Before that, relatives possibly came from somewhere in Virginia. My father was a jack-of-all-trades, a laborer. He had a full-time job when they were building Camp Butner. Prior to that, he worked as a manservant. The husband was an alcoholic, so they paid my father to sit with him at night to make sure he didn't get up or go out. My father also did carpentry work and he had a brick-making machine. He made the bricks for the chimneys of our old house. He would make them and set them out to dry. I remember him having my brothers help him mix the mixture and then put it into the machine. My parents had nine children. I was number six in line.

I began elementary school at the Cary Colored School. The school burned down the year that I would have been in the sixth grade. I was then taught at home for one year until I could go into the eighth grade at Berry O'Kelly High School. I graduated from there in 1940. I attended St. Augustine's College in Raleigh, and graduated in 1946.

I taught in Parmele, North Carolina for five years, and then taught at Goldsboro High School for seven years. After that, I went to teach French at Horris Mann High School in Gary, Indiana. I was one of the first black teachers that they hired to desegregate the faculty there.

When I retired I came back home to Cary. For the first ten years I was back, I worked with the AARP in different capacities, such as community coordinator, and working with the housing programs. I would be in San Diego one week and Memphis another, so it was quite a busy time, and I enjoyed it very much.

Then I set out to make sure the Cary Colored Cemetery was preserved. We had it surveyed and got it protected, and I registered it with the state.

Gwen Matthews: I was interviewed on December 9, 1999. I grew up the oldest of five children. I attended segregated East Cary Elementary, later called Kingswood, until the eighth grade. I then attended Berry O'Kelly High School which was also segregated for grades nine and ten. In 1963, I was chosen as one of six black students to be the first to desegregate Cary High School. I graduated from Cary High in 1965.

I went to St. Augustine's College in Raleigh for one year, and then left college and worked for six years as a keypunch operator. I realized I needed more education, so I went to Meredith College in Raleigh and majored in English. I was one of the first African-Americans to attend Meredith, and I was their first black graduate. So I was instrumental in desegregating two schools. I taught in high school for three years, and then decided to get my master's degree, so I went to Teachers College at Columbia University.

I taught at NC State University and in Virginia. Then I returned home to Raleigh and began teaching English at Wake Technical Community College. I stayed for twenty-eight years, retiring in June of 2009. I started out in the English department, then joined the academic enrichment department teaching developmental students. I was that department's head for fifteen and a half years. Then I joined the academic advising center where I worked until my retirement.

Deborah Matthews Wright: I was interviewed on January 3, 2000. I am eight years younger than my sister, Gwen Matthews. We grew up in Wake County, just outside the city limits, between Raleigh and Cary. I started school in a segregated school in Cary. In 1965, at the age of ten, I went into the fifth grade at Swift Creek Elementary School. I was one of three African-Americans to desegregate Swift Creek School for the very first time.

I went to Cary Elementary for the eighth grade. In 1969, I went to West Cary Middle School for the ninth grade. Then for grades ten through twelve I went to Cary High School. I also went to Meredith College, majoring in psychology with a minor in sociology. I finished my psychology degree and went to work as a college counselor at St. Augustine College in Raleigh for three or four years. At the same time, I pursued a master's degree in counseling from NC State University and finished in 1983. Then I started a career in human resources at NC State. Now I'm assistant director of human resources there.

I am a licensed minister, and a certified mediator. I have my own ministry for women, and I'm also married to a minister. I have one daughter.

Carolyn Sampson: I was interviewed on February 16, 2009. I was born in Raleigh. My African-American parents always encouraged education. They told us, "Get your education because I want you to do better than me." I have two sisters and one brother. I guess we all tried to make something out of ourselves.

My primary education was in all-black schools in Raleigh. I went to Hunter Elementary School, and then to Ligon High School. I never rode a bus, I walked to school. When I graduated from Ligon High School, for about two and a half years I went to St. Augustine's College. Then I worked awhile, got married and had a child.

My sister and her husband were working in training schools in the division for youth facilities in New York, and asked me to come join them, so I moved to New York during the summer program. From the summer program, I got hired at Tryon School for Boys, which is a school for "persons in need of supervision," (which means juvenile delinquency.) I started with direct service to children and adolescents, then I was the community involvement program coordinator, covering a twenty-county area. I completed my degree at State University of New York (SUNY.) Then they moved me from direct service to the central office in the community involvement program. I worked there for thirteen years.

I returned to Cary, and after awhile I took a job with the state of North Carolina as a contracts consultant for the daycare department in the division of facilities services, trying to exist as a black person in a white administration. Later, I was able to move into a position as one of two mental health consultants. We had a hundred counties to deal with. Our jobs entailed the licensing of mental health, substance abuse, and the developmentally disabled, for all substance abuse facilities in the state of North Carolina. All those programs that exist in the state of North Carolina have to be licensed by the group care facility bridge. There were two of us to do that job. It was an impossible job, but there had to be a way, so I worked out a plan in such a way that it could be done.

By that time I have three children and was still a single parent, doing what I could do. After that job, for a period I was doing research for a lawyer. In my previous job, I had created many of the records that I needed to look up for the lawyer, so knowing the system really helped me do the research. It worked out well for families who had causes, and for the lawyer who needed the details to wrap up his case. I eventually retired and now live in Cary.

Mary Shelton: My parents were born in North Carolina. My father was from Colfax and my mother was from Williamston. My mama is black and my father is white. They were both deaf and mute. They met at the only school for the deaf in Raleigh which was not segregated.

INTRODUCING THE WHITE COMMUNITY:

Charlie Adams: I was interviewed on February 18, 2000. My dad, Henry Adams, was born and raised in Cary. He spent his entire life there, except for when he went off to school. His family was originally from

Cary. If you trace them back far enough, they came from Jamestown, Virginia.

When my dad left Cary, he went to Trinity Park, which is now Duke University. He had a sister who had a drugstore in Durham and she heavily influenced him to go to pharmacy school in Massachusetts. When he came back he opened a drugstore in Cary. He ran Adams' Rexall Drugs until he tired of that and found out that I was not going to be a pharmacist after college. So he sold the store to Ralph Ashworth and he opened an appliance store. He had that store until he died. It is now Wolfe's Appliance on Chatham Street. So he spent his entire lifetime in business.

But his love was really education and athletics. Nobody ever loved Cary more than he did. He served many, many years on the local advisory board for Cary and quite a few terms on the Wake County school board. He was getting ready to run again when he died.

My mom, Ethel Adams, was born in Durham. They moved to Cary when she was about eleven years old. My mom was a long-time teacher. Her entire career was spent in Wake County. I think she started out at Millbrook High School, then moved to the old Green Hope High School (before it burned down), and then ended her career working for Carl Mills for many years at Cary Elementary School.

I was born in Cary and lived there my entire life. I went through grades one through twelve at Cary Elementary and High School. So our roots and our heritage are deep in Cary. We lived our entire life on Academy Street. We were two houses from the school where my mom taught all those years. In the middle of the block was the Baptist Church where my mom and I attended, and on the end of the block was the Methodist Church where my dad attended, and then the drugstore was across the street. So I tell everybody I had a very sheltered life, I never got off Academy Street.

When I got out of college, I was drafted and went into the service, and when I got out of the service I started a teaching and coaching career in Laurel, Delaware. My former principal, Paul Cooper, came down to East Carolina when I was finishing my master's degree and offered me a teaching position and head basketball coach at Cary High School. So I came back to Cary and coached and taught there for four years, and then went into administration in Garner as dean and assistant principal. I then was hired by the North Carolina High School Athletic Association in 1967, and I served seventeen years as an assistant. I've been the director of the Association since 1984.

In college, I majored in social studies and physical education. I taught sociology, economics and problems of democracy in Cary, and coached basketball, assistant football, umpired the baseball games and started the track meets. We did it all back in those days.

I am an only child, but I felt like I had all of Cary as my brothers and sisters. It was such a close community back in those days. Everybody who was born there stayed there so you knew everybody and went to school with them. There were guys and gals that I went to school with for all twelve years, so I had a really great family.

The Ashworths - Ralph: We were interviewed on August 5, 2003. Daphne and I are both from Wake County. Daphne was reared in Willow Springs and I met her when she came to Fuquay High School. Then I went to UNC-Chapel Hill, entering pharmacy school. (**Daphne**): I went to UNC-Greensboro for two years, then transferred to UNC-Chapel Hill, majoring in medical technology. (**Ralph**): We both graduated in 1955, and then in July of that year we married.

I was working in Johnson's Drugstore in Fuquay when we heard that a drugstore was for sale in Cary. We bought Adams Drugstore from Henry Adams in 1957, and renamed it Ashworth Drugstore. The drugstore was the center of town at the main intersection of Academy and Chatham Streets. Right across the street there was the town hall, the fire department and the bank. Everything was centered pretty closely to this intersection. The Greyhound and Trailways buses both stopped at the drugstore. We sold tickets for the buses and we also took in freight and put freight on the bus. We were the Western Union, and we took payments for the telephone bills and the light bills. So it was really the center of activity.

When we first started, Cary High School was still up the street. They moved three years later. In the afternoons, we would have all the high school kids filling up our drugstore and Mitchell's Drugstore down the street. This was before fast foods and everybody came in for snacks and so forth.

We started in the Hallmark card shop business in 1969. Now we have sixteen shops, one in Virginia and fifteen in North Carolina. When we started out, Cary couldn't support one card shop. Now we have five card shops in Cary.

(**Daphne**): Our son Paul is a pharmacist too, so he now runs the drugstore, and Ralph works for him. And our older son, Gary, is a CPA and he's in the card shop business with us. (**Ralph**): He's our comptroller.

Daphne and I got involved in many civic organizations. I joined the Jaycees, the Rotary, Cary's sister cities, and many others. A lot of us helped sponsor a youth program. Both of us got involved with Cary Visual Arts. Daphne joined the Jaycettes, the Cary Jr. Woman's Club, The Cary Garden Club, and others.

Tom Byrd: I was interviewed on January 25, 2005. I was born on July 28, 1932 in Duplin County, in the eastern part of North Carolina. My parents were farmers.

Four years after high school, I made my girlfriend, Janet Elaine Swenson, my wife and we started our family of three children. I have a son and two daughters.

My first off-farm job was in Wilmington, North Carolina with the railroad company, Atlantic Coastline Railroad, which is now part of the CSX system. After working there for almost two years, I joined the air force. After I got out of the air force I got a degree in journalism from University of North Carolina-Chapel Hill. I started working for the News and Observer newspaper and continued there for a short time. Then I was hired by NC State University in the department of agricultural communications. I prepared news releases on developments in the college of agricultural and life sciences. I worked on numerous publications, from newsletters to magazines, periodical publications, and "how to" publications. That's where I spent the remainder of my career. I retired in 1988.

Jerry Miller, the artist who lives next door to me, was an architect. He made his living designing homes, but he was also interested in drawing old buildings. He would not only make sketches of buildings that were in the town at the time, but he would make sketches from photographs of buildings that existed in the past. In the late sixties, he came to me and said, "Tom, I'd like to publish my drawings in a book, but I need someone to write a little something about these places to go under each drawing." We produced the first edition of *Around and About Cary,* the first comprehensive history that had been written of the town, in December of 1970. The second edition, which is updated and much more thorough, was published in January of 1995.

Paul Cooper Jr.: I was interviewed on March 19, 2009. I was born in Warrenton, North Carolina in 1936. My dad, Paul Cooper Sr., was the principal of the high school there. We moved to Cary in 1947 when I was in the sixth grade. I graduated from Cary High School in 1955, from the brick building on Academy Street. From there I went one year to

Hargrave Military Academy in Chatham, Virginia, and then went to the Naval Academy. So I was basically gone from Cary after 1955. I was either at the Naval Academy or in the navy. My first duty was in California. Then I served three tours flying from aircraft carriers into Vietnam from '65 through '73, the end of the war.

I came back to the east coast in '73. We went to Newport, Rhode Island, and from there we moved down to Virginia Beach and were on the east coast the rest of my naval career. I'm still here in Virginia Beach.

Daddy was the principal at Cary High School from 1948 through 1967. He was the principal throughout the time of desegregating the school, and then he retired in 1967.

Mary Crowder: I was interviewed on April 1, 1999. December 14, 1930 was my birthday. I lived behind the Page-Walker Hotel and also the Frank Page house on Wilkinson Avenue, the street that was named for my family. My mom came from Penny Road, the Swift Creek area. My granddaddy was Theopolis Lane Jones. The Lane in his name comes from Joel Lane who was one of the founders of Raleigh and who gave the land to build the state capital.

My mother attended the Cary elementary school, known originally as Cary Academy at that time. Her father brought the girls up either on Sunday afternoon or Monday morning by horse and buggy, and he picked them up on Friday. They stayed with Mr. and Mrs. Wiley Jones, Mr. and Mrs. Marvin Jones, and Mrs. Scott, whose house is where Ashworth's shopping center is now on Chatham Street.

My dad was born and raised in the Frank Page house which burned down in 1970. It stood on the site of today's town hall. Daddy was a mechanic, and owned the filling station that is on the corner of Academy and Chatham Streets. Mother and Daddy built the house on Wilkinson Avenue in 1929. I'm their only child.

I went to Peace College in Raleigh, and then I worked in lingerie in the basement of Belk's.

Bertha Pleasants Daniel: I was interviewed on July 19, 2000. I was born in 1915, right here, off of Cornwall Road. We had a farm that went from Cornwall Road back to the other side of Kildare Farm Road. It was about a hundred-acre farm. My father was married twice, he married sisters. He and his first wife had several children, but only eight that lived. When she died, he married my mother who had seven children. My father died in 1929, and my mother held onto the farm by the skin of her teeth during the Depression years. She had to hire everything done, because the boys were other places doing other things. We managed. She lived to be 95 years old.

We walked to school. We went to Cary Elementary and High School. After I married, my husband worked with the State Department of Transportation. I have two children, a boy and a girl. I worked with the Department of Transportation too.

Rachel Dunham: I was interviewed on November 18, 1998. I was born on April 4, 1904 in Pino, North Carolina. My sister and I came to Cary in 1918 to attend Cary High School because we wanted to take home economics, and it was one of the only schools that taught it. She and I lived in the Page-Walker Hotel while going to school. I graduated in 1924, and then I taught at Goldsboro for two years in the primary grades. Then, after graduating from Western Carolina, I came to Cary to teach in 1927. I taught the second grade mostly for seven years. My husband, Rufus "Dad" Dunham taught the boys agriculture at Cary High School for forty years.

Ruth Fox: I was interviewed on June 10, 1999. I moved to Cary from the Charlotte area in 1919 when I was only seven years old. My father was connected with the Seaboard Railroad. I married Charles Fox who had three children from a previous marriage. He taught poultry science. I went to Lewisburg College, the oldest junior college in the nation, established in 1787. Then I transferred to Columbia College, Columbia, South Carolina. I took my graduate work at Appalachia State University in Boone for three summers.

Cary High and Farm Life School was the first public high school in North Carolina, dating back to 1907, according to the cornerstone on the building. I taught the second grade at Cary Elementary and High School for thirty-four years. I began teaching in 1933. Then I became the first principal of Briarcliff Elementary School, from 1967 to 1973.

Robert Heater: I was interviewed on July 16, and again on August 6, 1999. I was born February 27th, 1929 on Dry Avenue. Daddy, R.O. Heater, had Heater Well Company and we had our shop in the backyard of our house. I started to help him when I was about twelve. During World War II, when I was twelve years old, I was trained for the Cary volunteer fire department. While in high school, I joined the navy reserve in 1947, my senior year. Then when the Korean War started, I was called up, and I served for twenty-two months. I did not get sent overseas. They found out I knew railroading, so they put me in the ship's company teaching railroading.

Daddy was also a developer. He developed the first sub-division in Cary, called Russell Hills. After I got out of the service, I did some developing too, and learned you can make money from moving houses. We bought two houses out of the Montgomery Ward catalog and assembled them.

I served four terms as county commissioner from 1974 to 1990. During that time they were merging the two school systems, city and county.

Esther Ivey: I was interviewed on February 22, 1985. I was born in 1890 in Wake Forest, North Carolina, and we moved to Cary when I was a small infant. We lived on Chatham Street in the house that has so many gables. I began school at a private school on the north side of Chatham Street in the dwelling of Miss Katie and Miss Sally Peale. The schoolroom was in their bedroom. Then I went to Cary Elementary and High School, and graduated in 1906. I attended Guilford College which was a Quaker school near Greensboro, for four years majoring in biology. Then I taught school at Roanoke Rapids for two years. I also taught in Holly Springs, which was one of four high schools in the Wake County system. I taught there nine years. Then I worked at the Baptist State Convention as a bookkeeper for the remainder of my career.

The Johnsons - Raymond: We were interviewed on September 30, 2001. I was born in what is now Cary in 1928. My father was a farmer. He died when I was eight years old. My mother, Pattie May, hired sharecroppers to keep the farm going while she raised us. I had four sisters, I was the only boy. Also to make money, she took in boarders. Even though she was a widow, my mother took in neighbor girls from two families when their mothers died and raised them. I had more sisters than I could shake a stick at.

We never went lacking for anything because we raised our food. And we were fortunate because just before my father died, they built this house. During the Depression, my father didn't lose anything because he had all his money tied up in the house.

Going backwards, my great-grandfather owned all the land around the intersection of High House Road and Highway 55, a tract of about 350 acres, and he had more land in Chatham County. He was a big landowner. Then my grandfather, W.C. Johnson, owned land in Cary. My father liked farming so he bought this farm just up Highway 55 from his father's land. Then he got married in 1915.

Highway 55 was built in about 1946 and it cut our farm right in half. I graduated from the old Green Hope High School in 1945. I don't remember what year that high school burned down. There were not enough people in the area to really support the school, so shortly after I graduated, they carried all the high school students to Apex. That's the reason the new high school is called Green Hope, it was named after the old school.

When I was twenty-one, I bought my two sisters out of my father's farm and I took over the whole thing and farmed it myself. I grew tobacco and grain like corn, wheat, and oats. Because they kept cutting the tobacco allotment, I could no longer maintain the standard of living that I wanted to maintain, so in 1976 I started raising eggs. We bought day-old biddies from a commercial hatchery when they were just hatched, 40,000 at a time. We raised them until they reached the laying stage at about sixteen to eighteen weeks. We were lucky to secure a good market for our eggs. In the course of trying to be productive cost-wise, I started making my own feed for my chickens. Eventually, we phased out the chickens and just sold feed. From then on our primary livelihood was selling feed. I eventually phased out making feed and retired.

(**Emma Lou**): I came to Cary in the middle forties from Morrisville to go to school. I came here to this farm as a seventeen-year-old bride when I was still a junior in high school, and I finished school after I came here. I graduated from Cary High School in 1953, then went to King's Business College. I got a job with the state and later went to Duke University and worked in admissions as a secretary. I joined an organization called Eastern Star, a fraternal organization, and eventually I became their Grand Matron in 1976. I worked for Eastern Star for seventeen years. In 1993, my son hired me for his automobile business. I have worked there for seven years.

C.Y. Jordan: I was interviewed on December 8, 2000. I was born on East Chatham Street, and went all the way through and graduated from Cary High School. I joined the navy when I was seventeen, and got out when I was eighteen, then went to NC State University and majored in civil engineering. I graduated from State in 1950.

I worked with the Seaboard Airline Railroad until 1955, with a short interval in the army. I had just under a year of navy service in World War II, then in the inactive naval reserve. They felt I had not given enough service. Some said I hadn't fulfilled my obligation, so they called me into the army in 1953. The Korean War ended pretty shortly thereafter.

When I came out, I went back to my job with the railroad which was in Savannah, Georgia. Then my brother and I went into the building business together which involved developing. We developed Meadowmont off of Kildare Farm Road, and then Tanglewood. I'm a civil engineer so my primary purpose was to physically develop the land. We did some of the properties on Chatham Street in the early sixties. That is when I left the railroad to come back here to work with my brother. Things slowed down and I became dissatisfied with it in 1967, so I went back to work with the railroad as an assistant division engineer. I worked there another ten years. I have a son and a daughter.

Sonny Keisler: I was interviewed on August 25, 2000. I was born in 1944. I graduated from Cary High School in 1962 and went to Wake Forest University, then the University of Kentucky. I came back for four years, then went to the University of Georgia and got my doctorate. So basically from the early sixties on, I was gone more than I was in this area.

My mother and dad, Polly and Clyde Keisler, moved here in the early forties. Dad became the manager of Kildare Farm back when it was a dairy farm. He and mother also made a lot of land investments all around North Carolina and Virginia while he was managing the farm. They would buy and sell timberland. He did a little bit of development in the seventies and eighties, some residential and commercial.

Dad was involved with the Lion's club for quite a few years, with the group that got the first swimming pool in Cary in the Walnut Street area. And he helped get Hemlock Bluffs established south of Cary.

Cary was a small town of about 1,500 to 2,000 people for most of the time I was growing up here. It was a fairly progressive group. People were trying to encourage growth and to have as many amenities here in town as they could, so Dad was part of the group that was providing Cary with educational amenities. Dad was one of the team to put the plan together to desegregate Cary's schools. He worked with Henry Adams to get that accomplished.

Guy Mendenhall: I was interviewed on March 9, 2009. I was born in Raleigh in 1936. In 1941, my parents bought 16 acres beside Ephesus Baptist Church in Cary, so we lived out in the "boonies." My parents sent me to Raleigh city schools until I was about to start in the tenth grade, and we decided we wanted to come to the Cary schools. So I went three years to Cary High School starting in the tenth grade. My class of 1954 graduated from the stage at the old Cary High School on Academy Street.

Then I went four years to East Carolina University and played basketball there. Charlie Adams was on that team. After graduation, I coached basketball at Enloe High School in Raleigh for twelve years. Then I came to Cary High School as athletic director in 1977. I also taught four history classes. At that time, Cary was the second largest high school in North Carolina. It had only grades 10 through 12, no ninth graders. I was athletic director for sixteen years, and then I gave that up and went back to teaching in the classroom. I taught drivers' ed. for three years and during the summer also. I retired in 1993.

Carl Mills: I was interviewed on June 30, 1999, and again on July 13, 1999. I grew up about twenty miles north of Charlotte. I finished Concord High in 1943 and immediately started classes at Wake Forest College which was then located in the county.

I was still seventeen years old when I volunteered for the service during World War II, and wound up as a marine. I had a military career in the Pacific with the third amphibious corps. We were a reinforcement group at Guadalcanal, but I did not get involved in the main action there. Then we got into various amphibious operations that culminated at Okinawa. My group went to the Philippines.

When I came back home I went back to Wake Forest College. I became a math/science teacher at Louisburg High and coached basketball and baseball. Then I went to Henderson to be an elementary principal and taught sixth graders full-time for just one year.

In the fall of 1953, I accepted the position of principal at what was Cary Elementary and High School. Paul Cooper was the district principal. A new high school was built and opened in 1960, and I remained as principal of the elementary school in the old building on Academy Street. I was principal of Cary Elementary and High School from 1953 to 1960, and then Cary Elementary School from 1960 until 1965, all in the old building. Then I decided to go into the county office as assistant superintendent. I retired in 1979.

In 1956 or '57, I got some of the folks together and we organized a Lion's Club for Cary. Later, when it was really needed, I called in the mayor and town representatives and said, "You're going to have to get a recreation department started." So when the population was about 15,000, the town of Cary took over what the Lion's Club had started.

Ned Perry: I was interviewed on March 30, 1999. I was born in Franklin County, a neighboring county to Wake, and lived there until I was twenty-one years old. I moved to Raleigh in 1958. I started my education attending North Carolina State University. I have attended the University of Georgia, the University of Wisconsin, the University at College Station, Texas - Texas A&M, and I attended classes at the U.S. Fire Academy in Maryland.

I started with the Raleigh fire department as a "tailboard man," and was promoted to a fire captain in charge of Fire Station #1. Then I learned that the town of Cary was looking for a fire chief, so I applied and got the job in October of 1975. In 1993, I retired with thirty-six and a half years of service.

Charlotte Phelps: I was interviewed on March 4, 2009. I was born in Angier. We moved to Cary when I had turned six, right before I started school. We bought a house on Academy Street which had a huge front porch. My dad eventually sold it after I left home.

I went to Elon College for one semester, and then to another school before I went to work for the Highway Patrol at the communications center. I married Louis Phelps and we eventually moved back to Cary. My husband was in the national guard for 28 years, and worked with DOT for 38 years. I have two daughters.

Bruce Roberts: I was interviewed on January 17, 2009. I came to North Carolina in 1955 to work for the Hamlet News Messenger as a photographer. It was probably one of the smallest papers in North Carolina. Then a year or so later, I got an offer from the Charlotte Observer as a staff photographer. During the late sixties, I was freelancing for various New York magazines: Time, Life, Sports Illustrated; doing assignments and so forth. Many were Civil Rights assignments in the South.

Billy Rogers: I was interviewed on August 2, 2000. I was born in Cary, June 13, 1935. Henry Adams was my uncle and Charlie Adams is my cousin.

My father became a self-employed produce broker. From his produce route, he opened a small grocery store. He operated the store from sometime in the forties until 1952. Then he sold his grocery store and opened a little restaurant called Rogers Restaurant and a motel on Chatham Street. In 1966, my wife Barbara and I bought the motel and restaurant from him. The motel had seven rooms and an apartment, and we built five additional rooms on the back in 1980.

The Seegers – Marie: We were interviewed on August 23, 2000. I came to Cary as an infant. My mother was a widow and had six children.

I went all through elementary and high school in Cary and attended the First Baptist Church.

(Fred): I moved to Cary in 1944 when I was going into the ninth grade. When I graduated from Cary High School, I worked with my father in the construction business. Then I went into the air force, and was sent to Cheyenne, Wyoming as a teletype operator/instructor. I volunteered to go to Korea, and I was there for twelve months.

In 1953, we married in the First Baptist Church in Cary. I decided to re-enlist in the air force and we moved to Cheyenne, Wyoming. When I got out of the air force, we moved back to Cary in 1966. I was a salesman for thirty-eight years. I was in the tobacco industry for ten years, and then I was in confectionery and food for the remaining twenty-eight years of my career.

Elva Templeton: I was interviewed on January 24, 1976. I was born in Cary on May 3, 1898. My father was Dr. James McPherson Templeton. He practiced medicine in Cary for about fifty years. He had a house where the elementary school is now. He had a little office right in the yard but he didn't use it too much. He went into the homes mostly, making house calls. He would go see the colored people just as well as he would the white folks. And a lot of the colored people said that they had lost a real friend when he died.

I went to college in Winston-Salem in 1916. I took straight A-B teachers' certification for two years. Then I went out to Kentucky to see if I liked home demonstration work. I did not like it, so I began teaching. I taught high school science, French, history and home economics in Arapaho, Pamlico County, and then in Johnston County before I returned home to Cary.

John Yarborough: I was interviewed on August 21, 2000. My grandfather was the superintendent at the blind school in Raleigh. He lived on Academy Street in the pink house, now called the Guess-Ogle house. My father, Dr. Frank Yarborough, built his home and his office next door to his parents. Before he built his house there, he lived on Dry Avenue about three houses down. His doctor's office was over the old post office downtown. He initially went into practice with Dr. Templeton, who died not too long after that, in 1932.

I graduated from Cary High School, and then I went to college. After I graduated I went to work for a pharmaceutical company and they transferred me to Virginia. Then I went to pharmacy school and graduated when I was thirty-five. I am now a pharmacist in Virginia.

PART I

LIVING UNDER SEGREGATION

CHAPTER 2

CARY BEFORE DESEGREGATION

CARY AND THE CIVIL WAR:

The book called *Born in Slavery, Slave Narratives from the Federal Writers' Project, 1936 to 1938* was published by the federal government as the result of a project conducted by the WPA during the Great Depression. The project put people to work going into the field and interviewing former slaves or their descendants. Within that book, six of the people interviewed were living in Cary at the time of the interviews. They recalled the time when either their parents, or they themselves had been slaves, who had owned them and where they lived, presumably in or near present-day Cary.

Valley Perry, who was 50 years old when interviewed, said her mother, Clarice and grandmother Josephine, were owned by Nat and Lucy Whitaker of Wake County. Lila Nichols, who was 89 years old when interviewed on May 18, 1937, said she was also owned by Nat Whitaker, and that Nat's father Willis had given her to Nat. She recalled the Whitaker plantation was in the Rhamkatte area of Cary. Martha Organ said her parents, Handy and Melissa Jones had also been owned by Mr. Whitaker, and later by Rufus Jones of the old Fanning Jones place.

John Beckwith, who was 83 years old when interviewed, said he had been owned by Joe Edwards, Marion Gully, and Hilliard Beckwith. After the war, both his parents remained on the Beckwith plantation until their deaths, and he stayed until he was sixteen before striking out on his own.

Last, George Eatman, who was 93 years old when he was interviewed on May 18, 1937, said he had been owned by Gus Eatman on the old Templeton plantation on the Durham Highway.

Tom Byrd: While researching Cary's history for my book, *Around and About Cary*, I discovered *The Slave Narratives*. In the 1930s, during the Great Depression when the federal government was trying to find jobs for unemployed people, they sent these writers out to interview people who were born in slavery. They did it in one-on-one interviews. They gave them a standard set of questions, like: Where did you live when you were a slave? What was your life like as a slave? Do you remember the liberation? What did you do after the war? These narratives, which were written in dialect, have since been printed and you can find them in major libraries. Fortunately I found former slaves in the book who had lived in this area with Cary connections, which added another dimension to the book and gave me some original material.

During and after the Civil War, Sherman's name became like a curse word to many older Southerners. He was looked upon as next to the devil, he had horns and all, but he actually was a pretty brave general, and what he did was extremely daring. It took a lot of fortitude to march an army through hostile country and get as far as he did, cut off from all supplies. He was pretty hard on people that he thought were determined to destroy the union, such as when he went through Georgia. He was trying to destroy the South's means of production. The Union generals questioned, was it better to kill somebody or to destroy their will to fight? Probably there are a lot of Southerners who survived the war because of what Sherman did in Georgia and South Carolina, places like that. If they had just fought the war the other way and turn every place into a battlefield and shot them, a lot more could have died.

In Georgia they were tearing up railroads and burning anything that could produce anything of value to the confederate army. They were destroying crops because they knew that armies had to have food and they didn't want supplies going to the troops. They didn't show South Carolina much mercy because they blamed South Carolina for starting the war when they fired on Fort Sumter, so they were pretty hard on them.

Of course, Atlanta was burned, Columbia was burned, and then when Sherman reached North Carolina, people were really afraid. After hearing about what Sherman had done elsewhere, here in North Carolina they thought they were next. One thing they worried about was that they knew union troops were coming through South Carolina, but they didn't know where they would cross into North Carolina. So the whole state was alarmed. Sherman could go anywhere he wanted to go, the South couldn't stop him. He came in through Scotland County. Around Laurinburg he crossed the border with 60,000 troops. They didn't all march down one road, they would fan out. They would get in four different columns and that made it easier for them to live off the land, spread over a larger area. Besides, it would take forever to put that many men and horses down one of the little dirt roads they had in those days, so they would use different roads as long as they didn't get too spread out, because then they might become vulnerable.

North Carolina was the last state to join the confederacy. There was a lot of really strong confederate sentiment, especially in the eastern part of the state. But the farther west you went, the less there was and the population in the Raleigh/Cary area was a little more evenly divided. Commander Blair led the corps that came to Cary. When he crossed the line, he issued some orders to his troops, telling them that the people of North Carolina are different from those of South Carolina, so they should be shown some consideration. Then he said, "You need to be especially careful about taking things from poor people so you don't leave them destitute." So there was some humanity and some mercy shown. But the stories that were circulated after the war were brutal, and there were a lot of them.

Sherman's first major tackle in North Carolina was into Fayetteville. He went there because there had been a U.S. arsenal before the war where they made and stored guns and ammunition. The South confiscated it when the war began and started making munitions for the confederacy, so he went there to destroy the arsenal. Fayetteville was known as a very strong secessionist town. They had a newspaper there that was very pro-South and anti-Lincoln. So he did hit that town harder than any other town. They destroyed some cotton mills, for example, when they headed into town.

You won't hear many Southerners say this, but the stories of the burnings by Sherman's army in North Carolina have been greatly exaggerated. In Georgia and South Carolina it was much worse. But when they got to North Carolina, the war was winding down and everybody knew it, so why keep burning everything. *The Slave Narratives* do mention some destruction of property. And the armies were living mainly off the land. That's the only way they could exist, because when they were marching hundreds of miles, they couldn't carry enough food, ammunition, fodder for the horses and all to keep going. They had to get what they needed from the countryside in order to survive. So the chickens were in danger, and the pigs were in danger, and the cows were in danger, because they were looking for something better to eat. I could not find any evidence of widespread destructiveness around here just for the sake of it. In fact, the commander of the corps that came to Cary and was stationed in Cary had attended the University of North Carolina, and he was somewhat sympathetic to North Carolinians. He made an effort to try to keep his guys in check. As the Southern troops were withdrawing from the area, they would go out and take things and think, "Well, we might as well. The confederates are going to take it so we'll take it instead."

Sherman went from Fayetteville to Goldsboro, and Goldsboro to Raleigh. It was at the end of the Civil War when there was a lot of troop movement through Cary. Johnston's army withdrew through Cary. Sherman's troops came through the town, and that kind of thing.

Before Sherman reached Raleigh, Lee had surrendered. By that time they knew the game was up. In fact, when Sherman came through, there was only one building in Raleigh that was destroyed. It was a railroad depot and it was destroyed by the Southern troops as they were withdrawing. So they didn't come through torching everything that came in their path. Sherman came into Raleigh and set up his headquarters in the governor's mansion, and then went over to Bennett's Place in Durham to negotiate the surrender of General Johnston. Lee only surrendered his army in Virginia and then Johnston was the commander of the troops that were in North Carolina and what were left in South Carolina and Georgia, so there was that second surrender of most of the rest of the troops in the field.

At the end of the war, I think Cary was mainly farm country. There were a few large plantations, but it was mainly small farms and people who had furnished their own labor. So when the slaves were freed, their labor force was not disrupted like it was for the big plantations. Then after the war, this area began to industrialize more so than the eastern part of the state that was more rural. It was after the war that the tobacco industry in towns like Durham got started. Reconstruction was difficult. It was made difficult because there were economic circumstances. There had been this tremendous loss during the war of manpower; lots of people were killed and lots of people came back maimed. Then you had this difficulty of working out some kind of accommodation between the races. The blacks were now free. You couldn't buy and sell them, but how were the two races going to live together now. It was no longer master and slave. Some of this problem is still being worked out, to some extent. So there were lots of challenges after the war.

Bertha Daniel: My grandmother, (we called her Nanny,) was the youngest one of a big family living in this area. Nanny's mother and father joined a wagon train going out west. They started on their journey, but I don't know how far they got when Nanny's mother had a sick baby that died. Further down the road, her husband got sick and died. How far west they were by then, I don't know. She was pregnant, expecting my grandmother. So she bundled up her children and came back home.

When Nanny's mother returned here, she had all these children to raise. So she bought a big farm between here and Apex and they farmed the land and paid for the farm. When Nanny was a young girl, her mother had already told her that when she got married, which slaves she was going to give her as a wedding present. She was engaged to be married when the Civil War came along, but her fiancé went to the war and was killed. Sometime later, she married my grandfather, but by then the slaves were all free, so she didn't ever get the promised slaves. My grandmother lived to be 87 years old.

The Johnsons - Emma Lou: Jacob Johnson and his wife Mary came here from Virginia. His will is dated 1761. Our family cemetery is near the intersection of High House Road and Highway 55. We have speculated that the grave in that cemetery of Albert Theodore was probably the child of a black family that they adored who lived on the farm. **(Raymond):** He probably wasn't a slave, because they had a different cemetery for the slaves. You know how the intersection at High House and Highway 55 used to curve around? The reason for that was because in the northwest quadrant there was a slave cemetery. When they straightened the roads out, they had to take care of that not long ago. They moved some of the graves. So Albert was probably a tenant farmer.

THE TWENTIETH CENTURY:

Bruce Roberts: I think the worst assignment I got as a photographer during the Civil Rights time period was, I was assigned to George Wallace's presidential campaign as a photographer. I didn't know it at the time, but Time Magazine really wasn't interested in many pictures of George Wallace's campaign. They wanted to have a photographer there in case he got shot. I wasn't there when he was shot because it happened about two years later, after the campaign was over. I have 10,000 pictures of George Wallace campaigning. It was really a pretty chaotic campaign. On one side of the street were his supporters and on the other side were all the anti-Wallace supporters. You just hoped they didn't start fighting each other while you were there. About halfway through the campaign, he was given Secret Service protection and they got the thing organized, so you had some semblance of order.

Not a single one of my pictures was ever published. Actually, the press paid for Wallace's plane. They sold tickets on the campaign plane for something like $12,000 for the campaign. That is how much Time wanted somebody there.

I also had an assignment from Life Magazine. Life was interested in doing a Klan story, and did considerable research on where the best constant Klan people could be found. It turned out to be the Klan in Natchez, the very famous tourist town. I met a reporter from Life Magazine at the airport and we drove into town. We were both a little nervous about this when the Klan took us out in the woods. Theirs was the only mounted Klan outfit in America. They were on horseback. They had beautiful robes, with a red robe for the minister and a green robe for the Grand Dragon. The rest were white. Going to a Klan rally, you always had prayers. It really is amazing how religion gets mixed into the meetings.

Progress was being made in the sixties, and most states had passed laws that the Klan could not wear face masks. They could not cover their faces for pogroms, or meetings or whatever. But in Mississippi, they still could. We saw the first Klansman come in and I got a really spectacular shot of him. It was springtime and the green of the leaves was just coming out.

The Klan meeting I remember the most was in Salisbury, North Carolina. The textile mills were beginning to be integrated. The Klan was always trying to take advantage of any opportunity for members, because that meant money. So their whole pitch to the unions was, "If you join the Klan, we'll stop the textile mills from being integrated." I don't think that succeeded. I think they would promise anything to get members. There was a sign on the South Carolina line that said "The KKK welcomes you to South Carolina."

The best story about a Klan rally was a few years earlier when I was down in Maxton, near Hamlet, North Carolina in 1958. The Klan decided that they would burn a cross on the front lawn of an Indian home. The Lumbee Indians are down that way. I think the Lumbee Indians are a mixture of Indians and Lost Colony people, because some of the same names appear in the Lumbee Indian tribe. The Lumbees didn't like the idea of the Klan coming down there. I got a call from the Grand Dragon in the area. He had a field outside of Maxton and had everybody there. They had a platform in the clearing with a loudspeaker and a hundred watt light bulb that was hanging over the platform, both connected to a generator.

The Lumbees that lived around there had worked out an agreement with the sheriff. If they wouldn't aim low and hit the Klansmen, they could shoot their guns in the air. Somehow the Lumbees got wind of the Klan meeting and the planned cross-burning in front of one of their own houses. They knew where the Klan met in the woods. So when the Grand Dragon started to talk, the Lumbees' first shot hit the light bulb and plunged the Klan into darkness. Immediately after that, all around in the woods, the Lumbees began to shoot off their guns. All the Klansmen heard were gunshots surrounding them, so they threw off their robes and fled. The story goes that the Grand Dragon had to pay $10.00 to a black man to drive him out of the area to his car.

I thought the Lumbee Indians should get grand status because they stood up to the Klan. The one thing that the Klan could not stand was to be laughed at. After the Klan fled, the Lumbee Indians picked up the Klan robes. Morey Rosen was the photographer who got the picture that ran in Life Magazine of the Indians dressed up in the Klan robes. He shot it from the back so you could see the cross and everything. The Indians were just turning around and smiling at the camera. It became kind of an icon of absolute humiliation to the Klan. They never really recovered from that humiliation. They got laughed out of eastern North Carolina. I always thought that the Lumbee Indians should have some kind of remembrance for what they did, because it brought about the absolute ruination of the Klan, and that was really when things changed in the eastern part of the state.

In 1960, the day after the Greensboro sit-in, there was a lunch counter sit-in in Charlotte. Nothing really happened, except it was the end of integrated lunch counters. So it worked. They closed the lunch counters for about a month, and then they worked out an agreement to quietly reopen them and serve everybody. It was probably the most successful in the sense that there was no violence. It did not get headlines, but it brought about the results that everybody wanted. Then about a month later the theaters ended up becoming integrated as well. They didn't close down at all, they just quietly admitted everybody who could sit wherever they wanted to sit.

Greensboro probably had the more violent episodes. There was the Woolworth lunch counter sit-in, and there was confrontation. I think someone was actually killed in Greensboro. After the sit-ins and the theaters were open, Charlotte had the reputation of being on a very moderate and pro-sensible course. South Carolina, of course, had the big fight over the confederate flag on the capital.

The other change was that all the segregated bathroom signs disappeared. One of the pictures of mine that ran as a double page in a book on the South that Life published was a picture of a bathroom in South Carolina in which you had three doors. One said Men, one said Ladies, and one said Colored. That was common back then. The colored bathrooms were unisex. But rather than Gentlemen and Ladies, or Men and Women, it always seemed to read, Men, Ladies and Colored. In Charlotte one day in the sixties, I passed an office supply store, and I went in to see if they were still selling white and colored signs for bathrooms. They had one set left and I bought it. If you want to see it, it is now at the Charlotte Museum. The separate water fountains were usually in different locations. Those signs just said "White" and "Colored."

I remember when they started integrating schools, particularly in South Carolina. A lot of the towns started private schools for the white kids and the black kids got the old white schools. It was kind of a strange time. In the smaller places, I think there were some special arrangements made so that all of the white students could go together to form their own private school. The community financially helped each other out. Originally it had been the "separate but equal" ruling in the Supreme Court. I thought, what really has happened here is that the blacks have gotten the good equipment and the good schools, and the whites now have not, out of their own choice.

A BRIEF HISTORY OF EDUCATION AND CIVIL RIGHTS IN NORTH CAROLINA:

The following is not a complete or comprehensive history of race relations, education, or legal decisions that affected citizens in North Carolina. Rather, a brief history of events and new laws is offered here for clarity and as background to the narrator stories throughout the book. This chapter also highlights many, but not all of the schools in Wake County that were mentioned by narrators.

In 1831, a federal law was passed that slaves were not allowed to be taught to read or write. This was done in part to prevent runaways from creating their own freedom papers.

Throughout the South, before 1839, the educational system for whites consisted of mostly private schools for those who could afford them. Few provisions were made for the poor, orphans or blacks. Then

Wake County voted to support the public education system for whites through modest taxes when they passed the Public School Law of 1839. However, the development of public education was very slow, and what was created virtually ended with the onset of the Civil War in 1861.

Following the Civil War, the Public School Law of 1869 was passed in North Carolina to provide for separate white and black schools. The system basically copied what had been in place before the Civil War. $100,000 was approved to support this law. It called for a levy of township taxes to provide a four-month term for all children if the township failed to make provision for the schools. The middle and upper classes considered public education to be charity for the poor. And white citizens were vehemently opposed to spending their tax dollars educating black students.

At the end of the Civil War in 1865, Congress established the Freedman's Bureau under the direction of the Army. Against violent Southern opposition, it built or supported the building of more than 4,000 schools, with more than 9,000 teachers for the education of 250,000 black students throughout the South. It was the first widespread free educational system in the South. At that time, one in ten black freed slaves could read and write. Encouraged by the Freedman's Bureau, thousands of white men and women from the North, mostly missionaries and Quakers, came south to set up schools and educate freed slaves. Most of them had to face extreme hostility from the communities where they established their schools. By 1867, almost every county had at least one black school attended by both the young and old. Raleigh's Freedman's Bureau was on the campus of today's Peace College. When the Freedman's Bureau was abolished in 1870, 21% of the freed slaves were literate.

In 1896, the U.S. Supreme Court ruling in *Plessy v Ferguson* established the premise of "separate but equal." Thus followed a number of segregation laws that became known as "Jim Crow," named after a stereotypical black song-and-dance man of that era.

In 1899, as part of a state-wide campaign for white supremacy that became known as the "red shirt movement," the state General Assembly re-drew Cary's boundaries in an attempt to exclude blacks from within city and town limits. At the time about one-third of the town's population was black. The white areas of town were within the boundaries, but the northern portion was excluded, with the exception of a small portion of land that contained the Page house (built by town founder Frank Page,) and half of the adjacent Page-Walker Hotel. In the 1900 census, the black population had been reduced to only 7% of the town's population. By 1915, once the movement had declined, the original one-square-mile boundaries were restored.

In the early 1900s, J.H.P. Adams began to sell home-sites to black families in a four-block area on the north side of Cary which contributed to significant growth of that section of town. There was also a black section just to the south of the town boundary near Cornwall Road where the black church and black school were located. And a third black section grew near Walnut Street where the very first black school had been built by Buck Jones. There were two named areas there; one was called "Little Washington" and the other was known as "Frogtown."

According to a Wake County statistical report of the county superintendent for the 1914/15 school year, white schools with an attendance of from 45 to 70 students were allocated two teachers with a salary of $40.00 per month each. With an attendance of from 70 to75 students, they were allocated three teachers, with one teacher receiving a salary of $60.00 per month and the other two at $40.00 per month. For black schools, attendance of 40 to 50 students were allocated one teacher at a salary of $25.00 per month. With an attendance of 50 to 60 students, they were allocated two teachers with salaries of $25.00 per month for one, and $18.00 per month for the second teacher. And with an attendance of 60 to 90 students, they were still only allocated two teachers, but the second salary could be raised to $20.00 per month. Another document from 1902 states that white teacher salaries ranged from $20.00 to $33.00 per month, while black teachers salaries ranged from $15.00 to $25.00 per month.

In the early twentieth century, Julius Rosenwald, philanthropist and president of Sears, Robuck & Co., met Booker T. Washington and together they discussed what could be done about the deplorable lack of schools for black children in the rural South. In 1917, using a system of matching funds, Julius established the Rosenwald Fund and provided $70 million in seed money. The fund's purpose was to build public schools, colleges, universities, museums, Jewish charities and black institutions. To qualify for a school, each community had to raise some of the money. The fund eventually ran out of money in 1948. By that time, more than 5,300 black schools, 200 teacher homes, and 160 shop buildings were constructed in 883 counties in 15 states from Maryland to Texas. Between 1918 and 1932, 800 Rosenwald schools were built and opened in North Carolina alone, the most of any other state. And by the end of 1932, Rosenwald schools taught one-third of all black students in the South.

In 1954, the U.S. Supreme Court decision in *Brown vs. the Board of Education* ruled that it was unconstitutional to have separate schools for the races. In 1955, following the *Brown* decision, the North Carolina General Assembly gave local school boards control over the desegregation of their schools.

Following the *Brown* decision, white supremacist groups such as Citizen's Councils sprang up across the South to apply economic pressure on African-Americans and whites to support the continuation of integration. Group members were from the white merchant, middle and upper classes. Unlike the Ku Klux Klan, they did not (openly) advocate violence. Rather, these groups used such tactics as shunning, boycotting or making threats to keep the races divided, and to defeat desegregation and the formation of unions. The black middle class was especially vulnerable to these tactics, which included refusing or calling in loans, and hampering their businesses. The groups targeted black people who were members of the National Association for the Advancement of Colored People (NAACP,) who registered to vote, or signed a petition to integrate the schools. The North Carolina group was called the North Carolina Patriots. In 1955, a labor leader estimated that there were 568 segregationist groups in the South with an estimated 208,000 members.

Also following the *Brown* decision, some states proposed upgrading all their black schools to maintain segregation.

In 1956, North Carolina adopted the Pearsall Plan which stated that no child in the state would be forced to attend a school with a child of another race. The Plan allowed North Carolinians to use state funds for tuition to private schools. In 1969, a federal court declared the Pearsall Plan unconstitutional.

In 1960, as part of the civil rights movement, a group called the Student Non-Violent Coordinating Committee (SNCC) formed on the campus of Shaw University in Raleigh. Their goals were to secure voting rights, and the desegregation of schools and public places.

On February 1, 1960, four black students from Agricultural and Technical (A&T) College staged the first-ever peaceful sit-in at the Woolworth lunch counter in Greensboro, North Carolina, setting off a trend that swept the nation. Ten days later, on February 10, 1960, protestors entered the lunch counters at McLellan's, Woolworth's, Kress, Walgreens, Hudson Belk and Eckerd's in the Fayetteville Street Mall in downtown Raleigh. Owners closed the counters "in the interest of public safety." Two days later, 41 students were arrested near Woolworth's in Cameron Village and two more were arrested at McLellan's. After ten days of protests, Kress offered stand-up service to blacks and whites.

Eckerd's opened with service to whites only. The rest remained closed. However, by April of 1964, all downtown Raleigh lunch counters, indoor theaters, recreational facilities, restaurants, and some hotels and motels were desegregated.

There were two separate school systems in Wake County until 1976. The Raleigh city school system was comprised of the inner-city, urban schools in Raleigh proper. The Wake County school system encompassed all schools in the outlying, suburban and rural parts of the county. Cary was in the Wake County school system.

As early as 1952, private Catholic parish schools in North Carolina began desegregation. The first school in Raleigh to desegregate was one of these. Catholic Bishop Vincent S. Waters ordered that Sacred Heart Catholic High School in Raleigh be desegregated for the 1955/56 school year.

In 1960, 7-year-old William Campbell was admitted into the second grade at Murphey School. He became the first black student to desegregate a white public school in the Raleigh city district. He was the only black student in that school for the next five years. Shortly thereafter, 400 white parents petitioned for reassignment of William on the grounds that integration was not in the best interests of the children. The school board failed to react. (Bill Campbell grew up to become the mayor of Atlanta, Georgia.)

In 1961, the Raleigh city school board assigned five black students to Daniels Jr. High, and three black students to Broughton High School to begin desegregation in those two schools in Raleigh.

In July 1964, President Johnson signed the Civil Rights Act which outlaws the segregation of public facilities, and racial discrimination in employment and education. This act enforced the *Brown* decision to desegregate the schools throughout the South. The Civil Rights Act required that North Carolina school boards had to report their progress of desegregation yearly to the U.S. Department of Health, Education and Welfare (H.E.W.) The first report submitted by the Wake County school board for the 1964-65 school year stated that seven black students had attended previously all-white schools. All seven were in Cary. One year later, the number had risen to 93 students in Wake County.

Also in 1964, the 24th amendment to the U.S. Constitution was passed which appealed the poll tax. Combined with the Voting Rights Act that was passed in 1965, voter registration opened up for blacks throughout the country.

In 1965, North Carolina adopted the freedom-of-choice plan which allowed parents to choose the public schools their children would attend. In 1968, a federal court ruled the plan was unconstitutional.

In August 1966, following a Ku Klux Klan meeting in Raleigh, the group Direct Action for Racial Equality (DARE) was formed by mostly NC State University students who were motivated to improve racial relations.

On April 4, 1968, Dr. Martin Luther King Jr. was assassinated in Memphis, Tennessee. The next day, Shaw University students ran down Fayetteville Street in Raleigh chanting, "Burn, baby, burn." Hudson Belk was set on fire near Shaw University.

In 1969, demonstrators at A&T University in Greensboro were fired upon. One was killed and five policemen were injured.

BLACK COLLEGES AND UNIVERSITIES:

In 1865, Shaw University opened in Raleigh as the oldest black private Baptist college in the country. In 1874, women were admitted. In 1882, Shaw Medical School opened as the first four-year medical school for blacks in the country. The medical school closed in 1918.

In 1867, St. Augustine's College was opened in Raleigh as a private institution supported by the Episcopalian clergy and the United Negro College Fund to educate teachers for black students. Today, St. Augustine's has been ranked in the top five of 117 Historically Black College or Universities (HBCUs) in the country. Also in 1867, Barber-Scotia College for Women was opened in Concord, North Carolina by Presbyterians to educate social workers and teachers for the recently freed slaves. Barber-Scotia became a co-ed college in 1954.

In 1893, the Agricultural and Technical (A&T) College of North Carolina was opened on the campus of Shaw University by a Shaw graduate. It later moved to Greensboro. And in 1910, N.C. Central University opened in Durham by another graduate of Shaw.

In 1951, after the decision was made in *Sweatt v Painter*, the (white) North Carolina State University (NCSU) Board of Trustees adopted a policy that black students would only gain admission if they were living in-state and applying for graduate programs that were not offered at an HBCU in North Carolina. In 1953, two black electrical engineering graduate students were admitted because they met those requirements. In 1956, the U.S. Supreme Court case *Fraiser v Consolidated University of the North Carolina Board of Trustees* ruled that black undergraduate and graduate students could not be denied admission to the consolidated university system because of race. Four undergraduate black students were then admitted to NCSU in1956. In 1973, the NCSU board of governors passed desegregation guidelines for admissions.

In 1955, University of North Carolina (UNC) in Chapel Hill enrolled three black students for the first time.

WHITE PUBLIC PRIMARY GRADE SCHOOLS:

In Raleigh: Needham B. Broughton High School opened in Raleigh in 1929. Swift Creek Elementary School also opened in 1929 in the Swift Creek area between Raleigh and Cary. It was later incorporated into Cary.

In Apex: In 1976, Apex High School opened as a fully integrated school.

In Cary: The first public school in the Cary area is believed to have been opened in 1847, with 47 students who attended classes for 73 days in a year. All education ceased during and after the Civil War. Following the war, the next free public school opened in 1872 with 17 students who were offered two 8-week sessions.

In 1870, a private boarding school called Cary Academy opened in a wooden, two-story building at the head of Academy Street. It attracted tuition-paying students from near and far to come to Cary to attend grades 1-11.

By 1877, Cary had established a School Committee, and they divided the town into two school districts. Their goal was to build four one-teacher public schools, one for whites and one for blacks in each of the two districts. It is believed that the two schools for District #1 were near Reedy Creek Road at North Harrison Avenue. The white school for District #2 was just south of the private Cary Academy school at the head of Academy Street. Alfred "Buck" Jones provided the land and a log cabin for the black school for District #2 near Walnut Street and Tanglewood Drive. The first public school classes began in November and usually ran for four months with three levels of instruction. When Buck Jones died in 1893, an agreement was reached that students from the white school would begin attending Cary Academy. Their school building just behind Cary Academy was then given to the black students and the name was changed to the Cary Colored School.

In 1896, Cary Academy was incorporated as Cary High School, still with grades 1-11. In 1900, the school had 248 students, including all of the boarding students that came from all over the South. Cary's population at the time was only 333 people, so the school and education became the centerpiece of the town. The school offered two five-month terms. By 1900, only about half of all children were attending either a public or private school in Cary.

Under Governor Charles B. Aycock, who became known as the "education governor" in 1901, three new schools were built in Cary Township. In District #1, a white two-room school was built called Reedy Creek, and a one-room school for blacks was built called Evans Grove. In District #2, a four-room white school was built on West Chatham Street called Cary Public School. Black students in District #2 continued to attend Cary Colored School.

In 1907, the North Carolina General Assembly voted to support public high schools. Up until this time, only elementary schools and universities had been supported by state funds. Shortly thereafter, the board of directors of private Cary Academy offered to sell the school to the state. The Cary School Committee petitioned the Board of Education to convert the school to one of the new public high schools to be supported by the state. The Board approved the conversion just eight days after the General Assembly vote to support high schools. This made Cary High School the first state-assisted public high school in North Carolina. The name of the school was changed to Cary High School. Even though it remained a boarding school, Cary High School became a model for public high schools throughout the state. This further enhanced Cary as the town for education.

In 1927, the students from Reedy Creek were transferred to Cary High School. By 1947, Cary High School offered grades 1-12 for all the white students in Cary. With town growth, a new white high school was built on Walnut Street which opened in the fall of 1960 for grades 9-12. The old school changed its name to Cary Elementary and Jr. High School with grades 1-8. It later became Cary Elementary School with grades 1-5.

Following the *Brown* decision in 1954, the assistant county school superintendent, Thomas Grimes, stated that the goal of school officials for desegregation was to, "make the change as fast as it would be accepted." By the early 1960s, the Board of Education adopted a "freedom of choice" plan. Students were allowed to attend any school in their district that had space available. Where space was limited, preference would be given to students living nearest the school. So in the spring of 1963, parents of twenty black students in the Cary district requested that their children attend previously all-white schools. Thus, all-white Cary High School was desegregated when six black female students from Berry O'Kelly High School were transferred to the Cary school. Cary High School was the first school in the Wake County school system to desegregate. (Several schools in the Raleigh city school system had admitted black students prior to that time.) A year later, Gregory Crowe, was admitted to Cary High as the first black male student.

In 1963, West Cary Elementary School opened and later changed its name to Northwoods Elementary. South Cary Elementary opened 1967. It later changed its name to Briarcliff Elementary. And Henry Adams Elementary opened in 1969.

BLACK PUBLIC PRIMARY GRADE SCHOOLS:

Throughout the State: The 1850 census for North Carolina shows 217 free Negroes attending school. Of those, 52 were from Wake County. By 1869, there were 257 black schools with 15,600 students in North Carolina.

In Raleigh: The Deaf, Dumb and Blind School opened in 1869 with a Negro department. The school was never segregated.

In 1869, a 69-acre reconstruction village called Method was started by a former slave, Jesse Mason. Located where the state fairgrounds stand today, Method became a suburb of Raleigh. As early as 1870, there was a colored school in Method. In 1895, that school was renamed Berry O'Kelly Training School after a prominent black merchant, civic leader and philanthropist who lived in the area and who was instrumental in the development of the school. By 1919, Berry O'Kelly was one of the first black schools to have a nine-month term. In 1923, Berry O'Kelly Training School became the first North Carolina accredited rural black high school in the state. Berry O'Kelly was in the Wake County school system.

The first black school bus was bought in 1929 with the help of the Rosenwald Fund. This bus started its daily route at Fuquay Springs, then went on to Holly Springs, Apex, and Cary before it delivered the students to Berry O'Kelly High School in Method.

John W. Ligon High School opened in 1953 as an all-black school. In 1971, it became a desegregated junior high school. In 1982, Ligon became a magnet middle school.

In 1962, William G. Enloe High School opened in Raleigh as the first fully integrated high school in the Raleigh city school system. It was named for Raleigh's first black mayor who was in office at the time the school opened. The school offered grades 7-12. In 1982, Enloe became a magnet school.

In Apex: In 1880, the Apex Normal School for blacks was opened by Reverend Matthew Brown, a Baptist minister, in a section of Apex called "Woptown." That school burned down approximately ten years later. In 1896, a new school was built for blacks called Apex Normal and Collegiate Institute. The new school offered grades 1-6 for students of both sexes, for an individual tuition of $1.50 per month. Students could board at the school for an additional $5.00 per month. The school was still in operation in 1913.

In 1914 there was a new black school called Apex Public School on West Street, which burned down in 1931. For one year, students attended school in the three different locations of the Tent Sisters Hall, the Odd Fellows Hall and a store. By 1932, a new Rosenwald school had been built on the corner of Tingen Road and James Street. It was called White Oak School #1. In 1942, the Apex Elementary School opened as the first Wake County school system Negro school accredited by the North Carolina Department of Education. A few years later, the name was changed to Apex Jr. High with grades 1-9. Grades 10-12 went to Berry O'Kelly High School in Method. In 1955, Apex Jr. High was expanded to a senior high school and the 10th grade was added. In 1956 the 11th grade was added. And in 1957 the 12th grade was added and the name changed once again to Apex Consolidated High School. In 1970, Apex Consolidated High School became Apex Elementary, with grades 4-8. Today, Apex Elementary School at 700 Tingen Road is a magnet school. The student body is comprised of 65% white students, 23% black students and 12% are students of other races.

In Cary: It is rumored that just after the end of the Civil War, a freedman school was opened on the corner of Dixon Street in Cary. As said previously, by 1877, Buck Jones had built a log cabin school for District #2 on the corner of what is today Walnut Street and Tanglewood Drive. Buck was a descendent of Nathanial Jones of White Plains, a Cary plantation owner. Upon his death in 1815, Nathanial Jones freed his slaves in his will. This was a shocking thing in those days before the Civil War. Nathanial Jones is buried in the old White Plains Cemetery on Tolliver Drive in Maynard Oaks subdivision.

When Buck Jones died in 1893, white students were moved to Cary Academy and their school building was given to black students. The name was changed to the Cary Colored School. It was also a log building, and stood near the old Cary Christian Colored Church on Holleman Street, which was a dirt road leading to Hillcrest Cemetery from Kildare Farm Road.

As part of an expanding educational system in North Carolina, in 1901 a one-room school for blacks called Evans Grove was built in District #1, which was believed to have been located near Reedy Creek. In the 1920s when the Cary Colored School was expanded by a second room addition and a second teacher was added, the Evans Grove students were transferred to Cary Colored School and Evans Grove was closed. Cary Colored School was now a wooden, two-room school with outside privies, and a wood-burning stove for heat. Annie Mitchell Meadows taught grades 1-4 in one room and Rev. J.W. Meadows taught grades 5-7 in the other room.

The Cary Colored School burned down in 1936. It is widely believed that the cause of the fire was arson, although it was never proven. When the school burned down, it was first proposed to bus the black students to an elementary school in Method. The justification was that there were few black students in Cary, and there was no land available to build a new school. However, Cary's black parents banded together and boycotted busing their children to Method. They demanded a replacement school be built in Cary. They eventually won their school. The original deed for the land on which the new school would be built just north of Chapel Hill Road is dated October 1, 1936 and was owned by Goelet Arrington, et.al. He was a prominent black landowner in Cary. The school was originally called East Cary Elementary School. The first building that opened in 1937 was a small wooden building. To fill the new school, it was consolidated with other schools in surrounding areas. The first school to send its students to East Cary was Shiloh, followed by Rhamkatte, then Asbury and Method elementary schools. In 1954, the original 1937 five-room wooden building was replaced with a brick building to add needed space to the school. Then in 1960, the school was expanded again to include a gymtorium, additional classrooms and a cafeteria. In the 1969/70 school year, East Cary Elementary School became a mostly white, fully integrated school and the name was changed to Kingswood Elementary.

In 1965, two years after Cary High School had begun the desegregation process, West Cary High School opened on Evans Road as Cary's first all-black high school. While still under construction, the Wake County Board of Education named this new school Clyde Evans High School. Clyde Evans Sr. had been on the black school advisory board for 22 years, and had been instrumental in acquiring the land for the school. Shortly thereafter, however, the board passed a ruling that schools would no longer be named after people from the community, so the school opened as West Cary High School. One year later, in 1966, Berry O'Kelly

High School in Method closed. Cary students who had not yet transferred from Berry O'Kelly then began attending West Cary High School. Other students were bused in from Method, Morrisville, Jeffrey's Grove, Millbrook, Rhamkatte, Bayleaf, Neuse, St. Matthew and Asbury to fill the new high school.

When the school year began in the fall of 1967, of the 25,000 total students in the Wake County school system, 9,000 were black. Of those, 300 black students were attending predominantly white schools. In the 1967/68 school year, West Cary became a desegregated all-ninth grade school with 340 students, and the name was changed to West Cary Junior High. J. Estes Byers remained as principal and Clarence Batts was assistant principal. There were 17 teachers and one librarian. Then in 1970, West Cary Junior High became West Cary Middle School for grades 6-8.

All Cary schools were fully desegregated in the 1969/70 school year in accordance with the deadline set forth in the Federal Desegregation Guidelines. In 1969, East Cary Elementary became an all-sixth grade school and converted from an all-black to a mostly white school, with an 88% white student body that first year. The school principal was J.W. Walters. There were twelve teachers and one librarian for 364 sixth graders. The members of Cary's school advisory council were Dr. Kenneth Keller, Dr. E.B. Davis, William Gardner, Katherine Sears, Haywood Jones, Richard Pleasants, Melba Collins, Clancy Cain and Herbert Barbee. Then in 1970, East Cary changed its name to Kingswood and became a fully desegregated elementary school for grades 1-5.

CHAPTER 3

AFRICAN-AMERICAN LIFE ON THE FARM BEFORE DESEGREGATION

SJ and Leonia Farrar - SJ: My great-grandfather was a local preacher named Farrar Green. My grandfather also became a local preacher, then my father became a local preacher, and now there are four or five of us in the ministry out of that Farrar clan. Mama and Daddy would take us to prayer meetings. We would walk two and three miles on a Wednesday night, and sometimes on a Saturday night, and we had to go through woods and valleys and whatever. We would have to walk on logs that were across the creeks, with no lights.

My father was a sharecropper. That's what 99% of the black people in that area were, we were share farmers. You kept half of what was left, not half of what was made. Sometimes we had nothing to sell to be able to figure out what was left. You had to take the landowner's word for what was left and be thankful to get it. You were allowed to work the land. We moved from farm to farm.

My father died when I was nine years old, and my mother was left with having to support us on her own. Leonia's father was a hard worker. She doesn't know what it is to eat the last biscuit because he was there to provide for her. That was different. What made the difference in sharecropper family lives was the number of children that they had. The larger your family was, the larger the farm you could work would be. A small family of children had a small farm. I don't remember our family ever having more than five acres of tobacco, and then corn and sweet potatoes. We couldn't sell the sweet potatoes, we had to have them for our own food.

Leonia's father always found work on a big farm. You talk about classes, that made them a class above us. My mother and father were considered poor and ignorant. Her father was not that poor because he could man more acres of land.

When my father died, my mother continued to work on the farm with all of us, under all kind of situations. We were just field hands. We didn't know where we were going to get the next meal from.

My mother was fair complexioned and nice looking, a beautiful lady, and the men owners would always want special favors from her. She wouldn't go for it. She made them keep their hands to themselves. She had to move every year, from very small farm to farm because she wouldn't put up with it.

As the children grew older, the boys would be "rented out." They would be hired out to the landowner of a larger farm for a certain amount of dollars per year. When we reached twelve, thirteen, fourteen, fifteen years old, we were "pulled out of the nest," and had to work for somebody else for just a few dollars. That was the only way my mother could make it. I had seven brothers, and the oldest two were already "working by the month."

My oldest brother, Odell, could do anything with his hands. He was a machinist, even though he was never trained to be a machinist. He was working with a man who operated a sawmill. Odell could take that sawmill completely apart and put it back together. Even though he was mechanically inclined, he worked for nothing. We weren't allowed to learn anything back in those days except just what we could pick up on our own. The more talented that you were, the more you were allowed to do if you could do it effectively, but you were never paid for it. It didn't make any difference what work you were performing as far as payment was concerned. Working on the machinery, you were in the shade. You would put the tractor or whatever under a barn, under a big tree somewhere and then work on it. That was a blessing, not to have to be out there behind a mule in the sun.

I have seen my mother beat the dogs to the hen nests to get the eggs. Then she would put them together until she had a dozen, and walk five miles to sell that dozen eggs for 15¢. Then she would walk another five miles back home and save the money until Sunday, then walk another five miles to church and put the 15¢ in church.

She had to walk, in extremely cold weather, to wash and iron, and her pay would be an old hog head coming out of the smokehouse with bugs in it. She would lay it out in the sun and let the sun run the bugs away. Then she would skim them off and cook it for us. That sounds horrible, doesn't it? But we survived.

(Leonia): Daddy had nineteen children, and I'm the seventh child. I was determined that I was going to better myself, so I asked Daddy, "Can you send me to school?"

Daddy said, "No, I cannot send you children to school because there are too many of you."

I said, "Okay, I'm going to get married." That was the thing for farming children, for girls especially to do. They would get married, because the father needed to thin the crowd out so there were fewer mouths to feed. So I got married to Farrar, and as a married couple we continued to be sharecroppers. I told him, "I want to make you a good wife and I want children. I want to stay home and be a good mother for these children." I'm the mother of eight.

(SJ): One year as sharecroppers on a farm, we had a good crop. Our tobacco turned out to be nice. The landowner tried to keep the money away from me. I couldn't take it. I said, "I'm not going to work my wife and our three children to death and then give somebody else everything we made." That was my turning point. It took a lot of courage and a lot of harassment. I had to leave the farm because I was considered a troublemaker.

(Leonia): When we sold the last crop of tobacco and they carried it to the market to sell, the landlord wanted all of the money. Farrar was determined he wasn't going to let him take all of the money, so he got a lawyer and they went to court. The court found that he was right, he deserved his share of money. The landowner had to pay the cost of the court and give us all the money we had earned. The judge told us, "If I were you, I would move from that farm."

And that's how we made it to Cary. He told me, "Honey, I'm going to find you a place and build you a house."

I said, "You can't build a house. How can you build a house?"

He said, "I'm going to put you in a house, Honey. I'm leaving this farm."

Carolyn Rogers: My parents, SJ and Leonia Farrar, were sharecroppers. We lived on the landowner's farm and tended the crops. My husband has often said to me, "For a farm girl, you are afraid of everything that runs, crawls and flies." And I am. We would have to go out to the fields to pick those big, fat, green worms off of the tobacco, because they would eat the tobacco leaves. I'm scared to death of them. They were just squishy, fat, and juicy. We would have to pick them off and throw them down on the ground in such a way that it would kill them. And we had to do it quickly because we have to get the entire field finished.

My brothers were out in the field "priming tobacco," which means they were breaking the leaves off of the stalk, putting those in what we called "sleds," and then the sleds were pulled by horses to bring the tobacco to the barn. I "handed leaves," which means that I would gather three or four leaves together and hand them to the person who was looping them. The looper's job was to wrap a thread around the leaves that I gave her and then wrap them onto a stick. The stick then was hung up in the barn so the tobacco leaves would be cured.

There were many mornings where, after the tobacco was cured, we would have to get up at 3:00 AM, take the cured tobacco out of the barn so we would be ready to refill that barn by 6:00 AM. Working in tobacco is dirty work. We would be dirty, the gnats were swarming around us, the mosquitoes were stinging us. It was not a beautiful job.

But I would not trade my farm-working days for anything, because those days made me who I am and gave me my work ethics. Being out there, looking up at the long rows that were never ending, chopping tobacco or throwing worms or taking the suckers off. Suckers are little things that grew off from the tobacco stock that impeded the growth of the tobacco leaves. So we would have to get up in the morning and pull the suckers off and throw those down. Or we would remove the flowering part of the tobacco plant. They called it "suckering," breaking off that top. We would go back home, and we were so tired and miserable, and we had goop all over us, gum from the tobacco, and it was just horrible.

The housing was provided by the landowner. Once we lived in a barn but my parents fixed it up and made it look like a home. They even painted the walls. But we worked the dry tobacco upstairs, getting it ready for market. When you took it out of the tobacco barn where it was being cured, you had to have somewhere to house the tobacco. Beneath us in the same barn where we lived was "the pit," what in a regular house we would call the basement. We would hang the dry tobacco in the pit because it had to be kept moist so it would not crumble when being handled. Once it was moist, we would take the tobacco from the pit in the basement upstairs to the attic so we could wrap it to get it ready for market. We had to take it through our living space, unless we took it around to the back and hoisted it up to the loft. You could do that.

Our living space had walls. There was a kitchen. There was a living room. There was my parents' bedroom. Then upstairs a portion of the attic space was our bedroom (for the three kids.) we always smelled tobacco upstairs, always. We did not smell like tobacco, but the smell of tobacco was always upstairs. My parents' first home was a pack house. And this home, which is where I grew up, was a pack house. When we went out our back door we went out into a horse pasture.

When we left the pack house, we moved to another farm and lived in a small house with maybe four rooms. Then we moved down the road from that house, still on the same farm. The new one was a nice, big, two-story white house, but it was filled with bats. We had bats for company all the time. I was always so afraid to go to bed because I could look at the mantle and see a bat sitting on it. I was scared to death.

That was the typical farm. We had the pasture with the big red barn, and cows and horses, (we called them mules,) and a pond. The tobacco barns were out from the pasture. I was afraid of the cow. One morning Daddy made me milk the cow. That cow swished me with her tail, and that did it. We used to kill chickens by wringing their necks, and I would have to pluck the feathers from the dead chickens. I remember watching the headless chicken hop around. Oh, it was just horrible. I remember sitting on the back porch churning milk until the butter came to the top.

There was no plumbing in any of these houses, so we had to draw water from a well. We would go out, let the bucket down into the well and draw the water up, then pour the water into another bucket and we carried it into the house. Or we had a pump outside the house where we would have to pump the water into the bucket. The water bucket stayed on the back porch on a shelf until it was empty. Usually we would keep two buckets of water there. We had electric lights that we could flip on at a switch. We had a wood stove so Daddy cut wood and we carried it inside.

Then we moved from there into a real house. I say "real house" because there were no bats. That was a nice house. It was painted, it had a living room, three bedrooms and a kitchen. We moved from that house to Cary. That's why Cary was city to me. Living in Green Level, we never knew that anything existed past 55 Highway.

It was romantic if you owned the farm, and even then those kids worked on the farm alongside us, and it was just as bad for them. Then when we moved to Cary, Daddy said, "I don't want you to feel like you are city slickers, so you're going back to the farm," and he farmed us out during the summer. So I and my two brothers continued to work on the farm from when I was in the seventh grade through high school. The summer I came back from my first year of college, I worked at Rogers' Restaurant instead. I said, "No more, this is it for me. I will never work on the farm again."

When I started dating and still working on the farm, I would call my mom in Cary, on Evans Road, and ask her to please run me a tub of water so that when I got home I could jump right into the tub to get all of that gum off of my hands and from beneath my fingernails. By the time my boyfriend arrived, I was just as prim and proper, and he never knew I had been in a field all day.

Leroy and Betty Farrar – Leroy: There were eight children in my family. When Daddy passed away, those of us still at home were sharecroppers; SJ and me, and three others. One sister and two brothers had already left home when Daddy died. They were in and around home but they weren't working on the farm that we were working. They were in the area where they could come home at night, but they were working with other people making a little money to help out. Before I got married I worked on the farm with somebody else, and then my younger brothers stayed with Mama on her farm. I got paid for what I was doing and I gave it to Mama to help take care of the others. That was kind of rough. The work part was not bad because I enjoyed farming, but I couldn't make any money. Then I got married and started a family.

When we were farmers, I didn't know anything that could be any better for us in those days. Some was good years and some was not so good. I enjoyed the farm life, but you couldn't accomplish anything because you were sharecropping. When you would work a day, half the day you worked for yourself and half the day you worked for the man that owned the crops, so half of the money that you made went to the owner of the property. We would plant the crop, and tend the crop, and harvest the crop, and take it to market, and then we had to hand half the money over to the landowner, and pay our bills out of the half we could keep. You got paid once a year. Even though I loved the farm, I realized I had to get out of there because by then I was married and raising a family, so I needed some money. The year that the storm Hazel came through, I quit farming. It was in the fall and the crop was already in by that time. We already had it harvested.

During Civil Rights, it did not change in my workplace. When I went to work, the blacks and the whites would work together just like brothers and sisters almost on that job. We had no problems. When I was on the farm we worked together too. Betty had a little different experience than I had on the farm because I don't think she enjoyed it as much as I did.

(**Betty**): With nine children in my family, we had a big farm. I got along fine on the farm. My mother didn't work out in the fields. She would help tie tobacco and grade it, but she mostly stayed inside and cooked and washed and ironed for people. She had about four or five families that she washed for every week, making a little extra money. I had two sisters and six brothers, and we all worked on the farm with my daddy. He was a smart man and he always wanted to be ahead of everything, setting that tobacco. He about dropped from it. He just couldn't stand to be behind anybody else, he always had to be in front. And he would work you to death.

We had fun, but I didn't understand how things worked. There were two young, white girls who worked with us in tobacco, and they saw us every day. When my sister and I would go to the store we had to pass their house, and they would come out and call us "niggers." They called to us, "Hey niggers," like they didn't even know us. That always disturbed my sister and me. We went on to the store and didn't change direction or worry with them but it did upset us. I guess what we should of done was to tell their parents, because we never had any trouble with the parents saying anything like that to us. We all got along. But we did go back home and tell our mama. That's the only trouble that we had.

When harvesting the crop, we would work from Monday morning until Saturday night. And we had to get up sometimes at 2:00 AM and pull out a barn of tobacco, run back home and eat breakfast, go back out and put tobacco back into the barn all day long from Monday to Saturday night. That was hard. During the summer we would pull the tobacco off the stalk and put it in the barn to cure it. That's summertime work. Then in the wintertime we worked the tobacco and to get it ready for market. By then we would be back in school. Our parents would take care of working the tobacco while we were in school and when we got home we helped out with it by pulling tobacco off of sticks until dark. That's the way that worked.

We had seven acres of potatoes one year and it took us two weeks to plant them. We had to stay out of school to do that. We had to get out there and tear up the ground. Then after the potato vines grew, we had to pull them up and turn them one way, plow along that side and put soda down, then turn them on the other side, plow and put more soda down. Then we had to spread the vines out so they could continue growing until fall. It was a whole lot of hard, unnecessary work because it could have been done when the vines were younger, but I guess they didn't have the knowledge at that time. So it was done the hard way. I would rather put in tobacco than have to do all that work.

When I was home, I handed leaves mostly. There was a lot of work to be done in tobacco, I'll tell you. We would get up early and go out in the fields. The tobacco would be wet sometimes, and we would get wet all over unless we wore an apron or something. Work, work, work. I thought we didn't get nearly enough money for all the time we had to put in it. (**Leroy**): We would make just enough money to barely make it. Sometimes we wouldn't even have enough money to make it.

During the winter months while I wasn't doing anything special on the farm, I would take a shotgun and go to the woods to hunt rabbits and squirrels. That's what we would eat during the wintertime. Our landowner would go to the curb market on Saturdays. I would give some of what I killed during that week to the landlady, and she would take them to the curb market and sell them for me. That enabled us to have a little money. We got along so well. She was glad to take them.

We had a house on her land. There was nothing elaborate about it but it was a nice place to live. Their kids would play with our kids. We had a real good relationship with our croppers. I go through there now sometime when I'm going to my church. My church is up near Jordan Lake. Every once in awhile, I stop by where we used to live and see those people, and a lot of them still live there. They're not farming anymore. I still respect that place because that's where we got started in a little two-room house there, the stack house. Our first home after we married was on that farm. It was a nice little house. It's still there today. Two of our children were born there.

After we got married, we went from one farm to another farm. These people were kinfolk and they lived close together. They were nice. The last farm that we stayed on, the man that owned it promised me, if I would stay there and take care of him and his wife, he would give me five acres of land. There was no house on it but it was five acres of good farmland with plenty of places to build a house. But he died and that was the last of that. He didn't have it in his will or anything. He was a good old man. He made furniture for us that we still have. He worked in a shop a lot and he could make anything. We all worked together with his son and his family, putting in tobacco and taking out tobacco.

The Johnsons - Raymond: I was born in 1928 on the farm on Highway 55. About 350 acres at the intersection of High House and Highway 55 belonged to my grandfather. My father was raised there, and he liked farming so he bought this farm just up the street. My father died when I was eight. My mother, Pattie May, hired sharecroppers to keep the farm going while she raised us. I had four sisters, I was the only boy. We never went lacking for anything because we raised our own food. (**Emma Lou**): Pattie May raised everything they ate, from chickens to eggs to hogs, and all the vegetables. She was a wonderful provider, and she did that all on her own.

(Raymond): The tenants lived in a separate house on the property. They didn't pay anything, they just lived there and Mother furnished the equipment. Because they didn't have tractors, she furnished the mules, plows, the seed, the fertilizer, and the land. They did all the work, and when they carried the crop to town, for their labor they got half, and for her input, she got half.

(Emma Lou): They were farming tobacco and also corn. During tobacco harvest, she had to hire extra help, and she would feed the extra people who harvested the tobacco. The back porch was screened in and she had a table out there where she would feed all the tenants. For some reason back then they didn't feel free to invite them in, so she would feed them out there, and feed the others in her kitchen. She cooked on an old wood-burning stove and she did all the cooking. I don't know how she did it. The first tractor they ever had on this farm was bought in 1951. They were plowing with mules when I came here before that.

During the Depression and after, there were a lot of hobos on the railroad that runs right behind our house. Pattie May said that for some reason they would come here and ask for food, and she would feed them.

(Raymond): When I turned twenty-one, two of my sisters and I got together and they sold me their shares, so I bought my two sisters out of this farm. When I bought the house, I just took over the whole thing and farmed it myself without tenants. We grew tobacco, corn, wheat, and oats.

Growing tobacco is a thirteen-month job. You started by clearing out the woods to get the best land. You would burn off the weeds and kill the grass. During the winter, you would pile tinder on the land where you were going to have a plant bed and burn it. Back in those days you cured tobacco with wood. All winter you cut what we called "flue wood" to fire the tobacco barn to cure the tobacco. Then when days were pretty, you would begin plowing your land to get it plowed up so you could have it ready for the crops. About March, you would start planting your corn to get it out of the way. In the meantime, you would be picking weeds off the plant beds, by hand of course. Then around the last week in April or the first of May, you would transplant tobacco into the fields where you had been plowing all winter to get them ready.

(Emma Lou): As the plants grew, another miniature plant would try to grow, but you need to pull them off, so that the strength of the plant would go to the main shoot. Today they have chemicals that control that, and also to control the worms. When I came here, we had to go out into the tobacco field and pull the worms off the plants. That's when I decided I would rather do public work. You had to pick the worm up with your hand and put it in a can or step on them. There were hundreds of these green, fat worms, and they had horns. They would spit this green juice out at you. Oh, they were terrible. They wouldn't bite you.

(Raymond): You had to keep the tobacco cultivated through the whole year to keep it growing and get it ready for harvest. Then you started harvesting somewhere in mid-July. It will take six to eight weeks to get your tobacco harvested and ready for market. During that time you would be in what they called the pack house, a barn where you would keep the tobacco stored after you've cured it. Then you would tie it into bundles, so many leaves together, and it would be sold like that at the market. They took pride in tobacco back in those days.

Now they just dump it into a big sheet and take it to the market. Back then we had to grade it. We had to get moisture into it so it was in handling condition, because it would crumble if you didn't do that. So you had to hang it down in a pit to "come in order," to get moisture into it. Under the barn was a big basement room called the pit. Tobacco was looped on a stick and then you would hang it in this pit overnight and enough moisture would accumulate in there to make the tobacco pliable.

The next day you would take it into the grading room which was up at ground level, and grade the tobacco into five grades - good, better, better, sorry, sorry. **(Emma Lou)**: Some leaves were still green, some that had over-cured and were black like a burnt biscuit, some that the stem didn't "kill out," didn't dry, it was still green. There would be some leaves that were a beautiful golden yellow but with a touch of orange on them and maybe had a few spots. And then you would have the perfect, golden leaf of tobacco. You got high dollar for it. When I first came here you made a wonderful living at it, but it was work, constant hard work.

(Raymond): Along with the tobacco, we had roasting ears when corn was in its wet stage. Then about October when they were still green, you would go out and pull the leaves off the corn before the frost got the leaves, take them to the barn to feed the mules. We also fed our mules hay. We had to have a field to grow hay. We harvested the hay the same time of year and took it to the barn. We had to have the barn full of hay when frost came to feed the animals over the winter.

(Emma Lou): We would heat this house with wood. There was a wood shelter right outside by the back door. They would have to cut the wood and stack it up for the winter to heat this house.

So we were growing everything we needed for ourselves, our family, our hands and our animals to live the year around, and we needed a cash crop. Tobacco was our money crop. And then we were growing hay and corn and vegetables, and we were harvesting the wood off the land, all just so we could survive.

(Raymond): In the early days, we cured our tobacco with wood which we cut all winter. We would fill a tobacco barn every week, and take it out on a six-day cycle. **(Emma Lou):** They would build fires in those flues. Then he would have to sit up all night and watch it, to keep it fired up. When we were young, I used to spend the night with him at the barn. That was real exciting back then in the barn, watching the fire, making sure the barn didn't burn. We have never had one burn, we were lucky. He slept a little at the barn, then the next day he had to be out in the fields harvesting.

(Raymond): Tobacco was our cash crop, but they kept cutting the tobacco allotment. To keep the price up, the tobacco companies had a program where you could only plant so much tobacco. Each farm was allotted so much. Back when my daddy was farming, you could plant as much as you wanted to, but then it got to where you couldn't plant but so many acres. And they kept cutting the allotment, cutting the allotment. In 1977 we stopped farming tobacco.

GETTING OFF THE FARM:

Between 1945 and 1965, it is estimated that 11 million southern tenant farmers, sharecroppers and small farm owners moved off the farms. In the South, black sharecroppers totaled an estimated 541,000 in 1940, but by 1959 that number had dropped to an estimated 121,000. The drop was largely due to the development of farming machinery and chemicals that took the place of human labor.

SJ and Leonia Farrar - SJ: After we had the big lawsuit with our landowner who was trying to take all our money, we left the farm in 1949 and went to Durham. That was our first attempt to leave the farm. I got a job at Duke Hospital, in the dietetic department. I started off busing tables for the nurses and doctors in the dining room, and I worked myself up from there into the storage room. When I left there two and a half years later, I was supervisor of the storage room. There had never been a black man that held that position before. I was making $22.50 every two weeks, and my wife had to make do with that amount, to keep the kids going, but she didn't ever give up. I used to work two and three jobs. I would come home, get a cup of coffee, shut my eyes and lie down, then go right back out to another job. She would help me clean buildings.

I would walk from East Durham to Duke Hospital in the dead part of the winter. It would be so cold. I would get on the railroad track and walk four and a half miles from my house to Duke Hospital. I didn't have a dime to get a bus token, so I would walk there and back. I made friends at the hospital who sometimes would give me a ride home.

When I left the hospital at the end of 1951, we moved back to the country, back to a farm in Apex.

There was an acre of land adjoining the land where we were farming. I went to the landowner and asked him to sell me that acre of land. He said, "No way am I going to sell you that land." But I was determined to buy some land.

He came to my house one day and asked my wife where I was, and she told him I was fishing. I had the crops and everything up to date, so this was my time to take a break and go fishing. It was our form of recreation, to go fishing, sit by the creek. He told her that I should be there on that farm doing something. She told me about it when I got home.

He ran a country store nearby. That made me mad, so I went over to the store and I walked in, and I saw him there with another white man. I called his name and he stood up, "What do you want, SJ?"

I said, "As long as I live, don't you ever put your foot in my yard and tell my wife what to tell me. You are to have enough courage to tell me yourself and not tell her."

He said, "I'll have you know, when I walk in your front yard, that's my yard. You don't own anything. That's mine and when I talk to your wife on the porch, that's my porch."

(**Leonia**): It wasn't his porch because we had rented the house from year to year. That was the law then. That was ours. He had no right to come over there and make demands. (**SJ**): But he had that attitude. And from that moment, I said to myself, a man will never again stand in my front yard, at my front door and tell me to be home. That really motivated and inspired me to get something of my own. It was the same man who I had asked to sell me that acre of land, and he said no.

So I went out and got a job off the farm, working at Southern Building Supply in Raleigh as a truck driver. I went from a truck driver to a cabinet installer/helper. The owner and the manager took a liking to me, and they would let me do things that whites weren't supposed to allow blacks to do at that time. I had gotten to the point where I knew as much about installation as the white installer. Soon I had his job. I learned all of that carpentry work from being watchful.

One day one of our contractor customers came through the area where I was working, and he said to my boss, "What's SJ doing around that table? A black man's not supposed to do that work."

The manager said, "He's learning the trade, that's what he's doing."

He said, "As long as you keep that 'nigger' in this shop with a hammer in his hand, I'll never buy another thing from you." Two years later, that same customer wouldn't let anybody do his work but me.

In 1957, I came to Cary and started looking around. Some people my mother and father knew years ago introduced me to the Evans family. Evans Road was nothing like it is now. It was just a dirt road, all mud and hilly. I think there were only three or four houses on the road then. We purchased some property from Tilton Evans. There were two Evans brothers, Clyde and Tilton. Clyde owned some of the land and Tilton owned the other part from here down. We purchased our land from Tilton Evans.

(**Leonia**): When we came to look, this spot was beautiful, it just caught my eye. It had great big, beautiful oak trees. I said, "Let's buy that lot, and my sister can buy the lot over there. I love this lot. Let's get this one." He built a four-room home on our land. (**SJ**): It was 28' X 36'.

My brother Leroy lives right next door. My brother Paul lived three doors down from him on the other corner lot. Dynasty Road wasn't there then. When we offered to buy this land, we didn't have the money to buy it. For this acre and three-quarters, we paid $225. And I had to borrow $10 from my boss to pay down on it.

When I was working in Raleigh at Southern Builders, Mr. Pat Garner was the owner and Rock Cummings was the manager. They had always liked me. I went in and asked, "Mr. Garner, I want to buy an acre of land. I want to build a house on it."

He asked, "What do you need?"

I said, "I need $10 to pay down on the lot." He reached his hand into his pocket and pulled out $10. Mr. Pat said to me, "You can pay me when you can." That was the Lord working. He was a nice man. He was always good to us, always. And Mr. Rock Cummings was a hard driver, that's why they called him the Rock. But he was always nice to us, just as nice as he could be. When his wife died, he called us. We went to his wife's funeral. We were the only blacks there and it didn't matter, we were treated just like family.

I dug the foundation of that first house on Christmas Eve with a pick and shovel. There were all of these rocks. (**Leonia**): Over the years,

Farrar kept building onto our house because we kept having children. With every child, he added on a room, until I had my eighth child.

When you have seven or eight children, a mother can see something in each child as they grow. I told him, "Now we have had a hard time, I mean a hard time growing up on the farm. Our children are not going to grow up the way we did." I could see in every one of my children what they were cut out to be. I kept telling Farrar, "We have to get these children in school."

I worked in these white homes, cleaning. What little bit of money I made I would give to him. I was often paid with clothes.

I told him, "After I get our children in school, I am going to better myself." I love to fix hair, so after my last child started school, I wanted to go to beauty school.

Most of our children are educated. (**SJ**): What a struggle it was to get them through school. Carolyn was in college. Leonia was in beauty college and doing day work on someone's farm in the summertime. We kept sending our children on to school and sure enough, Carolyn accomplished her goals. She did it without a lot of fanfare. She never had a scholarship, she never had any money given to her, and never had any welfare. We never accepted any kind of social benefits, never. I wouldn't accept it. I wouldn't even apply for it.

(**Leonia**): The house that he built burnt down in 1885. Then we rebuilt our house on the same foundation. And we built a house close by for our daughter. We bought an existing house for her and had it moved onto an extra lot we had. When we had been here five years, his brother moved in next door. There are a lot of us in this area now.

(**SJ**): Once I got some training in cabinetmaking at Southern Builders, in 1972 I went into business for myself. We made it by being careful. The Lord had given me special talents and I built my business from them. I built the building at Old Apex Road and Chatham Street for my business. That used to be Farrar's cabinet shop. The tax base in Cary is high, and eventually it went beyond our profit line. So I sold that building and we moved out to a less populous place. Then I retired and turned it over to my sons.

I had no schooling. My wife had no schooling. All of our schooling has come later. I worked day and night. Then I decided to become a minister like my forefathers. I took my seminary courses on Saturday mornings when I should have been home resting, instead of sitting in a classroom, dead tired. I started in the ministry in 1957, the same year we moved to Cary. But we had all these kids in school. Since we sent Gwen through college, our youngest graduated from Livingstone College. That is the AME Zion church school which is fully accredited.

(**Leonia**): After Gwen finished her first year of school, I asked him to pay for my schooling at beauty college. He scared me to death. He said, "I'll send you to school, but you better not flunk. If you flunk, I'll kill you." When I graduated, I was the valedictorian of the class.

(**SJ**): At that time, I had been promoted to superintendent of 23 churches throughout the district. She would go with me and study while I would drive. It was 126 miles to my further point. I was working ten and twelve hours a day. (**Leonia**): I came out of school in 1971. After I graduated, I set up my own beauty shop right there, in my home. From then things started getting better and better for us. My husband built that beauty shop for me and I worked there for thirty-two years. Then I retired because I was sick of hair.

If you keep God in front of you, he'll open doors for you. I didn't have any idea I would be as far as I am today, and I wouldn't be if it weren't for him. I applied to be a teacher assistant for Gwen, my baby, in 1962. The Wake County Board of Education called me and said, "We need you to be out in the field. We're going to send you to school for about two or three months for training. We need you to go out and find all of the children that cannot go to school because they don't have the clothing or the shoes to go to school." They gave me a thick book of names and addresses. Most did not have phones back then. I took that book and went out and talked to the parents to see why their children couldn't go to school. I had to transport those children back and forth to the clinic myself. I was out there in the field doing social work. I did that for about two and a half years.

Then they wanted me to be the PTA president for East Cary Elementary School. I stayed on the list for twenty-three and a half years, and then they made me the district president. Then I was the PTA chaplain for West Cary Elementary School for two years. (It is Northwoods Elementary School now.) I guess the Lord knew what he wanted me to do to support him, because he is the preacher, I'm just the missionary. (**SJ**): She preaches to me.

She's the conference president of Missionary Outreach. We have 327 churches and she's chairman. (**Leonia**): I'm the conference director over the missionary department. I go out into the field to find the homeless. (**SJ**): She finds families who need food. She has a food bank in an out-building in our backyard. She finds food for people who don't have the resources to buy their own food. She tries to get clothing. She collects money and distributes it. (**Leonia**): I send money to famine, flood, or fire relief. I have even helped the Red Cross. I do all of that type of work.

Leroy and Betty Farrar – Leroy: In 1953, my brother-in-law was working in Raleigh for Farmer's Exchange. He knew I had planned to get off the farm. We were getting a crop of tobacco ready to go to market, and we had one more barn of tobacco to get ready when he came by to get me for a job in Raleigh. Betty said, "If you want to go take a job, you go ahead and the kids and I will finish this tobacco." Reynolds was Southern State Iron and Roofing Company at that time, it was not Reynolds Aluminum yet. So I went to Raleigh and started working with Reynolds Aluminum Supply Company. I drove a tractor and trailers for them for twenty-three years. I retired from Reynolds, and I'm still there working part-time. I plan to keep working until I get ready to go to heaven. I enjoy working.

I was a truck driver and warehouseman all together at Reynolds Aluminum. We would go out one day and deliver. Then we would come back in and put up stock in the warehouse. Then I would load my own truck in the afternoon and go back out the next day. We worked one day out and one day in. That was interesting, but a lot of hard work, driving all over North Carolina and some parts of South Carolina and some parts of Virginia. I got to meet a lot of people.

My brother SJ moved here one year before I did. He built his own house. I bought land right after he did and I started building mine too. But because I was driving a truck, I didn't have much time so we hired somebody to finish building our house.

Our house burned. His did too. Our house caught fire four years after it was built, in 1962. Then we rebuilt it and enlarged it somewhat. Betty was here when it happened and I was in Elizabeth City on the truck when it burned. (**Betty**): It started at a gas hot water heater that we had in the closet. When I got the children up to go to school, I discovered it was burning, so I called the fire department, and by the time they got here, there was lots of black smoke. You could hardly see in here. I tried to come back in to get some things, but they said, "No, you can't go in there." But they put it out before the house burnt down to the ground. The fire did a lot of damage inside. (**Leroy**): We had to rebuild it, so we added onto it. Things work out for the best at times, because we needed a little larger house. Our kids were growing up, so we took advantage.

I have five brothers that have built houses in this area. My brother Paul lived down the road before he passed away. I have a brother across the way. So we've come a long way. God has been good to us. We've had some ups and some downs.

I sing gospel too, all over the country. I do solos and then I sing with two groups in my church. My baby son is a minister and he has two kids that are ministers. Then I have another grandson that is a minister, and our oldest daughter, Berma, is a minister. We have a lot of ministers in our family and a lot of them sing too. All my kids and most of my grandkids sing. Tim plays the organ. I sing a cappella. Sometimes when he's not far from where I'm going to perform, I ask him to come and play for me. I recorded a record and he played for that. I recorded one record. My reason for doing that was because my father was a minister, and I don't have one sermon or song of his. He was a good singer, and I don't have anything of my father. I don't even have a picture of him. I decided I was not going to let that happen to me. I'm going to have something left when I'm gone for the kids and my grandkids. That's the reason I recorded that record, so I'd have something to leave for others, letting people know that I passed this way. I've had so many people ask me to continue to record and I don't want any part of it. I've been asked to go out and just sing for a living, but I don't want to live that way. That's kind of a hard life. I know it has to be hard.

CHAPTER 4

OTHER AFRICAN-AMERICAN OCCUPATIONS IN CARY BEFORE DESEGREGATION

George Bailey: My Evans ancestors came from Wales and settled in Yorktown. An Evans genealogist documented her family to when they started marrying Indians. We branched off from the white Indian side of the Evans' and we can trace our family all the way to present, based on those documentations. So we go from Wales to Yorktown, and then throughout North Carolina, with descendants starting in 1675 when the first Evans was born in York County, Virginia. When they moved from Virginia as landowners, they moved to Chatham County, North Carolina to buy land.

The Evans' were never slaves, not that I know of. They married free Indians who married freed slaves. Most people don't know that there was a lot of inter-marriage between people in the 1800s. It was not just a black and white or Indian society. The Evans' came from England, married whites and married Indians here. Indians married blacks, and they married whites. My great-grandfather Charlie was Indian and part white. His wife was Indian but looked white. Now their children married Indian or black, and then other generations have married Indian, white, black, or whatever.

Our basic history starts with my great-grandparents, Charlie and Mathilda Evans, who settled in Chatham County, North Carolina. Charlie and Mathilda moved from Chatham County to Cary. Charlie was an entrepreneur, a horse trader and a horse doctor. Charlie purchased a total of 100 acres of land. They bought 75 acres of land initially for $10.00 an acre. He purchased 25 more acres later. His land is on Old Apex Road, near High House Road. The original blocks of land are over near

Duchess Village, which is the subdivision my brother Herbert and I developed, and where the family cemetery is located. My grandfather, Clyde Evans Sr., bought a hundred acres on Evans Road. Then his brothers, Herbert Evans and Loveless Evans, migrated to Evans Road too and bought land either from Clyde or from somebody else. When Clyde Sr. died, he passed his land on to my mom, his daughter Mamie Bailey, and all the relatives. The Baileys, as with my grandfather Evans and his father before him, had been very tied to the land. We have tried to retain land ownership as one of our basic principles.

My grandfather Clyde never called himself a farmer. He disliked that. He was a pulp-wood man. Now, he did a lot of farming, he had a big garden. He had corn, he raised tobacco, he raised pigs, and he sold his produce as well, but he was not a farmer. He was a pulp-wood man. He just could not relate to being a farmer as his occupation. He did deal in a lot of timber.

Evans Estates is on my grandfather Clyde's land, so, there will always be an Evans on Evans Road. When we tore my grandfather's house down, I took a log from that house and put it in my house. It carries the point load from the foundation up to the ceiling which supports my roof. So I have now established a foundation that was from my grandfather, from the base of my house to the base of the roof.

Clyde Evans Jr.: The Evans family is of Indian decent. We came out of Chatham County. My grandfather, Charlie Evans, had taken up many acres of land between High House Road and Highway 54. Then when my father and other members of the family were grown, he cut the land up into plots and gave each one twenty-five or thirty acres of that land. It all stayed in the family.

My grandfather was tall and light complexioned. He was a horseman and he worked for rich folks. His job was to dress up real nice and haul these people from one place to another in a carriage, as a carriage driver.

My grandmother's father was a Blackfoot Indian. He was dark, not black but dark and weighed about 140 pounds. He had a braid down his back. He owned two or three hundred acres of land in New Hill. There were very few black people in that territory. Most of them were half-Indian, half-white, half-breeds. My grandmother was a midwife. She appeared to be white with long, blonde hair. Mathilda was her name, and my grandfather was Charlie Evans. He dealt in timber and firewood. My father, Clyde Evans Sr., got into that business.

I was raised in the woods with forestry, logging, pulp, and lumber. My father stayed away from home some. He dealt in veneer timber used to build furniture. Huge trees were cut into five-foot lengths. They used to load the lumber right there on the Southern Railroad track. Our agent was from Highpoint, from the furniture factory. If someone had a hundred acres of land, he would go and crew the timber. They called it "crew" the timber, which means to find out how much timber on the land is valuable. Furniture used to be built out of poplar, now its maple and so forth. We dealt in some maple, but not too much. Daddy had to go where the trees were, and he went by horse and wagon. If it was ten or fifteen miles away, he couldn't get home, he had to find a place to stay near where he was working, and come home on weekends. He used to do a lot of work around Wake Forest. Daddy and Buck Jordan's father used to work together. He'd hire Daddy to go with him, and that's when Daddy learned how to crew timber. The Jordan family came into Cary and developed it.

There used to be two or three sawmills around Cary. Today the timber is hauled to the mill, but the mill used to come to us years ago. He would buy a section of trees, choose the trees he wanted and cut them down. Then there were folks who would move the sawmill to that place. He would haul them to the mill by horses and mules. I remember my father with carts, bringing them out to the road, loading them on a wagon, carrying them up to the mill. That was a long time ago. He dealt in timber all his life. We children would do the farming, what little farming was done. He kept us busy all the time doing something. Most of the blacks in Cary didn't own property. Most of them lived on white people's properties, as tenant farmers and so forth. But we weren't tenant farmers because we owned our own land.

I used to take care of Henry Adams' yard. He was living in what you would call an old slave house between Cary and Morrisville. I believe that house is still there. It was a big two-story house, small in diameter but tall. The first time I ever drove a car was Henry Adams' car. He ran the drugstore, and he had a nice, fine car. My sister used to work at Ashworth Drugstore. Ralph Ashworth is a very fine fellow. The Heater family drilled wells over this whole territory. I worked for R.O. Heater. I used to know everybody in Cary by first and last name, white and black.

Linda Evans: Daddy, Clyde Evans Jr., loved working on automobiles and he was a lumber man. He could go out and cut a tree, and lay it within inches of where he would want it to fall. He was really smart, even though he did not have much education.

Daddy would say, "These Evans' were some hard-working men." My granddaddy, Clyde Sr., taught them how to work. Daddy built the oldest side of this house fifty-five years ago and brought the family here. This land, which is one and a half acres, is land that was given to him by his mother and father. They allotted so much for each child. When they moved into this house, my sister Gail, the third child, had already been born. Then as the family grew, Daddy decided to add onto the house. There are eight of us. He did a really good job.

My daddy used to have a club in our basement of the house on Evans Road, called the Pasadena Club. People still talk about that club to this day because it was their entertainment. Family, friends, and people we knew in the area would come. Daddy had live bands, and they would jam. And the food he had was magnificent. He had a bar down there, with beer and liquor. I remember the big jugs of hot sausages and pickles. He would have bags of potato chips hanging from little metal hangers. Of course, we would sneak down there sometimes and steal a pickle. It was a very popular club.

The club wasn't anything official. Everybody came and it was packed every weekend. I think Daddy ran the club for fifteen years. Sometimes Mama would go down and cook some of the food, fry chicken or whatever. He charged people an admission charge, and he also charged for the food, so that was a way of making a living.

I remember the jukebox. I think it cost a nickel to get a song. I wish we still had that jukebox. Sometimes the music would get loud, and there we were, kids upstairs trying to sleep. So Daddy said any time it got too loud, we should take the broom handle and hit the floor, boom, boom, boom. We should hit it three times and he would cut the sound down. I remember having to hit - boom, boom, boom – because it was getting too loud. Then they would quiet down a little bit. He had that club in the fifties to sixties. It was just open on weekends. I remember the cigarette smoke. People parked in the bigger parking lot at the side of the house. It was something.

It provided a way of making a living. Daddy had eight kids to feed, and he provided for us. Daddy would make a way. He put the roof over our heads and made sure there was food on the table.

Bertha Pleasants Daniel: My brother Robert was the sheriff in Cary until he retired. Robert was a real good guy.

Clyde Evans Jr.: I owned a nightclub. I have a full basement under this house, running from front to back, as large as the house. One night, the sheriff of Cary for 35 years, Robert Pleasants, came out here. We always talked and discussed things. He said, "Clyde, you know we're segregated and we've got a problem. I want to make a bargain with you."

I said, "Yes, I'll listen to that."

He said, "Clyde, what I want you to do, we want to keep all you black folks on this side of Cary. If I keep all the black folks on this side of Cary, we won't have any problems at all." And he was right.

The Evans' and the white people understood one another. We associated with them and developed with them. They left us alone to tend our business, and they didn't bother with us. The black folks were treated very nice by the white folks of Cary. There was no tension in Cary at all. I've never known an incident that happened in Cary between the black and the white. They left us alone. We stayed in our own district.

Herbert Bailey: My grandfather had no formal schooling or training, but he acquired reading skills and some math skills. As I recall, he died with $10,500 in cash (to him, "plenty of money,") and his original farm tract today is worth approximately $10 million. That figure would have boggled his mind if he had lived to see it. He bought the farm for $10.00 an acre. He cut the timber on the land to pay for it, and earned the full purchase price of $1,000. My grandmother promoted the deal, because she was a real lover of land.

I harvested tobacco for my grandfather Evans from the time that I could physically manage the job. I probably began working for him at the age of ten or twelve. I worked for some other people too, tending tobacco.

In the fifties, our primary source for fuel to heat the house was wood. At the dead-end of Evans Road there was a sawmill. We could go down there and get slabs of wood for free. Slabs were the part of the log cut off to make the wood square so it could be cut into boards. There are four slabs from every log. We drove down there and hauled slabs back home. My grandfather, Clyde Evans Sr., had a '36 Ford truck. If he jacked it off the ground on one side, he would put a belt across the rear tire and put a circular saw on the other end of the belt. We would start the truck up and the wheel would turn the saw. Then we put it on a platform with a handle and we lifted the platform and pushed the slabs into the saw. It would cut off 18" pieces of slab pine wood that we used for cooking and to heat the house. Timber was cut off the farm land to build and to heat my father's house. My parents finally got an oil heater. We had gardens, chickens, and some livestock. We were, and continue to be, proudly self-sufficient.

My father, Joe Bailey, was a chauffeur for the government in Norfolk, Virginia for his first job. My mother, Mamie Evans Bailey, was a welder in the Norfolk navy yard, working on aircraft carriers and destroyers during World War II. They met there and married, and I was born there in 1945. I was only a few months old when we moved back to the farm in Cary. We stayed with my Evans grandparents for about two years.

At that time, Evans Road was unpaved. When my great grandmother, my grandmother's mother died, they had to carry her out on a stretcher to Highway 54 because the weather was bad, with snow was on the ground. Shortly after this event, my mother and father built the house on Evans Road.

My first recollection of working was for my dad as a plumber. He installed plumbing in country houses which were generally very close to the ground, so he had to dig a trench under the house to the area of work. Indoor plumbing was becoming more available, and he installed all the pipes under the house.

They only had cast iron pipe at that time and it had to be cut. The joints were lead and oakum. They didn't have any kind of rubber seal yet, so they had to use molten lead to seal the joints. Molten lead melts at about 700-800 degrees, and it cools very quickly. To melt the lead they used a propane "lead pot." While the lead is molten, we had to very quickly carry it to the needed place. My job was to bring the molten lead to Daddy, and I had to get it to him faster than it would cool. So I would crawl down the trench that he dug underneath the house. Because lead is extremely heavy, I had to hold my left hand with my right hand to be able to carry it, and do a kind of leapfrog crawl, where I would move it in, set it down, move it in and set it down until I got to where he was working.

Being from the other side of the track, sometimes jobs were hard to hold. One morning in the 1950s I asked him, "Dad, why did you have to leave so early?" He said he had to make sure he could get to work on time because the jobs were really valuable. He indicated his salary was $50.00 a week. I asked him why he had to leave in the dark. He said he left so early so that, if his pickup broke down, he could still walk to work. He worked near the intersection of Wade Avenue and U.S. 1.

One morning, I said, "Dad, where are you going today?"

He said, "I'm going to NC State University to work, and I really don't want to go. I've been there four months and I've got four months to go."

I said, "What are you doing?"

He said, "I'm digging a ditch."

I said, "How deep is it?"

He said, "I don't know, but I can tell you, I have to throw the dirt three times before I can throw the dirt out of the ditch." So he had to dig that ditch three times.

I asked, "How long is the ditch?"

He said, "It's from NC State University to Cameron Village." It took him eight months to dig that ditch with a pick and shovel, by hand.

I said, "Dad, why don't you quit?"

He said, "Son, I have five kids."

As a child, my dad experienced prejudice to the –nth degree. He grew up in a family who did not like him. His mother died when he was nine, so he was raised by aunts and uncles on his mother's side, in Faison, North Carolina. My dad said he had seen times when he would have to steal fatback out of the frying pan at home to eat.

My dad is gone now, but he was probably one of the most intelligent men that I have ever met, and he had a drive that was stronger than a locomotive coming down hill with a full load. He was unbelievably relentless; he was always hustling. He was an entrepreneur and he was a survivor.

In 1963 I graduated from high school. My graduation day was on a Saturday, and my mother graduated from Shaw University on Friday, the day before me. After high school, I went off to college and graduated, and all four of my sisters and brothers behind me, (Constance, George, Ray, and Carolyn,) graduated from college too. We were among the first college-educated Evans generation of children.

George Bailey: My daddy tried to get his journeyman's card in the city of Raleigh as a plumbing contractor. They had a series of tests which required you to pull and wipe some lead joints. He knew that he had passed this exam, but he had to take it over three times. The third time they finally gave it to him. It was his persistence that allowed him to get his license and to make his livelihood. From there, he started Capital City Plumbing.

My dad used to tell me stories. This is not one of those good stories, but it tells you how he played in the scenario of segregation. My father was always an entrepreneur and owned his own companies from about 1963, starting with plumbing companies that worked in major complexes. He was basically doing utilities, running underground water pipe and sewer pipe. Daddy had a contract with one of the largest builders in North Carolina. One day, he was on one of his jobs, and he met the developer who had a group of other white men around him. During the conversation that ensued, two or three times the developer called Daddy the N-word. The conversation was pertaining to something on the job. "You blah blah this, you blah blah that." At that time, segregation and Jim Crow were heavy in Raleigh, North Carolina. Daddy had had problems several times in Raleigh.

Daddy was a very shrewd man, and for somebody who only had a ninth grade education, he excelled in business. The unique thing about my dad is that he always knew when he couldn't handle something, and when he would run into a problem. He had several businesses in which he had a white partner. Daddy owned 51% of the business, but he was not out in front on any of the business deals, he was in the background. Being black, you couldn't be out in front on a major business deal in North Carolina. That just wasn't going to cut it. As times got better, he had partnerships in various companies where he was out in front. When he passed away, I'll put it this way, he wasn't poor.

At one time there was a big sign out in the field on I-70, "Johnston County, the home of the KKK." I grew up with that. My daddy had a job at the prison in Johnston County at that time, and he had three pieces of equipment there. Somebody poured sugar in the fuel tanks, which actually makes a piece of equipment worthless if you run it long enough. You can't repair it, you have to basically throw it away. I know what it was, it was racism. There were a lot of people down there who didn't like that my father won the contract, so they put sugar in his tanks.

Mama basically handled the office, and Daddy had to work the system. Daddy had contacts with everyone in the town of Cary. He donated money to the fire department and so forth, but during segregation, we were kept under toe. We went to all segregated schools. We were never out in the forefront of anything. We constantly worked so we didn't have time to be politicians. The Evans' weren't really politicians as such, out there in the forefront of the desegregation movement. We experienced it, but we were sheltered from it by our upbringing. Daddy had to confront it every day in his businesses when dealing with people. Mother only confronted it on small occasions, because she was not out there in the business world.

<u>Sallie Jones</u>: During World War II, my brother was drafted into the service. A number of the guys were called up for the draft. The people used to put a star in the window letting you know they had somebody serving. I know that everyone here out of our community came back, but some of them were never the same because of what they had seen and experienced.

My brother was a mechanic in France, working on tanks. He was involved in the Battle of the Bulge. At that time, black soldiers were not trained to fight, but the units were losing men so fast, he said, that they just came by and threw them all guns and said, "Come on." Most of them had done some hunting and knew something about a gun.

My younger brother was drafted in 1944 and was stationed in Germany. One of the stories he told was that, on a weekend break, he and some of his guys had decided that they were not going to go off base. They were so tired from working all week that they decided to stay in their barracks. Just about dark, some MPs came in, pointed at my brother and said, "That's the one." They took my brother into the woods in the snow and abandoned him. They just left him there, and he didn't know where he was. He had to wander back on his own, and he couldn't speak German. A person who was in the barracks with him came looking for him. As he was running, trying to find his way back, his friend found him, and led him back to the barracks. Otherwise, he said he would have frozen to death. They must have found out that he was the wrong person, because he didn't get out of service until he had fulfilled his time, so he must not have been in trouble with the army. He knew he hadn't done anything. He had not been out of the barracks all day. He was never the same after he returned home.

Carolyn Rogers: My dad's older brothers were all sharecroppers. My Uncle Willie, who was the youngest of the brothers, worked for Roy's Rental for awhile. My Uncle Leroy is the talented singer. My dad is a minister. I come from a long line of preachers, singers and musicians. When Uncle Leroy left farming, he still had a huge garden in his backyard. He ended up working for Reynolds Aluminum Company. Uncle Calvin is a minister too, and lives on Rochelle Road. He used to work for Mayflower Moving Company. Uncle Paul worked for J.C. Penney in Durham. They all left the farm when they moved to Cary and have led very successful lives.

Leroy Farrar: When I left the farm the first time, I went in the army and stayed for six years during World War II. I served in the European theaters; Germany, Belgium, and France. I was on my way to the Pacific when the Japanese surrendered. We were on the way to Japan and we had just reached the Panama Canal when the Japanese surrendered. I had a German guitar at that time, and I play a little bit.

When we heard that news, we had a ball on that ship, because we knew we were going to be sent home. We didn't know it was going to come that quick. Our ship turned around and came back to New York, so I didn't ever have to go to the Pacific.

I was in the quartermaster outfit. We transferred backwards and forwards, but I didn't ever have to go to the front lines. We could hear the battles going on, though. A lot of my friends didn't come back home, but I was one of the blessed ones that came back. One of the most frightful things while I was in service was the snipers. They were back behind the lines and they were there to die or to kill you. I was never shot at by a sniper, and I never had to shoot anybody either.

Then I came home and eventually married Betty. I've known her all of her life. She was eighteen when we got married and I was twenty-two. We got married in 1948 and continued on the farm as sharecroppers for maybe five years. Then we left the farm and moved to Cary. We bought land and built a house here, and we've been here ever since. We have six children. We have fifteen grandchildren and four great-grandchildren.

Gwen Matthews: I only knew my grandmother on my father's side. Down Lake Wheeler Road there used to be peach orchards and tobacco. I recently found out that my grandmother and her children worked those farms. They went from place to place picking peaches, and did not have a house to live in, per se'. They lived on whatever farm would take them in and they worked there until they moved on to the next farm.

I grew up with an extended family surrounding me. Whoever had money or food, we all shared what we had. We lived on the same road. Our house was on the corner, and next door lived my grandmother, and next to her lived my father's brother, and next to him lived my father's other brother. Then Daddy's sisters lived a little further up the road. We weren't poor in the way that people might think of being poor. We had no money. There were times when we ate a lot of very simple foods. We had very little meat sometimes, but it wasn't anything we thought about because everybody we knew didn't always have meat.

My grandmother always had food because she cleaned homes. Every home she worked in considered her part of the family. She could ask any family whose home she worked in for anything and they would give it to her, so her Sunday meals were great. We all ate Sunday meals at Grandma's house, because she had chicken and all kinds of things. They also had a small farm so we were able to get food there. It was a very simple way of life. My father had a car. So we weren't poor, but we really weren't middle class by any stretch of the imagination.

My father worked in plumbing and at a fabric place. His last job was at a blueprint company. When he was young, my father wanted to be a lawyer, but he said at that time there was no such thing as integration. I think that was why I had to go to Cary High, because there were things he wanted to do but he felt that because of the system that was in place, he could not do them. He did not have the money to go to college, anyway.

Daddy was a very intelligent man. He could have been a good lawyer because he had a way with words. I used to be in 4H, and my father would write my speeches. If I wrote a speech, I might get second place, but if my father wrote it, I would get first place every time. He was just wonderful with words, and can hold a conversation with anybody on any subject and know exactly what he was talking about. So he was a very bright man and it's a shame that he couldn't become a lawyer.

Robert Heater: Our housekeeper, Geneva Edwards, is 75 and has been working for us now for forty years. Her daddy worked with us until he died. During the Depression, Daddy couldn't pay him. They'd work together, and on Saturday they'd go to the grocery store and Daddy would buy groceries for both families. I don't know when Herman started working for Daddy. When I was young, Herman would get after me just like I was one of his children. I've got pictures of him, and he was a really good looking man. Sometimes Daddy would ask Herman to drive us somewhere. Herman would go home, take a bath and put on his suit and necktie. He looked smart as a whip.

During the war, they sent him out to drill a well at Hurdle Mills between Hillsborough and Roxboro. He was well respected in that community. They would contract with him and they would pay him to do the work and he'd bring it home. He saved money for three years doing his own contracting and collecting, and for a black man to do that in those days was unheard of. Herman was as fine a human as ever walked on this earth. Geneva is as fine a woman as ever walked this earth. They just don't come any better.

The Seegers - Fred: When the mail came through and was dropped off at the depot in Cary, the Cottons had a little cart that they pulled. They would bring the mail from the depot up to the post office. The mail came twice a day. So Cotton and Evalina, an African-American couple, would bring the mail up to the post office in the cart, and it was sorted and put in the boxes or general delivery or wherever it should go. If you wanted to know if the mail had come yet that day, you would just ask around if anybody had seen Cotton and Evalina today. If somebody had seen them, that would mean that they had brought the mail up from the depot to the post office.

(**Marie**): During the war, Evalina was the person who delivered the telegrams. All the people in Cary that had children in service lived in fear of her coming to their house because most telegrams were for people being notified of casualties from the war. Any time they ever saw her walking around with a telegram, they immediately knew that it was terrible news. My mother had two sons, one in the army and one in the navy. My younger brother, who was in the army, was in forty-eight battles in the European theater. Even as little children, we were always so afraid when we saw Evalina because she might be bring us very, very bad news.

CHAPTER 5

THE SEGREGRATED COMMUNITY

Bruce Roberts: When I moved to Birmingham, I noticed there is such a difference between North Carolina and Alabama in that the old South is still there in Alabama, whereas North Carolina just had a different feel about it. A large part of that, I think, is that there are mostly small farms and not the big plantations like those in Alabama. I was told when I came here, North Carolina is a "valley of humility between two mountains of conceit," (meaning Virginia and South Carolina.)

Ralph Ashworth: We didn't have much of a black community in Cary, but here in the segregated South, it was very bad. It was segregated until sometime in the sixties, and we got here in 1957. At that time African-Americans did not sit down and eat at our soda fountain. There were no signs or anything. It was just understood that they shouldn't do that, but they could carry everything out. Those were the bad times. But African-Americans did come to Ashworth Drugstore to get their drugs.

There were no black businesses or stores in Cary when we first got here. There may have been some in the early days. Many of them were farmers, and they didn't live right in town. There were a couple of churches that still exist, right down the street and one on Evans Road that were active and still are.

The schools were still segregated when we arrived. I guess things really started to change when the schools integrated in the sixties. It just changed gradually over time, when the Civil Rights movement really began. In the South, you started to see 'white only' and 'black only' and public restroom signs taken down. Then the sit-in in Greensboro took place. When all these events were going on in North Carolina, it just kind of faded away. There was not one specific day when it ended. It just evolved to being much better. That was not a good time in our history.

THE AFRICAN-AMERICAN EXPERIENCE:

Mary Shelton: My mama is black and my father was white. My father was born in Colfax and my mother was born in Williamston, North Carolina. They were both deaf and mute. They met at the only school for the deaf, the Governor Morehead School for the Deaf, Dumb and Blind in Raleigh. There was only one deaf school, and it was not segregated. They stayed there nine months out of the year, and then they went back to their perspective farms three months a year.

As a mixed race couple, they were not allowed to get married, they wouldn't get permission. So they moved to Michigan, and waited until both sets of parents died on both sides, and then they got married in Michigan. So they didn't get married until they were in their thirties.

My mom didn't work, she was a housewife. My dad made ball bearings for cars. At the deaf school, he learned carpentry, and he built his own home when he was sixty-five. It was just amazing that he could remember all those carpentry skills that he had learned in North Carolina when he was young.

My mama is still alive, she is 95. My dad passed away in 1998. I buried him in Colfax, North Carolina, next to his mom and dad in a private cemetery. Even though they lived all these years married, his family refused to allow my mother to be buried next to him. And that was in 1998.

Clyde Evans Jr.: Cars were rather scarce, and poor people basically didn't have a car until the latter part of the twentieth century. If you couldn't afford a car, you used a wagon and horses. You had horses to ride, and a mule or a horse to pull the wagon. I went to church many times in a two-horse wagon. We tied the horses up in front of the church, right on Kildare Farm Road. When I was young, our school and our church were behind old Cary High School. The church moved to Evans Road later. It was an independent church at one time, but it is now the United Church of Christ.

When I was about ten or twelve years old, I would catch a train from Cary to Raleigh for ten cents. I couldn't understand why they would stop a big train like that for a few dimes. We went to the movies in Raleigh and then caught the train and came back home. The movie cost about fifteen cents. All the theaters in Raleigh were segregated, though.

We appreciated more in my early days. We appreciated morning, noon and night the food we had to eat. We would eat certain foods only on Sunday, because it was a special day. I was here before the

Depression, in Hoover's time. My father would go take care of a neighbor who maybe had a problem with his crop. People would get together and have a corn shucking, or to build tobacco barns or a house. We would sit up all night long shucking corn, or building a house or a tobacco barn out of logs. People would combine as a unit to build all these things and help a neighbor.

It was hard times here but we survived them. Fatback was two cents a pound. Hamburger meat was three cents a pound. You would work a whole week for a dollar and a half, two dollars.

We kept to ourselves. We were not allowed to be out at night, we were supposed to be home. At night you would never catch us away from home. We'd start running hard if it was on the verge of getting dark. I never got caught. We'd be punished for that. They wouldn't punish you physically. They would just say, "Now, you didn't do what you were told. Now you aren't going to go out after dark anymore." That was the punishment they gave. We were only associated with brothers and sisters and cousins. We liked going to the baseball game sometimes, but we had to be back by dark. Everywhere we went had to be within walking distance. We had no other way to get there unless we could ride a horse or get on a wagon.

Dr. Templeton was a little, short fellow. He owned land from the school on Academy Street to Raleigh on the south side of Highway 54 and Western Blvd. My father was a caretaker for their land. He was our family doctor. Dr. Yarborough was a heck of a fine doctor. He was my daddy's doctor, and we'd take care of the Yarboroughs, by keeping them in wood and so forth. My daddy told me a story once about how Dr. Yarborough said, "Clyde, when did you have a physical?"

Daddy said, "I've never had a physical, why? Do I need one? First, let me run something past you. I've got two children I have never paid you for."

The doctor said, "Clyde, I don't care about that, but I will give you a physical." I don't know if Daddy ever took that physical or not. Daddy died in 1993. Dr. Yarborough had two offices, one for the black race and one for white. He had a walk-through from the house to his office.

We lived in isolation more or less, from other people. We lived in a kind of circle with our neighbors who were black folks. My father didn't like to associate too much. I never ate a meal away from home until I was over twenty years old. All the Evans' were well thought of.

My mother appeared to be white with long, blonde hair. Now in our family, we have a lot of folks who could go for white just as well as they could go for black. I know of several incidents where they were stopped by police. They had a lot of black children in the car with them and the officer would question them. He said, "Are you going to lower yourself to that extent, to say you're a black person and you're white?"

She said, "I'm not white. I might look white, but I'm not, I'm black." Well, you don't pay any attention to it. That's just the officer's opinion.

In this territory, we were treated extremely well. We would always segregate ourselves with black and white. We'd associate with both, but when it came to family, we huddled in a group. But to achieve certain things in life, you have to leave your domain and venture out. You can't do it in your own circle. You had to live with someone with greater experiences to teach you those things.

I built this house when I first got married. I built it by myself and with help from the community. My father gave me this land when I got married. He gave all his children a lot of two acres of land right on Evans Road. We sell land here now. We have a development down the street called Evans Estate.

I cut the trees out of that road. There was an old stagecoach going through here. My father bought a hundred acres of land here. I was reared right down the street. I was about ten or twelve years old when I came here. My old home was down the street, an old log house that was converted to part plank and part logs. It was built a long time ago. When they put in the Evans Estate road, they tore the house down.

I treasure that part of my life. I was living on High House Road from birth until I was ten or twelve. Then we moved over here and I lived in that old house until I got married. I plowed corn at the old home place. I sold some land across the street to a developer. We had land to Highway 54. The school is on Evans property, and it started out as a segregated school, as West Cary High School. Then when the town changed its philosophy, it got to be a mixed school.

We have a family cemetery on the corner of High House Road and Old Apex Road. All our people and some outsiders are buried there. I expect to be buried there too. My grandfather and all my uncles and aunts are buried there. It is named the Evans Internal Cemetery.

We always said Evans' were rich. We were rich in heritage, not in money. Our heritage made us rich. We were never highly educated people. I have a few in the family now who are highly educated. I have eight children. I have twin boys who live in Raleigh, one daughter in Atlanta and two more in Raleigh. My daughter Linda is working on her degree. She is living next door. Two of my children have died. My daughter in Raleigh finished at the state college out of Greenville, North Carolina.

Linda Evans: Evans Road was just a dirt road with only a few families on it. My father's parents and some of the brothers and sisters lived just down the road. Not all of them settled here, some moved away, but we were very close as a family. My Aunt Sally is Mamie Bailey. Her sons developed Evans Estates. She has children that are just a year apart from each of us. She had five children, and we grew up together and we would play.

The property right next to us was vacant, so we would build see-saws. We didn't have all the toys and everything. We didn't know any different. We didn't even know we were poor. We lived off the farm, off the land, so we always had something to eat. We never went hungry, and I'm so thankful for that. My grandfather farmed so our table was set. We always thought we were rich, we really did.

We didn't have a lot of association with the outside world. Our life was on Evans Road and the school we went to, and our neighbors. We grew up together, we played together, we fought together, we went to school together, so it was a close-knit community. We had a lot of fun.

Granddaddy farmed some tobacco. He had a mule that would get loose and run up Evans Road like he was on fire. All of us kids would be outside playing, and we would scramble to get in the house because we were so afraid of that mule. Then here would come Granddaddy on his tractor, coming to track down that mule. Then we would see him going back down the road on the tractor with the mule pulled behind.

I remember going to Winn Dixie for groceries, where Sorrell's is now on Harrison Avenue. Our parents would park behind the store and go into the back door to get the groceries, and then come out the back of the store and fill the car up with bags. I think the store was segregated because they would come out the back.

I remember a small grocery store on Highway 54, right across from the American Legion, called Terrell's Groceries. My mother would go into that store for groceries sometimes, and she walked down the aisles. It was owned by a white man, but James, who worked in the meat department, was black. My mother would go in there to buy meat and other things.

I remember going to King's Department Store in Raleigh when we lived in Cary. King's Department Store had segregated bathrooms, for colored and whites. They had separate water fountains too, one for coloreds and one for whites. Going there was the first time I had ever encountered segregation. My sister and I drank from the white water fountain, so that was our little private way of saying, "Pooh. I can drink anywhere I want. I can drink water from anybody's water fountain."

When we were small we used to love to go to Raleigh to visit my mother's parents, because that was an outing for us. All of us would get in the car, Daddy would drive of course, and we'd go to Raleigh to see Grandma. It seemed as though it took hours to get there. The streets were paved but there were no houses. There was only one road going into Raleigh, lined with trees. When we got into Raleigh we would see houses. Going to Raleigh was exciting because it was like a trip out of town.

Mom would shop in Raleigh, going to the different stores. My mother did a lot of sewing and she would make our clothes. A lot of times my mother would go to a second-hand place called the Bargain Box in Cameron Village. We didn't have a lot of money, but she knew how to be thrifty, and how to take a dollar and turn it into something really beautiful. She could get us a pair of shoes, and they would be used but she would clean them up, and to us they were brand new. We really appreciated what we got.

Occasionally we went to the movies, to the Ambassador Theater in downtown Raleigh. It's not there anymore. We would sneak in there and watch the movies. That was exciting.

When I was eleven years old, we left Cary and Evans Road, and moved near my grandparents in Raleigh because my parents were getting a divorce. Daddy stayed in Cary because of his ties here. He could not leave his land. He built this house, it was his. My mother was from Raleigh, so of course she felt more comfortable at home. They bought a house in Raleigh for us, and we grew up in Raleigh.

We never had a problem mixing with the white kids. And we never seemed to run into a lot of the racial slurs or the racial problems until integration time. Of course, our schools were predominantly black, so we didn't have a mix there. We had some neighbors that were white, but they were just our neighbors and it was okay. But my family is mixed. We have a lot of Indian and a lot of white blood in the family, so some of us are fair-skinned and some of us are brown-skinned, some have long, pretty straight hair and some have short, curly blonde hair. So a lot of people, some black people and some white people, thought we were half-breeds. We didn't consider ourselves to be so segregated because we had such a mix already within our family. Then when the Civil Rights movement began, we really started to see what was going on out there in the world.

Raleigh was the city, and Cary was "country." My mother never could get acclimated to living in Cary. She was part of the reason we had streetlights on the road. She went out and fought for them. She said we needed streetlights, so we got streetlights because she petitioned for them with the town of Cary. She initiated a few things to kind of civilize this part of Cary, because she was from Raleigh where they already had those things.

In Cary, when night came we would do our homework and then go to bed, because there were no lights on the street, so we went to bed early. When we moved to Raleigh we could hang out on the street because there were streetlights. We could sit out there on the curb and have our little parties right there on the corner. It was fun. Isn't it amazing how things can be so different from just right up the road.

Our entertainment was mostly centered around activities going on at school. If there was a dance or something, we'd be excited about going. I picked up my mother's trade of sewing, I love to sew, and I began to make my own clothes. When there were some big events coming up, I would always make my outfits for them. There were social organizations like the Blue Review and they would have dances and little fund-raisers for the young kids. I got involved in a lot of things like that, and they were fun.

Very few of us had access to a car. You were really bourgeoisie if you had a car and drove it to school. You were considered rich if you had a car to drive to school. Most of us came to school on the bus or we walked.

Herbert Bailey: I remember when Maynard Road didn't exist and when Kildaire farm was a farm. I remember when Harrison Avenue was called Allen Hill, or whatever it was, and it dead-ended. I remember when the center of town was the area around Ashworth's Drugstore and Hobby's Appliances, and when Cary had only one blinking caution light. I remember when Cary was a southern town, and was not occupied by the North.

I can only speak for my side of the track where it was an isolated, neighborly place where we knew everybody. If your house burned down, the neighbors helped to rebuild it. My father's barn burned down and the family helped build another one. When the barn caught fire, our white horse was inside, standing at the door. He would come to the door but then back up, start toward the door and back up. Finally the barn was consumed with the horse still inside, so he died. A horse was a valuable commodity back then.

I remember when the cross-country gas line came through, and I played in the ditch in the evenings when the gas company crews left. That gas line runs very close to the intersection of Silvergrove Drive in the Silverton subdivision, it goes through the Food Lion intersection of Harrison and Maynard, and finally it runs close to Crabtree Bridge in Morrisville. There was a creek that was in the Silverton area, and on that creek there was an extremely large bank. The gas company crews had a massive excavation there. You hear about how in past times, Indians always lived on a creek. After that gas line went through, for years and years we found arrowheads on that gas line route. I found ten or twenty myself. We collected them and saved them. The creek has changed and the subdivision has been built on it now, so all of that is gone.

As a child, we had to walk from here to Highway 54 and Maynard (but then there was no Maynard.) Evans Road at one time dead-ended into Highway 54. There was a place on that corner called Stone's Barbeque, a combination barbeque restaurant and grocery store. We would save our money all week long to buy a Tootsie pop at Stone's Barbeque. I remember once I got off the school bus and headed to Stone's to get a Tootsie pop. The bus drove away and I took off up the street behind the bus, when a car hit me. I remember going up in the air, and coming down, and the man who hit me was panicked. When I woke up, the man loaded me into his car and said he wanted to take me to the hospital, but I said, "No, no, no. Take me to my granddaddy." And so he drove me to my granddaddy's house. I wasn't badly hurt.

Carolyn Rogers: I remember going to a movie once in Apex. At that time it was segregated, so you had to go upstairs to the balcony. I think it cost 10¢ for the movie. There was a store in Apex we would all go to called John Beasley's General Store. Many blacks would go there because they could trade there. It was a general store where you could get barrels of molasses, or anything you needed. The Beasleys welcomed the black farmer. You would go in, select the needed items, and then put your name on the book for credit. When the tobacco season came in, you went in and paid your debt. That's the only store I can remember going into in downtown Apex. I don't think we were allowed to go into the other stores, but I was a child so if we could go into other stores, as children, we would not go inside.

In Cary, I never went to the Rexall Drugstore, or to Hobby's, or to any stores in Cary. Terrell's Grocery Store was at the corner of Academy Street and 54 Highway in what is now the Baptist church parking lot. That's where my parents got groceries.

Evans Road at that time was just a red dirt road that dead-ended. To get his family off the farm, my dad said he borrowed ten dollars from a man in order to buy the land from Tilton Evans so he could build our house. He and my two brothers, James and Ernest, built the house themselves, by hand. It was just a simple five-room cinderblock house, but it was beautiful to me. It was a mansion.

Before I saw the house, my dad told us we would have a bathroom inside. I could not believe that, because I was accustomed to outhouses. To think of a bathroom inside of the house, to me it was an outhouse inside the house. I thought that the house was going to smell so bad. So he actually had to take me to the house to show me how the bathroom actually worked so you would not have unpleasant smells in there at all. I was amazed.

After my dad bought the land on Evans Road, his brothers followed. Now I have a sister who lives next door to my parents, and a brother who lives behind my parents. My dad's brother lives next door to him. His son lives next door to him on the corner of Dynasty and Evans Road. Then my dad's older brother lives across Evans Road down on Rochelle Lane.

We had a wonderful life in Cary. I was insulated from all of the ugliness of segregation and what goes with it. My dad was such a patriarch, because he completely insulated his kids from all the horrors of segregation. I remember seeing the colored-only signs and the white-only signs, but it meant nothing to me because we didn't have to hear all of the remarks. It was natural to go to the "for colored only" water fountain.

We missed a lot of the derogatory remarks from whites during segregation because Daddy and Momma would take us shopping on Pettigrew Street in Durham, which only had black businesses. We would go there to do our shopping. Mom and Dad would put all the kids in the car and go down to Chavis Park in Raleigh for recreation. Because there were so many kids in that big old station wagon as we drove along, we would hear kids yelling, "Here comes Pharaoh's army." Little did they know that our last name was Farrar (pronounced almost the same way.) Chavis Park was the park in Raleigh for blacks. Pullen Park was for whites. So we stayed in our own little world. We were insulated from all of the outside derogatory remarks. Dad and Mom made sure of that.

We went to church, but we didn't go to church in Cary. We stayed at our home church in Apex, in Chatham County, to the Holland Chapel AME Zion Church, which is African Methodist Episcopal Zion. That's a lot to say, and is a history within itself. There were two black churches in

Cary at that time. One was AME Union Bethel, and the other one was the Christian Church. I don't remember if Mt. Zion Baptist was located on the corner of 54 Highway at that time. But because we were Zionist, we stayed at our home church in Apex. We never moved our membership to the churches in Cary.

Evans Road was predominantly a black neighborhood, and there was another black neighborhood over by Kingswood Elementary. That was primarily where we stayed and where our interactions were.

George Bailey: In my family, we were not out there in situations where segregation slapped us upside the head. At the time when we were being raised, we didn't go out to eat. We ate at home. There were so many elements about being raised in this area that my family didn't do. I was raised when the road was gravel, so the bus picked me up and carried me to school.

Gwen Matthews: The Lake Wheeler Road and Tryon Road area has always been home to my father's side of the family, for my grandparents, my father and his siblings, and for me. That is where they settled and they're all still there. There are cousins who have moved away, as I did at some point, but grandparents, aunts and uncles are all still there and that is home.

I grew up on Tryon Road. That was a very carefree environment, and it was a community in which there were whites and blacks. We had our own churches, but children would play together. Across the street from me was a white young lady named Sandy and we played together. We did not go into each other's house per se', but if there was an opportunity for us to be together, we would play, and we were always waving at each other. So that little area where I grew up was fun. I had a large extended family there, with grandparents, aunts and uncles, and first, second, and third cousins I could play with. I had cousins who were much older than I was, and they would take me off to places and we would do things together. If I got whipped at one aunt's house, I got whipped at the other one's house because I had no business doing whatever I did up there, and by the time I got home I had had two whippings. I was very mischievous, I really was. I enjoyed my growing up years.

I remember going downtown Raleigh to Hudson Belk with my grandmother on Saturdays. The water fountains and the bathrooms were segregated. One was labeled "Colored" and one was labeled "White." The colored bathroom was always filthy, just dirty. And you didn't want to drink out of the water fountain either. Oh, the crud that was down in there just wasn't clean. So we would sneak a drink out of the white fountain when no one was around. If we had to go to the bathroom, we waited until we got home.

Deborah Matthews Wright: I had grown up in an all black community, gone to an all black church and had only been around black people. When I was four or five, my mother and I went to Hudson Belk department store in downtown Raleigh to shop. I remember telling her that I had to use the bathroom. I remember her saying, "Okay," and she began walking across the store.

I said, "But I have to go now."

And she kept walking while she said, "I know, I know, but I have to find the colored bathroom."

I remember thinking, "What is a colored bathroom?" She had to explain it to me later because I didn't understand. We finally found the colored bathroom. When she made that statement that she had to find the colored bathroom, it was the first time I realized that things were different, and things were separate. Before that, I didn't know that there was a colored bathroom.

We were so segregated in our personal lives, living in the rural areas, that I don't have a whole lot of stories about the colored water fountain and the white water fountain and that sort of thing. I really didn't have the opportunity to experience those distinctions in my personal life until I was in school. My first experience was with the school being integrated.

Sallie Jones: On North Academy Street across the street from our house there was a ballpark, and we had a ragtag ball team. Some Saturdays a team would come and play them and they'd go play somebody else. That would be entertainment for awhile.

We could go to Raleigh on the train at that time for fourteen cents. For fifty cents, you could go to Raleigh and come back on the train and go to the movies. We would get on the train, go down Hargett Street and go to the movie, and then come back home. Our parents knew when the train ran. When we were walking up this hill on our street, you just see our heads. So when the train passed they knew we were coming, and they would stand out front and watch for us.

We all played together. The boys played, and as boys do, fight. Sometimes you would have to go break up a fight. They'd all be in a little gang. One had said something and the other one had disputed it and repeated it, and they would get into a brawl. But then after it was all over and we had broken it up, they would be sitting there again just like nothing ever happened, friends again.

There was a Rogers Grocery store near Hobby's Grocery. We would always go to Hobby's to buy candy, because then you could get penny candy and two cents candy. Mr. Hobby had this black guy working with him named Russ. We used to go in there and look for Russ when we bought candy, because if you got penny candy from Russ, you gave Russ your nickel and you may get five pieces, or you may get six. Mr. Hobby didn't mind. I know he knew Russ was doing that. And there was another man working there, I think he was Pete Murdock's father who ran the grocery business with Mr. Hobby. He used to be generous too, so we wouldn't look for Mr. Hobby. We'd go look for either Mr. Murdock or Russ to buy our candy.

When I was growing up, we looked forward to Saturdays, because on Saturdays we got our nickel. At Adams Drugstore, we could get a cone of ice cream for five cents. If we had done well through the week, we would earn a nickel and could go on Saturday afternoon and get that ice cream.

We bought food mostly at Hobby's Grocery Store. We didn't have to buy a whole lot because my grandfather had a farm, and after he passed, his sons ran the farm. And right across the street where the church is on North Academy Street, they had a huge garden. They had everything in it that you could want, so they didn't have to do too much shopping. And they had hogs. We had hog-killing time. My grandmother had a smokehouse, and after they killed a hog, they would smoke the hams and meat in there. They would stuff the sausages and hang them in the smokehouse and let them dry. My grandmother also had a cow, so we had our milk and our butter. So we didn't have to buy for a lot of things, just sugar, flour, staple things.

There was a man who lived here named Ralph Moore, and he had an automobile. Until my brothers got theirs, there were few automobiles in this area. There was the A&P in Raleigh, and my mother used to make out her shopping list on Saturdays and go to Raleigh to the A&P and buy a lot of things that we needed. You could buy in bulk and get things much cheaper there. Ralph Moore would come by and I guess she would pay him a dollar, or fifty cents or something, to take her to Raleigh to the A&P.

Leonia Farrar: I know when we came to Cary, I thought you had to be dressed nice. Right after we moved here, my neighbor down the street sent me up to a store in Cary. I knew I looked good, because I had my beautiful black dress on. I walked in the store my very first time and I said, "Hello." They looked up at me with a sour look. I said, "I came for some hot dogs, please."

One of the ladies said, "I'm sorry, we don't serve black people."

I said, "What?" I went right back home and told my neighbor, "They said they didn't serve black people."

My neighbor is real light skinned and has that pretty hair. She said, "What? I'm black myself. Come with me." She caught me by my hand and we went back up there. She said, "I am disgusted with you people."

They knew her. They said, "What is it?"

She said, "This is my friend and my neighbor. We went to school together in Apex before they moved to Cary. I am disappointed. I've been coming in this store ever since I moved to Cary. I may be light like you, but I am a black woman." That must have shocked them because they thought she was a white woman. She said, "My husband is just as black as she is. I am a black woman." From that day until this one, they treated me nice. It's been beautiful. They never refused to serve me again. They apologized. They said that they were sorry that this happened.

From that point it has been getting better and better. I'm glad I lived to see it come. It's not there yet, but it's better. It's nothing like it used to be. It used to be that a black man could not look at a white woman or he would have been killed. But we're getting away from that, so it's better.

Jeanette Evans: When I grew up, we couldn't go to the Cary lunch counter and sit down like we can now. We could go in and buy anything we wanted, but we couldn't sit down and eat it, we had to carry it out. There was another place in town too where we could go get a hot dog, but we had to go around the back and knock on the door. My mother said, "If I ever catch you doing that, it won't be good for you. I can make you a hot dog here at home. You don't have to go to anybody's back door because you couldn't go in the front door." It was just a little place on Highway 54. It's torn down now. But we couldn't go inside, we had to go behind it.

And if somebody we knew died, we would go to the church, but we had to go upstairs or in the back row if we wanted to stay. We couldn't sit in the front like you can now. Those days existed when I was growing up, but I didn't pay any attention to it. I just knew what I couldn't do and knew what I could do.

The grocery stores didn't have a place for us to sit down so we could go inside. We could buy anything we wanted, as long as we had our money to pay for it. If we didn't have the money, we could charge things. They would extend credit to us and we would pay them later when we did have money. We had at least two grocery stores in Cary where they gave us credit. We didn't have any problems with that.

Cary was nothing but a little one-horse town, with one policeman, one stop light and all dirt roads except the main street in Cary. We really didn't have any problems, black or white, because we all knew one another. My parents grew up with white folks in Cary, and as we came along, we grew up with their kids. We got along fine. If something happened with my parents, they were right there. And if something happened to them, we were there for them. I wouldn't say all of them would help us, but we didn't have any problems. If one was hurt, everybody was hurt, if they knew you. I guess it was probably worse when my parents were growing up. They didn't talk about it too much.

Black and white, some will always have problems. There are problems today, but I've never seen it in Cary. As long as you treat me right and I treat you right, that's all that counts. I was raised around whites, they were my neighbors and we were best of friends. They sat at my mother's table, and I sat at their mother's table.

The only trouble that I can remember was with two white girls who were my neighbors. If I saw them in town with some of their friends, they pretended that they didn't know me. When they did that the first time, I told my mother what happened. Later their mother came over and wanted to know why I stopped coming to their house. My mother told her what her girls had done. So she said, "You come with me. This is not going to ever happen again." She straightened them out. And to this day, we are the best of friends.

Everybody knew one another because Cary was so small. I could roller skate with my Cary friends on Highway 54. Every now and then a car might come by. Now I call this "small New York." Now you don't know anybody like we did. My life wasn't all that bad growing up. When the schools were integrated together, then everything was fine. My kids had it better than I did, because they didn't have to go way out of town to go to school.

Phyllis Cain: Basically growing up in this area, all of us came from close knit communities. Everybody knew everybody, prior to a lot of people moving from the North. We would go to different churches from ours and we knew everybody in that church. If one community had an event or an activity, we would go. Other schools would have their junior and senior proms and we would get invited, and we would go. So it was just a lot of fun growing up. After desegregation, I don't recall it being really much different, because at that time West Cary High School closed and we went off to college.

THE WHITE EXPERIENCE:

<u>Elva Templeton</u>: I'm just recalling some names of some of the colored folk. Bun Ferrell was a very noted colored person. I think he was on the school board of the colored people. There was Nas Jones. There was one they called Uncle Logan, and Richard Jones. Those are some of the prominent colored people in Cary.

There was a little place where the colored people lived near the corner of Park and Walker Streets that was called Frogtown. And then farther down on that same street south was another settlement called Little Washington. And then the others were just scattered around Cary.

We had a colored family who lived right behind us. Their property joined ours. Her name was Martha, but we called her Babe Jones. Handy Jones was her father. Momma would always give them all the fruits they wanted. They never bothered anything. They were good colored folks.

We called the older colored people aunts and uncles. We didn't dare call them anything else, being disrespectful to them. We had a good element of colored people, and we had a very good relationship with them. I don't think we ever had very much trouble with them, not more than we do the whites. I think whites sometimes are meaner than they are. We played with them when we were kids. We weren't allowed to sass them or be ugly to them or we got into trouble at home.

We had two horses and a wagon which we used to take our dirty clothes to a colored woman on Monday morning. The kids would get up before school and take the little van to her house, and then go pick them up that afternoon.

Uncle John Beckwith used to ring the school bells for us. He would watch while we would go to the store down the street to get candy. When the last bell started ringing, Uncle John would ring that bell until we got there so we wouldn't be late.

Before a funeral, they would toll the bell according to the number of years the person was old. Old Uncle John Taylor, a colored man, used to ring the bells for Sunday school, church and funerals. And nobody could toll the bell like he did.

We had an old colored man who had worked for us for twenty-five years or more, and he was getting kind of feeble. On Christmas morning,

Mother wouldn't let us get our Christmas presents until he came. We would go out on the porch and watch down the road for him. We would see him coming and we would run and meet him and try to make him hurry up. We didn't get anything much for Christmas, candy, an orange and maybe one or two toys, and they were all the toys we had during the year.

Esther Ivey: I had a kind feeling in my heart for the colored folks. We had a nice group of colored people in Cary. If you'll notice, we still do. I have friends that I cherish among the colored folks. We used to go to the colored church once in awhile, and they would always give us a good seat. We didn't ever stay to the closing of the service, and after the service we could hear them singing.

The Cary Colored School was near our house. There were some colored folks in the black community called Frogtown. I don't exactly know where Frogtown was, but the colored people lived there. They also lived where they do now, near Kingswood Elementary School.

My mother had so many children, we always had a cook and we had a colored man who came around. He could always get in and he would start the kitchen fire. He was a Northerner left behind by the Civil War, and he settled in Cary. He would start the kitchen fire and warm his feet in the oven. I think he lived on Walker Street.

The clothes were washed by hand. When we lived at our old home place, Aunt Dora came and did the washing. She would come on Mondays to wash the clothes outside. She had three or four tubs, and a pot that she heated the water in outside. Aunt Dora would come back and spend another day ironing.

My mother always trusted Aunt Dora. My mother would take the horse and buggy and go to Raleigh and leave us with Aunt Dora. We always called her Aunt Dora, and we called the older colored men uncle when we respected them. That was a term of respect. Mama would leave us with Aunt Dora and we knew to obey her too. I thought a great deal of her children.

Bertha Pleasants Daniel: I had a colored girl that helped with the laundry. When I went back to work, I had to get somebody to come in. She came in and kept the children and did some of the housework. She still lives in Cary. We picked her up every day and took her home every night. She worked for me when we lived on Wood Street in town, and then when we moved further out of town, she still stayed with us. She would walk and be here when the children got home from school, so she wasn't here all day every day. One day a week she cleaned, and two days she came and stayed all day when she had work to do. Then the rest of the days she would get here in time to be here when the children got home from school.

She was real good. I was real blessed to have such a nice colored girl. I talked to her not so long ago, I called her one day. She's real arthritic, and she was even then. She never had any children, but she was real good with my children. She had a sister who had a son and a daughter that were about the age of mine. I knew her sister but I didn't know the children. But our colored girl would tell my children about what her sister's children did, and being the same age, they did similar type things. They were always real interested and so was I.

Marie Seeger: Dr. Yarborough was our family doctor. He had built his home so that his office was attached to his home with a breezeway. They had two waiting rooms. One was for the white people, and one was for the black people. If you had an emergency, then he would have you come in the back where the black people were. You'd go around there and you'd get to go in really quickly.

Billy Rogers: Mrs. Young opened the first theater in Cary, sometime in the mid-forties. The movies were distributed by a company out of Charlotte. When it was time for the movie to change, they would bring the huge reels in on a big truck. Back then they were on real big reels, almost the size of an automobile tire. That building had two stories because the projection room had to be upstairs, and because the blacks sat upstairs in the balcony.

Rachel Dunham: We would go across the railroad tracks to the old station that used to be there. What a tragedy that the railroad station was torn down. It was right across from the Page-Walker Hotel. They also had a way to send telegrams there.

They had a separate waiting room for the colored folks and they had another room for whites.

Sonny Keisler: My dad was Clyde Keisler, and he was manager of Kildare farm which had a thousand acres, and he probably rented another four to five hundred acres of land through the latter years. His operation was a self-contained economic and social unit in the earlier days before Cary grew, until the early seventies. I think there were about seven families who lived on the farm. It was always difficult to keep employees on the farm. This area started growing, and you could make more money off the farm than on the farm, so people would come down from the mountains, stay a few years and then get another job and leave. Keeping employees was probably the biggest single job Dad had. Probably the next biggest job was keeping the equipment repaired. It would always break down.

Since he was self-contained, all the food stuff for the cattle and the flock of chickens was grown on the farm. Most of the people who lived on the farm grew their own vegetables, so they would take time off to tend their own gardens. Most everybody got milk from the dairy and raised their own pigs and chickens and cows, so they didn't have to go to the store to buy meats or vegetables. They made their own bread. When we were little kids, chicken feed would come in feed bags made of cotton with patterns on them. Bags would be distributed and people made clothes out of them.

The Kildare family owned the Pine State Creamery. All the milk and cream and dairy products that were produced on the farm went to Pine State. The chickens were primarily layers, they produced eggs. There was an egg market in Cary at the time. Our eggs went to the market in Cary, and then they would be distributed from there to various stores in the area. Kildare farm had about 30,000 chickens. At that time it was a pretty good-sized flock. These days you have 100,000 in your flocks. That's pretty much what Kildare farm was all about for forty some years.

In the fifties, Kildare Farm Road was a dirt road, so it was pretty isolated. Then the road was paved when developers crept down into that area. Slowly the farm was enclosed by subdivisions which lent to the decision to sell out. Dad was asked to become part of the development company.

John Yarborough: Daddy, Dr. Frank Yarborough, built the office at the present location on Park Street that was connected to our home. He practiced there throughout his entire career. The cars would line Park Street on both sides of the street from morning until night. And when I say night, I mean eleven o'clock, twelve o'clock. His office hours at night were Monday, Wednesday and Friday. Then on Tuesday, Thursday, Saturday and Sunday, after he cleared everyone out of the office, then he would make house calls. And then it got to where Monday, Wednesday and Friday office hours became Monday, Tuesday, Wednesday, Friday and part of Saturday office hours.

He was also the doctor for the county. He called on the county home and the county jail. Back then they had doctors for the Seaboard Railroad. I think he just saw the Seaboard employees at various times in his office. And he went to the hospital two, three, four times a week to do his hospital rounds.

Sometime in the early fifties, I remember he wrote a little sign he put in the waiting room for his patients that stated, due to circumstances and due to inflation he was going to have to raise his office visit fees from $2.00 to $3.00. You better not have anything else to do when you came because you were going to have a wait, unless it was an emergency, and then he would tell you to come to the back door.

Back then they had segregated waiting rooms. The white waiting room was a little larger, and it was at the part of the office that faced Academy Street. The colored waiting room opened up into the treatment room, and that was the part of the office that was adjacent to the driveway of the home. There weren't as many colored patients as white patients, and they would come around to the colored waiting room. Then if anyone had an emergency, they would come around to that part of the office and knock on his back door. He would either acknowledge you or let you in his little office that was not part of the treatment room that was also adjacent to the colored waiting room. It worked out real well, as I remember. Of course, times and mind sets were different back then, and I don't ever remember anyone complaining about having to wait.

Daddy's patients loved him. His Christmases from his patients were something to behold. It seemed like three-fourths of them brought something or gave him something. He was often paid in kind, especially before the fifties. It would not be unusual for him to get a ham or something in food. Patients were always bringing him food.

He died in 1957, before integration came in. He never experienced any problems. His colored patients loved him just as much as his white patients. He was like a member of the family. He treated everyone. He had no color perception at all when it came to his medicine.

I don't know if you've ever heard of Charlie Cotton and Sun Cotton. They were two black guys that were friends and patients of my father's. And another guy, Frank Woods, was also a patient and did a lot of work for Daddy around the home and things like that. They all had a horse and wagon. All the wagons had the tailgates that came out the back then. I don't know the function of the two by four that came out of the back of their wagon. Whenever they would come down Academy Street, we kids would all jump on the back of their wagon on that little tailgate and ride it down the street. By the time we got down to U.S. 1 there were three or four kids on the back of that wagon. It was just a dirt street back then. Charlie Cotton plowed everybody's garden every year. I think he had a big, beautiful work horse. Charlie used to drive his wagon right down the middle of the street. He knew we were jumping on the back. We were all great friends. When he plowed the garden, we kept him in water.

It seemed like most everyone knew each other very well, but we were all pretty good friends. But Charlie and Sun Cotton, they were two characters. Thinking about them brings back some good memories of that time when things were so much slower and so much more laid back, and the pace was so enjoyable.

I had the benefit of coming along in the fifties when times were so serene and seemingly honest and laid back. It was such a peaceful time to be in high school. To come along at that time is a very fortunate opportunity. It was a great time to live and a great time to grow up. I'm so glad I was a part of all that.

Mary Crowder: The black children went to Kingswood Elementary, except it was a smaller school then. Then they went to Berry O'Kelly High School which was down on Berry O'Kelly Road, near the state fairgrounds on the way to Raleigh. Part of it is still standing as a community center now. Most of them lived on the other side of the Durham Highway, and they have the little church that is on the corner of Highway 54 and Academy Street. There were two main black churches.

We had no animosity against them. They were friends and they worked in my home, and they did yard work. We thought a lot of them. May Hopkins worked for my grandmother Wilkinson, and I thought the world of May. And Will Boyd worked for my granddaddy as well as for my family. He was just a humble man. When my granddaddy died, they all came to the funeral.

He had his funeral at home. Back in those days you had funerals either at home or in church. You didn't go to funeral homes to have funerals. Papa's was at home. Black people came and they were welcome. The people that attended the funeral were in the living room and dining room area and in the back hall. The preacher preached his funeral. Then the procession went over to the cemetery and they buried him. We went back when the flowers and things were put in place. Brown Funeral Home conducted his service.

C.Y. Jordan: On several occasions, we, the white boys, played baseball against the black kids, and there was never any problem. It was one team against another, just kids who made up a team. We played a lot of baseball back then. We would choose up sides and get up a team and play, and there were never any arguments or disputes about it. We didn't have any referees. Today, you have to have umpires for Little League baseball, and the parents argue. We didn't argue. If you were out, you were out, you admitted it. And if it was close enough that you weren't sure, you settled it. You made an agreement, and reconciled it one way or another. You accepted that okay, I was out if you say I was. I don't think I was, but so what. We'll go on. That's the way we played it, and that's the way I recall playing with the black kids. I still have some dear friends out of that group.

The Evans' out on Evans Road are a big family, and they were dear to our family. I knew old man Clyde Evans Sr. He died a few years ago and he was up close to a hundred. He told me that his father was my grandfather James' foreman. He was in the logging business and old man Evans worked with him.

When Clyde was in his nineties, I would stop by to see him. His house was way down along a path off of Evans Road. I would drive down there, we would go inside, sit down in the house and talk. He would tell me all sorts of things.

Incidentally, he drove all around town on his little farm tractor when he was younger. He had a little box up on the side for his little dog to ride with him. He would put the dog in the box and to town he would go. That's the way he came to town.

I went by to see him one day. He was in his nineties and he was out there on that tractor with a chain behind it, and he was pulling down his barn. He had an old feed barn there. He would take that chain and hook it to a post and pull it out and everything else came with it, and he would drag it way down in the woods. He had it about half torn down when I went there to see him. He stopped and came to talk to me. I asked him, "Clyde, what in the world are you doing?"

He said, "I'm tearing down this old barn. It's about to fall down, it's ugly, and I'm getting rid of it." So we talked awhile and I left. A few days later, I went back by there and there was no evidence of any barn ever having been there. It was plowed up and was already sprouting grass. He had cleaned it up completely. And he was in his nineties.

His younger son John worked with me when we were developing Buckhurst housing development. We were putting in water and sewer lines ourselves. He's a very good mechanic, very talented laying sewer pipe or putting water pipe together. So we put in all the water and sewer lines, he and I down in the ditch laying pipe. Later on, John said, "Daddy plants that field of corn out there every year." This was just before he died. John said, "I asked him, Daddy, why in the world do you keep on planting that acre of corn?

He said, "Well, I've got to do something."

Old man Clyde told me, "I get out there and work. That's what it takes to keep you going." That's the reason he planted that corn every year. He probably didn't harvest it to a great degree. It was just something to do and to watch it grow.

Robert Heater: In the gym on weekends, we had boxing matches. Back then we had a first-class boxing team in Cary. A lot of schools around here had boxing teams and ours was by far the best. A lot of our graduates went on to fight in the Golden Gloves tournament.

The Golden Gloves are boxing tournaments that are held all over the United States. It was promoted by the Raleigh Times newspaper and the Raleigh Exchange Club. Daddy at one time was State Boxing Commissioner.

On Saturday nights, they would put ten black men in the ring at the same time, blindfolded. The one left standing won the prize. It might have been $20 or $100. That was one of the things they used to do. The men were not made to go into the ring, it was just for whoever wanted to fight. I don't recall any betting, but there very likely was some going on.

CHAPTER 6

SEGREGATED AFRICAN-AMERICAN SCHOOLS

SJ and Leonia Farrar - Leonia: I went to a colored school in Apex. We had to walk ten miles to catch the bus, five miles one way, and five miles back. SJ went to Clark's School, Bell's School. (**SJ**): Bell's School was the name of that one-room school where I went on the Wake County and Chatham County line in a little place called Fearrington. My first year in school was in a one-room school. The teacher had to teach all of us. We were farm children, hard headed boys. We would go out there in the woods and pick up sticks and whatever kind of wood we could find to fuel the big potbellied heater sitting in the middle of the floor that she had to keep us warm with in that classroom. We boys would keep that heater going.

Our books came from the white schools, when they were done with them. By the time they got to us, the backs would be gone, pages were torn out, and what was left was all torn up. The teacher had to be brighter than a white teacher to know what we were missing.

Leonia's family was living closer to Apex and we were living closer to Pittsboro. We went to the closest school to wherever we were living, because we would have to walk to get there. The only way the black schools would have a bus was if the PTA would buy one that was broken down after white kids were through with it. We would be walking to school and the white school bus would drive past us. The white children on the bus would spit out the window on us, and throw paper and trash on us. I know you think we're painting a sad picture, but every word of it is true.

After elementary school, we went to Apex High School. The first name was Apex Colored School, and then the second name was Apex Consolidated School, which means they consolidated Friendship School,

Clark School and New Hill School. That's when they put all of the children in Apex together in one school and called it Apex Consolidated School, and they closed all of those smaller schools. We would either walk or ride the bus. We would ride the bus for two or three hours to get to school, and again to get back home. Then once we were home, we would work out in the fields until dark, and then work by lantern light.

Leroy and Betty Farrar – Leroy: I had to quit school because my father passed away and Mama had to take care of all of us. After he died, I couldn't go to school. I think I only got as high as the ninth grade in Apex Consolidated School. I kind of educated myself after that as I went along.

Betty beat me in school, she went longer than I did. She went to high school. (**Betty**): We went to Apex Elementary School and then I went to Berry O'Kelly High School in Raleigh.

George Bailey: When I graduated, I was in the last class of Ligon High School in Raleigh that was an all-black school. Ligon became integrated in 1969. After Ligon was integrated, my brothers and sisters went to Enloe High School because we lived near Enloe. That stopped the chain of all-black schools right there in our family, with my brothers and sisters. I'm the middle child. My older siblings and I went to all-black schools, and my younger siblings went to mixed schools. And all of my kids went to mixed schools.

In my mother's family, education has been very important, because of the segregation that she experienced and we experienced growing up. My mother and father educated all five of their children. We all finished college. My mother went back to school and got her degree too. Now my father only had a ninth grade education, but he was a very successful businessman. My brother and I are in similar businesses right now.

BERRY O'KELLY HIGH SCHOOL:

Esther Ivey: We voted for bonds to pay for the first paved road to Cary. In order to get Method, which was at that time a colored area, to join in with us we had the road divided and a section went around by the Berry O'Kelly store. That was something extra. The road goes across the railroad tracks right there at the fairgrounds, and then it joins in a little bit farther down. Mr. Berry O'Kelly was Method. He had a big store there and so he ruled the roost at that place. They had to vote for the bonds too to pave the road at the Method end.

Clyde Evans Jr.: I graduated from Berry O'Kelly High School in Method. I built the first school bus for the black high school which cost Cary $1,800, and the state put money with it. It was a Model A wooden school bus, the top of the body was wood. The route started in Fuquay and picked up all high school students and took them to Berry O'Kelly. When we finished elementary school in Cary, there was no other place to go but to Berry O'Kelly. The only black school in Cary was an elementary school. Of course, it was a segregated school system.

We had an outstanding African-American named Berry O'Kelly. When they were paving the roads, Cary had so much political pull, they paved his road first, then it continued on as Number 1 South. When Number 1 South reached Cary, the paving stopped and the road proceeded as dirt.

When I was going to school, I had one of the finest educations any person could have during that time. I was taught by the finest teachers at Berry O'Kelly. They didn't play with us. We had to do exactly what they said. We conducted ourselves accordingly. If a teacher said something to you and you didn't do it, your parents would know about it that day, and you would be punished at home as well as at the school. "Spare the rod, spoil the child." We would get a whipping in school and the teacher gave us a note to take home to our parents, so when we got home, we got another whipping. Now if you put your hand on a child in school, they'll put you in jail. That's why you've got so much trouble in schools, no discipline. At sundown nobody would catch me away from home until I was eighteen or twenty years old.

Herbert Bailey: After eighth grade, we went to Berry O'Kelly High School in Raleigh. We would catch the bus to the elementary school, and sometimes we would disembark and get on another bus to go to Berry O'Kelly. Students from the Jeffries Grove area and this side of Wake County went to that school. During my senior year, my father and mother had a conflict with a teacher and the principal at Kingswood Elementary in Cary concerning my baby sister, so my mother and dad took four of their kids and packed up and moved to Raleigh, and they left me here. I stayed with my Evans grandparents on their farm in Cary so I could finish my senior year of high school. At some time during my senior year, my grandfather broke his leg. That is the only time I've ever known him to be injured. I stayed there and helped him with his animals and did whatever I could, and I also drove the school bus. The route started in Morrisville, then went to Cary Elementary School to pick up students, and then it went to Berry O'Kelly. We had to leave about an hour and a half early to get to school on time. For those staying after school for athletics, no school or county-provided transportation was furnished. There were no activity buses.

The schools were desegregated two years after I finished high school. They also shut down Berry O'Kelly two years after I graduated.

Gwen Matthews: I attended East Cary (now Kingswood) Elementary School, when it was segregated, until eighth grade. For my ninth and tenth grade years, I attended Berry O'Kelly High School in Method. The school no longer exists, but the gym is the community center for Method now. Those first two years of high school were fun years because I was very active. I was head cheerleader, I sang in the choir, and I was in lots of clubs. I ran track, and one summer I ran the regional and local sixty yard dash events. So I had a really good time at Berry O'Kelly.

Carolyn Rogers: When I started at Berry O'Kelly High School, because of segregation, the black kids would then catch the bus to East Cary Elementary (now Kingswood) and ride the bus from there to Method. Berry O'Kelly was right across the street from the fairgrounds off of Beryl Road and Method Road. Mary G. Carter was my English teacher, and I admired her so much that I wanted to emulate her when I went to college.

CARY SCHOOLS:

Elva Templeton: I just barely remember when there was a free school in Cary. It was supposedly a school that was opened in 1866 for the freed slaves. It was facing Dixon Avenue, on the corner of Dixon and Chatham Street.

There was the Cary Colored School, a two-room school, on the road to the colored cemetery off of Shirley Drive and Harrison Avenue, next to the Christian colored church. Ada Ruffin was one of the teachers at the Cary Colored School. She was a very fine colored person. She had her mother with her, Aunt Millie. Ms. Ada Ruffin used to talk about how the house on the corner at the Winn Dixie parking lot burned down one night during a big snow. Aunt Millie was a very religious old lady, and according to Ada, she was outdoors praying because she saw the snowflakes coming down with fire reflecting on them, and she thought they looked like drops of blood. She thought Judgment Day had come.

She was the most religious woman you ever saw in your life, good old soul.

Robert Heater: The black elementary school off of Kildare Farm Road was right behind the first house on Shirley Drive. It looks like there is an old driveway there, but back there was a black Christian church and a black elementary school. The Cary Colored School was a wood-frame building, and it had a little pot-bellied stove in it. I have never been inside it, but our housekeeper, Geneva, has talked about it at times.

Clyde Evans Jr.: I went to elementary school at the Cary Colored School which was a two-room school. We walked down Academy Street and over to the school. Reverend Meadows and Ms. Ada Ruffin were our teachers. The preacher was also the teacher. He married me.

The school board was an all-white school board. We also had a little black school board, and my father was on that board. They made a decision about what they wanted to do with their schools, but they had to take it to the white school board to approve it. The white schools in Cary got maybe $200,000, while the black schools only got maybe $1,000 or $1,500, but we had to take everything in stride.

C.Y. Jordan: I remember when the schools were not integrated. The black elementary school was just beyond where the playground is behind Cary Elementary School, just before Shirley Drive. There was a little trail that used to go through there to the cemetery. The Cary Colored School was right there, a little frame building. I don't remember any incidents going on prior to integration. I do remember the days when the black children would be walking up Academy Street going to their school and we would be walking up Academy Street going to our school. I've read in the history books that there might have been some remarks made to and from, and there probably were some, but I personally don't think that there was ever any serious conflict here. You know how kids are, they're going to say things. The Cary Colored School burned down in 1936, and then they built the school over here which is now Kingswood.

The colored Masons had a lot over on Boyd Street. They were planning to build a Masonic lodge there. The county owned a lot that the school was on off of Kildare Farm Road. When the school burned down, the county and the Masons swapped lots so that the county could build a school over here on Boyd Street, which is now Kingswood School. The Masons never built anything on their new lot. There wasn't any reason why they couldn't build on either lot. They just didn't get around to doing it, I believe is the way it was.

Sallie Jones: I began school here in Cary. The Cary Colored School used to be behind where the Cary Elementary School is now. The church that I attend now was located next to our small, three-room school. The school burned down the year that I would have been in the sixth grade. There was arson, but nobody would really admit that it was arson.

We used to walk down Academy Street and then down Dry Avenue to go to our school. There was a pathway through there. My cousins owned land next to the Dry house where Mr. Dry, the principal of the Cary Elementary School lived, and we would go down through there, past their house to our school. There used to be a building on the side of the Dry house that belonged to the school. It was the boy's dormitory for Cary Elementary which was a boarding school. There would always be some boys there, and as we would go through their school some mornings, they would throw rocks at us. Sometimes they would call us names too. Of course our parents told us, just keep going. When they threw rocks at us, we wouldn't stop to throw rocks back. The strange thing about it was, they would throw rocks at the girls as we walked to school together. The boys in our school would usually have gone on before us. They would stop sometimes and throw rocks back, and sometimes there would be a tussle.

I have always thought that when the school was burned, even though nobody ever said anything more about it, it was understandable what happened. There was always something being done to the church next door, which was vandalized many times. Water was poured into the piano, windows were broken and things like that. The church finally sold their land, and they are now on Evans Road. The new church was built in 1968, and the original church building was torn down.

When we finished elementary school here, we had to go to Method to go to high school. At that time, the state used to give you tests, I think at the end of the seventh grade, and if you passed the tests then you went into high school. High school only went to the eleventh grade then for all of Wake County, until the twelfth grade was added in 1947.

The new school, what is now known as Kingswood, is right in the neighborhood where I was born and still live. When our school burned down, they were not going to put another school in Cary for us to attend. Instead they decided that we would be bused to Method to go to elementary school. But my mother and my uncles and other families in the neighborhood decided no, we were not going to go to Method. They wanted our own school in Cary, so they boycotted. Some of the parents wouldn't let their kids go to school in Method. I was one of those, I didn't go to school, and my younger sister didn't go to school, and many others. Some had other means to be schooled. I had brothers and sisters already going to Method, so my mother had me use their books and study whatever they were studying. In the spring when they gave the test to see whether or not you could go into the eighth grade, my mother sent me down to take the test with the class in Method, and I passed. So I never was in the seventh grade. I went into the eighth grade at Berry O'Kelly High School. I went eighth, ninth, tenth and eleventh grade there, and graduated. My two younger siblings went to Kingswood Elementary, but I never did.

They kept saying they couldn't find land to build a new elementary school in Cary. My mother, Emily Jones, and my uncle, Goelet Arrington, owned some land where the gym for Kingswood stands today. When they heard the complaints that there was no land available, they decided to give their land to Cary to build the school. I asked my mother time and time again, why did she do that, but they wanted a school so badly that they gave their land away. The thing that disturbs me now is, they say they have no record of that gift, and they are crediting somebody else for the land, but it belonged to my mother and my uncle who made it possible to build the school. My mother said they got a token $100 or something for it. But I know what happened, she gave up her land, and he gave up his land for that school. The original building was placed on that land.

Jeanette Evans: The first black elementary school in Cary burnt down in 1936. Some said it was set afire, but we never had any proof. It burned down the same year that I was supposed to start school there. We had to wait until they built our new school.

My father, my mother and some old friends from church worked very hard to get a new school in Cary. Loveless Evans, Bun Ferrell, and Clyde Evans Sr. were all on the black school board. They all worked together for a new school. They did what they could at the time. I eventually went to Kingswood, the school my parents helped build.

Later, when they built a school on Evans Road, they were going to name it after Clyde Evans Sr., but it was decided they didn't want a school named after a person, so they called it West Cary High School. Now it's West Cary Middle School. And when they built the new black elementary school, they were going to name it the Bun Ferrell Elementary School. But when they decided to never name a school after a person, they first called it East Cary Elementary School, and later it was changed to Kingswood Elementary. So they named a street that runs alongside the school after Bun Ferrell instead. Both of those men worked really hard to get a new school, and Bun Ferrell sold the land that the school is on. The street beside the school is now called Ferrell Street, just like Evans Road was named after the Evans family. When they named a street after him, the town couldn't take that away from Bun Ferrell.

The first school called East Cary Elementary was just a one-room brick building. We were all in one room, every grade. That's the building where I began school because I was first in that school. We were small, but they kept on building the school. Later they built new school buildings there. I remember Ms. Logan and Ms. Hope. They just had three teachers at the time because the school was so small. It went from the first grade to the seventh grade, and then we went to Berry O'Kelly. I was in that one building until I finished the seventh grade, and then went to Berry O'Kelly. We didn't have a high school, so we had to go about six miles to Berry O'Kelly in Method.

Herbert Bailey: At Kingswood, there were three classrooms, a cafeteria, and of course the bathrooms, all in one building. Milk was supplied at lunch, when we would get a half pint of milk for three cents. I remember that because my job was to sell the milk. The teachers were Ms. L. W. Logan, Ms. Ligon, and Mrs. E.H. Hope. Mrs. Hope was a principal also at one time. In the history of my schooling, I have never been in an integrated school. I have no idea what it is like to sit down beside a white person and be educated.

The first addition built at Kingswood was a gym. The next thing they built was the cafeteria which was in the same building with the classrooms in the one building. We had potbellied stoves that burned coal for heat, and it was always a pleasure to get the coal. Something I could always do to please the teacher was to get the coal, which was in the northwest corner underneath the building.

The Wake County school board eventually built the school that is below the hill there. I graduated from the eighth grade at Kingswood. My principal's name was E.F. Rayford, and there were other principals as well through the years.

We had a playground with a maypole and another piece of equipment called a giant stride, which was a single pole that had chains with bars on the end of the chains, and we could go out to its perimeter and swing around the pole. We had a baseball field so we played a lot of softball.

There were probably between fifteen and twenty kids per class, and there were three classes in the same room. The one teacher taught all three classes. My teacher was Mrs. L.W. Logan in the first grade, and she taught first, second and third grades.

I remember coming out of our school and walking or riding down Academy Street and seeing this great big, white, pretty school building for the white students. There was always the separation, separation of the money and the resources and the quality.

Billy Rogers: I remember we didn't know that it could be any other way. The elementary school for the black kids was across Highway 54, and the school for the whites was at the head of Academy Street. Our school had first through twelfth grades. When school was dismissed in the afternoon, we would be going this way downtown, and some of the black kids lived over this way so we would cross. And they were our friends. We'd been taught, and our parents were taught that we were not supposed to go to school together. And we didn't go to church with them either. We still don't go to church together even now. I go to First Baptist, and if I would see one or two blacks there then I would be surprised. I don't know if the blacks want it or the whites don't want it, but we still aren't really mixed except where we have to be, generally speaking. That's a hard thing for me to understand.

Linda Evans: I went to East Cary Elementary (Kingswood.) Mr. Rayford was the principal at the time. One of the teachers was Ms. Williams-Vinson, who wrote the book *Both Sides of the Tracks*. Other teachers were Ms. Logan and Mr. Roseboro.

I wasn't that familiar with segregation, because I went to an all-black school where we played with each other and did not have a whole lot to do with the outside world. We watched a little TV and that type of thing, but we didn't really get out there. When I moved to Raleigh, it was during the time of the first real integration of the schools. I'll tell you, that was really a trying time. I went to Lucille Hunter Middle School and then I went to Hugh Morrison Middle School in Raleigh.

Deborah Matthews Wright: I'm one of five children, and we grew up in a rural area in Wake County. At that time it was considered the country, just outside the city limits of Raleigh, between Raleigh and Cary. As a result of decisions that were made, we ended up going to Cary schools rather than to Raleigh city schools, when Cary was in the county school system as a rural school. I first started school in the segregated school of East Cary Elementary.

Carolyn Rogers: Our East Cary Elementary days were just delightful days. Mr. E.F. Rayford was my principal there. He would teach us how to write correctly. I remember him saying, "You use your entire arm to write, not just your hand." He had beautiful handwriting and he wrote with such a flare. We all would be mesmerized watching him write on the chalkboard. Mr. Roseboro was my seventh grade teacher, and Mr. Davis was my eighth grade teacher. I remember the white building across from the main building where the cafeteria was housed. We had some classes in that building. It was just a white plank building with wooden floors, but we had some delightful times in both of those buildings. I remember May Days when we used to wrap the maypole. Those were beautiful days.

Herbert Bailey: West Cary High School was going to be called Clyde Evans Sr. High School, to be named after my grandfather. But then the school system wanted to get away from naming schools after individuals, so they changed it to West Cary High School. My grandfather orchestrated the deal for the county to purchase the land.

Phyllis Cain: My freshman and sophomore year, I attended Berry O'Kelly High School, which has a long-standing history. It was the high school my parents graduated from, and the high school I really wanted to graduate from because it had such a tradition. But it closed in 1965 and they built West Cary High School. We hated to see it close because so many of our parents had attended Berry O'Kelly. And the way the auditorium was built, it slanted downward, so when they had graduation, the graduates would march down from side to side. And then when they left, they were going uphill, in the auditorium. It was one of those old auditoriums. I always wanted to do that but we missed the chance.

At West Cary there were four classes; the freshman, sophomore, junior and senior classes. There was a class that graduated in 1966, and then our class, which was the last graduating class of West Cary High School, was in 1967. It was a segregated school. There were two or three white students that were bused over to our high school to take auto mechanics and carpentry. Also, there was one white teacher that taught at West Cary. Basically all of my friends stayed together when we moved to West Cary from Berry O'Kelly. The year I started as a freshman at Berry O'Kelly was the first year they integrated Cary High School, so six students from Berry O'Kelly went to previously all-white Cary High. One person who was in my class all the way through elementary school was chosen and five others that were older.

I think a lot of us were depressed that we didn't get to finish Berry O'Kelly, but once we got to West Cary High, it was fine because it was a very close-knit school. There were only 300 and some students in the whole school, so we were like a family. The person who really stands out is our principal, Mr. J.E. Byers. He instilled in us that we were the great West Cary High, so we had the philosophy that we were just as good as any other students at any other school. There was a larger high school in Raleigh, Ligon High School, but he instilled in us that we were the best, so we became a big family. I guess the most exciting thing that stands out for me was when we beat Ligon in basketball. We were arch-rivals and we finally beat Ligon High School, so that was a very exciting time.

We didn't have football, so the main sport for us was basketball. We had track, and we had drama club, and 4H. Of course we were segregated, so we had our own state-wide, African-American honor society called the Crown and Scepter Honor Society. We had a conference at St. Augustine's College on March 18, 1967, and Ronnie Harris, who was a member of my class, was elected president. He gave the president's message, so we were very proud of Ronnie. "The Crown and Scepter goal was, "Success through knowledge, leadership, character and responsibility." I was a member too. To qualify, you needed to maintain a B average, I believe.

We had our pep squad, student council, French I and French II, home economics, agriculture, and we always had homecoming which began with a basketball game, and a queen and king were crowned. Then we would invite the queen and king from the rival high school to our homecoming as well. We had a junior and senior prom with a D.J. in the high school gym. We hadn't moved into the hotels like they do now. Those are our activities that I remember. Ronnie Harris was the president of the class for several years, as well as the president of the Crown and Scepter Club. I was a reporter for the newspaper that we had our last year. We didn't have a yearbook, unfortunately. We joked around and played pranks. We loved to do that. We skipped school occasionally. I never did that, I was too scared.

One of the quotations our principal always said was, "We did not come here to play, to dream, to drift. We have work to do and loads to lift. Show not the struggle..." I don't know the rest of it, and I don't know the name of the person who wrote it. We would always have to say that in assembly.

I remember all the teachers. They were very concerned about us. They knew our parents and our parents knew them. They communicated well together. There were PTA meetings, and we knew that if something wasn't right at school our parents would find out at those meetings.

We still keep in contact with some of our teachers. Some of them are now deceased, but we still have contact with most of the ones that are left. They look just like they did when we were in high school. It was a very small school. I will name some of the West Cary teachers that are still living. Mary G. Cotter taught English. Doris Holloway was our librarian, Lilly Pearl Jones taught science. Jocelyn Archer taught chemistry. Mrs. E.M. Thomas taught history. I think she relocated to Charlotte and we've lost contact with her. Mr. Lockemore taught auto mechanics, Ella Smith was our French teacher, and James Joyner was our basketball coach. Some of them transferred to West Cary from Berry O'Kelly.

I can't speak for the other classes, but ours, the class of '67, was a very tight-knit group. There were only 53 of us so everybody knew everybody and we knew each other's parents. We really enjoyed the games a lot. I really can't think of any negative experiences, just very fond memories. Everything was a lot of fun. We hung out together on weekends. If you went downtown Raleigh on Saturday you would run into everybody from school. That was before the subdivisions and all the other shopping centers were built.

For graduation in 1967, they had something called a baccalaureate sermon which was held on Sunday May 28th, and then the commencement program was in the gym on May 30th. It was just a flat floored gym. Our graduation activities were very dignified. You could hear a pin drop, because if there was any noise, Mr. Byers would have probably escorted the noisemakers out. It was very dignified, very quiet. You got to hear everything that was going on. I loved that. We wore cap and gowns.

We had a one-year reunion, a twelve-year reunion, a twenty, a twenty-five, and a thirty-five year reunion. Four of our classmates are now deceased. Paul Pope always was the master of ceremonies at our class reunions. We always invited our teachers back as our guests to all of our reunions. They really enjoyed coming and reminiscing with us.

The last reunion that we had was at the school. I was the coordinator of that and so I thought it would be nice to tour the school. We had a banquet at North Carolina State Faculty Club. The next Saturday we toured the school. And on that Sunday we went to church together and had brunch. We manage to get together and keep in contact with each other. There are twelve to fourteen of us who used to go out to dinner and celebrate birthdays.

The majority of my classmates are still in the state. Quite a few have retired. I don't know how many went to college out of the 53, but there were quite a few. Some of our different careers are social workers, teachers, accountants, ministers, and engineers. Others went into businesses of their own. Some work in television broadcasting, employee relations, and one is a successful gospel singer. There were couples in the class that have dated since the eighth grade.

PART II

DESEGREGRATING THE COMMUNITY

CHAPTER 7

DESEGREGRATING THE COMMUNITY BEGINS

Charlotte Phelps: After we married, my husband and I lived in Raleigh, right down from the governor's mansion on Edenton Street. Our apartment was on the third floor, and in the sixties, during Civil Rights, we could actually see the demonstrations that went by in the street. We would sit on the porch and watch them going by. During the time when all that was going on, there were quite a few demonstrations. They would march down by the capital and then they would come around and go down in front of the governor's mansion. The demonstrations were basically peaceful. There were a few incidents where people got ugly, but for the most part I think they were pretty peaceful. I know they did have the National Guard called out, because my husband was in the National Guard and he thought one time he was going to be called out for downtown Raleigh. He was called out for a couple of others but they weren't here. He would actually know when they were going to occur. We had moved to Cary when Martin Luther King Jr. was assassinated so we did not see what happened in downtown Raleigh then.

Gwen Matthews: I was attending Meredith College when integration became much more noticeable. I did take part in some of the events that were taking place in Raleigh. Before integration, there was a theater in downtown Raleigh called the Ambassador, and blacks had to sit in the back seats. I remember having to sit there. I also remember marching for the integration of that particular theater. The marches were fairly peaceful. There were policemen and guards and hoses, but they never turned the hoses on us. We would be out there saying our chants, and the police would just be standing there. When I was marching, the dogs lunged at us but the police did not turn them loose on us. The only time I remember it getting violent was when Martin Luther King was assassinated, and then downtown became a whole different world, but I did not partake in that. I had friends who did, and they said it was not a pretty sight to be involved in what was going on downtown at that time. I think there was only one night of demonstrations when they found out that he had been assassinated, just a twenty-four to forty-eight hour period, so it wasn't an extended period of anger and violence being wrought upon the city. It was quite a time, a difficult time, but Raleigh seemed to have weathered it relatively well. Other than that particular time, I don't remember extreme cases of violence in this area during Civil Rights.

Linda Evans: The demonstrations and the riots that I remember happened when Martin Luther King was killed. There was so much going on at that time. They were rioting in the streets, throwing bottles, doing all kinds of crazy things when he was assassinated. I didn't want to get involved in it, so I stayed home and hid in the corner. Of course, in Raleigh it was minor compared to the other larger cities. I couldn't understand why they would go out and burn their own community. This is stupid. I know the man was fighting for our rights and everything, but you shouldn't go out and destroy something you've built. It was not real bad in Raleigh. The police came in quickly and they didn't allow a whole lot of violence to happen.

I had a boyfriend at the time was involved in burning a building. I don't remember which building. He was arrested, and I was so embarrassed. He got out of it, somehow it was settled. It seems as though once that happened, we weren't together anymore. I didn't want to be involved in anything like that, so I backed off from him. At that time, you didn't do a lot of talking about things. The gossip and the talk, we kept it hush hush. We didn't want everybody to know what was going on. So I just went on to school and minded my own business. It was not a very good time, but there was a lot of excitement. There were some disturbances that night after Martin Luther King was killed. That were a lot of ups and downs in the country, because of J.F. Kennedy and then his brother Bobby, and then Martin Luther King all being killed. Change is not easy.

Bruce Roberts: I guess the last physical sign in downtown Charlotte of segregation was in the theaters where the blacks still had to sit upstairs and the whites had to sit downstairs. There was a demonstration that followed perhaps a week or two after the lunch counter sit-ins. The demonstrators had signs saying that they wanted to be treated equally. About twenty of them were in front of the theater. The theater building was one of the older buildings on Tryon Street in Charlotte. What was ironic was that back in 1864, it apparently had been a bank building and was the place where the last meeting of the Confederate cabinet was held. The cabinet left Richmond and got to Charlotte about the time of the final surrender of Joe Johnston. The interesting thing about that particular spot was that when Jefferson Davis came out of the building at the end of the meeting, he was greeted by a dispatch writer who told him that Lincoln had been assassinated. So that spot was marked with a bronze plaque embedded in the concrete sidewalk to commemorate that event.

During Civil Rights a hundred years later, here were the demonstrators just a few feet away from that very spot. There were some white teenagers who were heckling the demonstrators and throwing pennies at them. It was most interesting to see the pennies roll around by all the feet, so Lincoln's face was all over the place. I don't think my photo of that ever got published.

Carl Mills: My life as an educator in Cary was fairly well balanced in that I was also a member of the First Baptist Church in Cary. I was an ordained deacon, and taught a Sunday school class for a number of years during the time that integration came along, I'm afraid the Baptists were not too fond of integration as far as the congregation was concerned. It was an internal situation, and perhaps the congregation was not too aware of what was being said among the deacons. They met and discussed how they would greet minority races at the front and side doors. The feeling was that they may not be as welcome as we would like for them to be. But to me, integration was the law of the land, and I took the same attitude that we did at the school. This is something that we need to work out and not really fight too much. Incidentally, no minority race people attempted to attend services at that particular time, so it wasn't really a problem. But to hear the deacons talk, they were just not to be too cordial if a minority couple showed up. I guess the southern attitude was, "we don't really know how to handle the situation." We would rather have things status quo instead of changing to some other social order.

It's just unfortunate that, among the churches, they say the 11:00 hour on Sundays is the most segregated hour of the week. There are not many large Negro churches in Cary. There is the one on Highway 54. But the majority of the blacks want to attend their church, so the integration is just not there. As you overlook the three services at the First Baptist church now, very seldom will you find a black couple or individual. Those few who do come are likely to be from a college and show up from Saint Augustine's or maybe a black student from NC State University.

There was no real tension, except the feeling that we don't want to interrupt the status quo. Dad Dunham was the chairman of the board most of those four years that I was deacon, so he was a calming influence. My comment to the deacon board was that I would ask the black couple or black individual who came to the door, "Did you come to worship?" If they said yes, I'd seat them anywhere they would want to be seated in the auditorium. But I had this comment to make also. If they came just to see if they could get in, I would invite them to go down to the Methodist church on the corner. So the only tension would be opposition of the change to the status quo.

Fred Seeger: I was in the air force during Civil Rights, and even in the South, the air force was fully integrated, so I became accustomed to that. I lived on base when I was stationed at Frances E. Warren Air Force Base in Cheyenne, Wyoming and also at Maxwell Field, Alabama. It wasn't unusual to have a black family living next door. In fact, one of our very good friends, a black couple, did live next door to us. It was something that I had become accustomed to, being in the air force.

When I was in Korea, I had four or five guys of color that lived in my Quonset hut with me. They were no more foreign to me, maybe not as foreign as my very best buddy from Chicago who was Italian. I had never even tasted black olives or pizza, things of that nature that Italians eat, as a backwoods boy out of North Carolina.

Integration is something that just evolved. In fact, when I came to Raleigh as assistant division manager, I trained black guys to work in the territory in Eastern North Carolina as salesmen for the tobacco company.

So many people have the wrong slant on desegregation and segregation in the South. People who didn't live or grow up in the South think we would say, "There's a black guy. Look out, he's going to kill you." And it wasn't like that at all. One of the guys that I grew up with and knew very well in Cary was about my age. He lived just down on Harrison Avenue, but he didn't go to the same school I went to. We would go out and do things together. I brought him with us when a group of my friends would go to Silver Lake to go swimming. He really wanted to be a part of my group of friends. So it wasn't like so many people have portrayed that the South was so extremely segregated back in the forties.

The Ashworths - Ralph: Cary's Centennial Celebration was held in 1971. We had women's groups, we had men's groups and we had parties and functions. We all dressed up and we had different names for the groups, fashion shows, and a parade. So that was a big time. (**Daphne**): We should mention there was a real effort to make sure that the African-American community was involved in all the activities, because they had had a big part in the creation of Cary. They were an important segment of the town. The blacks had a group too. A lot of the receptions were all together, which was good.

Ned Perry: Things have changed rather dramatically in Cary's fire department over the years. When I came to Cary in 1975, it was a combination department. We had eleven volunteers and fourteen paid personnel. As we grew and demand for fire protection increased, we obviously needed more people full time. So I started a program several years after I became fire chief to begin to reduce the reliance on the volunteer people. That program took eight or ten years to transition. We didn't release any of our volunteers, we kept them all until they chose to retire or to move. They were eligible for a retirement program under the North Carolina Firemen's Pension Fund. Several of the volunteers in Cary completed twenty years and are drawing that pension today.

One of the things that I'm very proud of is how we developed a very specific program of selecting our new recruits which enabled us to cross over barriers; the racial barriers, and the sexual barriers – male and female. There were no blacks in the fire department when I came here. Now we are well integrated. We were able to bring in blacks and other minority or protected groups into our program in a legal way that has been without problems. I'm particularly pleased with that because it has been very fair to the people that we brought into the program, and has enabled us to continue with these promotions and transfers that are very much an integrated part of our service. Our department is very highly integrated today and it runs very smoothly.

There were also no females in the department when I started, and I brought the first females into the program. That gets a little bit complicated when you have people staying all night and sleeping at the fire station. In most fire stations at that time, all of the fire fighters slept in one dormitory except for the officers, and they had a private bedroom. After we took a hard look at this challenge, other fire chiefs and I decided to do away with the officers' room. So what I did was to put all of the people in the one dormitory to sleep, dressed in a standard uniform at night.

In the area where the showers were, we had to redesign fire stations to have separate bathrooms for men and women. Then when it was time to go to bed, men and women would go to their bathrooms and dress for bed in the attire that was standard for everybody. Then they would go to bed.

When the bell rings at night, bright lights come on, the bells go off and you're awakened instantly. When that happens, you get into boots that are lined with wool so you don't have to put on socks, and your pants are already over the boots so when you step into the boots, you're dressed usually in less than ten seconds, and ready to get on the truck. This happened with men and women alike. It worked extremely well in Cary.

CHAPTER 8

THE PLAN TO DESEGREGRATE THE SCHOOLS

Prior to 1965, the Wake County School Board was divided into districts, separated largely by race, and each district was headed by a committee. The local district committees became very powerful over the years. In the 1940s and '50s, Henry Adams was a leader and a driving force on Cary's Advisory Council, which successfully improved facilities and brought in amenities for the schools.

In 1965, exercising a new level of authority granted by the state, the Wake County School Board abolished the districts, along with their committees, and created one district divided into attendance areas. Henry Adams was elected to the board. Six schools were placed in the Cary area. The white schools were: Cary Elementary, Cary High, West Cary Elementary, and Swift Creek Elementary. The black schools were: East Cary Elementary (Kingswood) and the new West Cary High. The new areas were headed by advisory councils that were weaker than the district committees had been. Cary's representative for the Advisory Council to the Board of Education was, once again, Henry Adams.

In an article in the Cary News of 12/29/99, Ella Williams-Vinson was quoted as saying that when they were boys her father, Arch Arrington Jr., and Henry Adams were close friends, something unusual between a black boy and a white boy at that time. Later, when Ms. Williams-Vinson was a teacher and Henry Adams was on the council, she recalled how Henry worked side by side with E.B. Ferrell and Clyde Evans Sr. from the black community to improve the black schools as well as the white ones.

Tom Byrd: If you are looking for things that were truly significant about the old days, what jumps out at me was the emphasis that local people put on education. This was a time when educational status was locally funded, to a large extent, and locally controlled. They were not getting a lot of resources from the county or the state, or even the federal government as they do now. Schools were largely the result of the effort that the local people put into them. I think that gave the town a sort of character that the typical little rural southern town did not have, and led to a lot of the positive things that later happened in Cary.

Carl Mills: East Cary Elementary (Kingswood,) was the black elementary school for the district, and Berry O'Kelly was the high school for the black kids. Berry O'Kelly was annexed into the Raleigh city system, and at that time Wake County paid tuition charges for the black kids in the area to go to Berry O'Kelly. Then what is now West Cary Middle School was built to house the black kids in the Cary area, with grades nine through twelve. That was to counter the charges the city of Raleigh and the Raleigh public schools placed on students attending Berry O'Kelly. There were only about ninety black kids involved from Cary in the late fifties. There were such a small number of black kids in the Cary attendance area that the feeling was that this was an ideal time to integrate. This meant thirty black kids went into the ninth grade, and about sixty went to the high school, a very token situation. But that's all there were.

Part of the story needs to be told about the Advisory Council in Cary during the fifties and sixties. It was about as powerful as the Board of Education. We met in the current library at Cary Elementary where there was an auditorium that sat over nine hundred people, and there would be standing room only. Folks came from Mount Vernon, Swift Creek, the Cary area, from all over and packed the place. I found out very quickly that the Cary Advisory Council was very forward looking. If you explained to them what you wanted to do pretty thoroughly, in other words you didn't pull their leg, they would give their approval, and they would raise the money.

I'll tell you, desegregating the school operated so smoothly in Cary, you wouldn't believe it. You would have had to experience it, and the key to me was the Advisory Council which was very important. Whatever we got into, if there was a vocational program, a new athletic program, what-have-you, they would raise the money to get it started.

At that time, there was a bitter battle between the city and the county school districts. Cary was in the county district during the time of desegregation, administered by the local Cary Advisory Council. Later, in a bid to even out the racial imbalances, in 1975 members of the House of

Representatives that lived in Raleigh presented a bill to the General Assembly to merge Wake County, Stevenson and Raleigh city schools into the city school district. It passed in 1976. However, minority percentages in the inner-city schools continued to rise thereafter.

Charlie Adams: My dad, Henry Adams, had such a passion for girls and boys and education and athletics. I don't know that he had all the advantages when he was growing up, so he wanted every boy and girl in Cary to have better opportunities, and more advantages, and a better school system. I've never known anybody who worked longer and harder at an avocation than he did to try to get things for Cary and for the Cary schools. At an early age, as a kid, I remember him just night after night being involved with the local politics and the Cary Advisory Board. It seemed like he served on that forever. He wanted to make sure that Cary had the best school in Wake County, and that they had what they should have had. I heard a lot of people over a lot of years talk about how they had never seen anybody fight for their school like he did. There was a lady from Garner, Mary Gentry, who was on the school board at the same time, and I remember her remarking that if everybody had the passion for their community that Henry Adams had, Wake County would be the finest school system in the country.

I think he felt that when he had done what he needed to do for Cary, it was time to try at a different level. They had encouraged him for years to run for the Wake County Board of Education, which he had always put off, because his love was Cary and he wanted Cary to get these things. I think somebody told him that if he would get on the Wake County board, Cary can get even more. So he ran, and he was elected pretty much by a landslide. He was well respected all over the county, and as a businessman, everybody knew him. I can't remember how many terms he was on the Wake County board.

I am really proud of all the things that people tell me that he did. I guess the thing I'm most proud of was that he was so ahead of his time in Civil Rights, and was concerned about separate but "so called" equal, which were not equal schools. He was on the Board of Education on two levels. At the local level, he saw the black schools and the white schools, and he knew we had the haves and the have-nots. Then at the Wake County level, he saw that it was even worse than that, and all those things bothered him greatly. I heard him in conversations with my mom, talking about how it was just not fair. One of his goals was to do everything he could to try to create a more equitable situation, and one of them was to start the integration process and get the black kids going to Cary. So he gathered a group of people together to develop a comprehensive plan to desegregate the Cary school. My dad told the principal, "We can't integrate Wake County until somebody is willing to step forward and do it locally. As a member of the school board, if I'm trying to integrate Wake County, I can't give it lip service and not do it in my own hometown." So he felt very strongly that Cary should be the first, and that in Cary desegregation could go smoothly. And then the rest of the county could follow suit.

Desegregating the schools was not a popular thing back in those days. There weren't many people who believed that blacks were equal, or that blacks should have equal opportunity. I can remember overhearing phone calls and hearing my dad's response, and realized somebody on the other end was really unhappy about him pushing to integrate the schools. I have read articles and I have heard people talking. In fact, one of my best friends who grew up with me and spent a lot of time at my house, and thought my mom and dad were just wonderful, actually turned against Dad because of his position on wanting to give the black children the same opportunities that white children had. Later that person came back to me and said, "Your dad was right and I was wrong. It upset me so badly that I quit going to see him and wouldn't have anything to do with him."

I said, "He had a lot of that, but it never bothered him. Deep down, he knew he was right, and he was willing to take the flack that came from a primarily white community during the days of segregation, because he felt so strongly that it was wrong. I'm most proud of him because he had tremendous vision. He was a very wise man who looked down that road, which most of us are not capable of doing, and realized that this was coming eventually, but somebody had to begin to do something about it. So he did.

My understanding is that my dad, Mr. Cooper, two or three of the local advisory people, a couple of the Wake County people, and the Evans family and the principal of the black school sat down and actually developed a game plan of how many students would come the first year, who they would be, and where they would come from. Obviously the black community put some of their best kids forward. And then each year there were supposed to be a geometric progression of the black kids coming to our school. So they had a really solid game plan that was overseen by the Wake County Board of Education, the Cary Advisory Board, and all the key players were involved.

They had decided that "X" number would come the first year. They would see how this worked. Then quadruple that number the next year, and then they hoped by the third year it would be a full-fledged attendance. I was there from about 1962 to maybe 1965 or '66, and each year it got bigger and bigger. I started out with a black student in my homeroom, and then I had several in sociology the next year, and then the following year I had quite a few. Then I went to Garner the next year to get into administration. So they had a good game plan. They just didn't send the entire black community over and say, we're integrated. There was a great deal of rhyme and reason given to this plan by the black community and the white community. It was well planned so it wouldn't backfire and it wouldn't fail.

I remember in our den, in our kitchen, meetings being held with Mr. Cooper the principal, and a couple of the county board members, and my dad and a couple of key players in Cary, black and white. They knew they were going to have to address a game plan with the H.E.W. I remember them working night after night after night putting this thing together, reviewing it, laying it aside, going off, coming back, picking it up and looking at it again. The H.E.W. in Atlanta had to bless the plan before it could be put into practice, because it was just the beginning of desegregation and they didn't want to see it fall on its face. I remember I was sitting there one night watching TV, and I was listening to my dad out of one ear, and he was very cautious in saying to the group, "We've got to dot every "i" and cross every "t" because we don't want anything to happen to set us back or to unravel this thing or destroy it." So they were very meticulous in putting together what now would be looked at as a model plan for integrating schools.

The H.E.W. did not come in and tell Cary how they should go about integrating their schools. They never got anything from Atlanta or from Washington. Because they were voluntarily desegregating the school, they were never under any fire or guidelines or ultimatums like many other cities and counties operated under later when they were being forced to integrate. Here it was voluntary progression. And then when they submitted it, I remember how delighted they were when they got the word back that the plan was totally acceptable. They were just told, "What you're doing is good, we applaud you, proceed." And that doused some of the fuel to the flames in Cary because they knew it was coming sooner or later. And they were getting pluses and thumbs up all the way along the line. When it came out of Atlanta that this plan was thoroughly approved and supported, I think then things really started to move.

There were several white people in Cary that my dad worked with to develop the plan that I can remember. There was Clyde Keisler who managed Kildare farm. There was W.C. Creel, who was the commissioner of labor who happened to be my father-in-law. And there was a Mr. Green who lived in Morrisville. There was a Ms. Phillips who lived down on Park Street, and there was the principal, Paul Cooper. I think Paul Cooper and my dad were the ones that did the most. I knew what a good man Mr. Cooper was. He had a South Carolina background, which would probably have made it even tougher for him to take the stand that he did, rather than if he had a North Carolina background, but he never backed off of it. Those are the white people I remember who worked with my father.

From the black community, there was the Evans family, which was a very prominent family in Cary. There was the principal of the black school in Cary, (probably J. Estes Byers.) He was the man that my dad had the most confidence in, and met with night after night when they were trying to develop the plan, along with the Evans family. My dad had a tremendous relationship with the blacks in Cary. They trusted him as a pharmacist and an appliance man, and they believed that what he was telling them was in their best interest and was right, and he would never let them down. As a result, it went a lot smoother because they did trust him and thought that he was taking them in the right direction, and they believed in him. All of their families knew him, a lot of them had worked for him, worked with him and they respected him. They thought he was okay.

The black community did not fight against desegregation because they saw the advantages to it. They realized that, for example, athletically the white students never knew whether we were better or worse than the black students, but we played in the nice facilities, we had the nice uniforms, and we had all the publicity. I remember how I would play backyard basketball with a lot of the black kids growing up, and they always were very envious of where we played. We would always play a preliminary game in Reynolds Coliseum before a state game, and then they would read about it in the Raleigh News and Observer or the Raleigh Times. We were undefeated in football, or won the state championship in basketball and got publicity that, had they done the same thing in the black school, you would have never heard about it. So I think they saw tremendous advantages in what we had as opposed to what they had.

And the black community was much more receptive because Cary had a good black population. They were good people. They were not racists and they were not radicals. They were just good, solid citizens who grew up with good work ethics and got along with the white people, and they realized this could work. I think the people who found it most distasteful were the white people who resisted, those who were the most racist and did not believe in equal facilities. My mom and I used to talk about how there was probably about a third of the Cary population that was very accepting of the idea, and probably another close to a third that were just waiting to see what was going to happen, and then the other element fought it and fought Dad, and tried everything they could to keep it from happening.

There were two school systems at that time, the Raleigh city schools and the Wake County schools. They were not one system like we have now. I don't know about the Raleigh city schools because we did not have anything to do with them. But in Wake County, Cary was the first school to officially and formally integrate and had the first black students. Cary was absolutely being watched by other communities. I remember all the articles in the News and Observer and the Raleigh Times that were both pro and con about Cary getting out front and integrating first. There were those who thought Cary was progressive and then there were those who thought Cary had sold out. But I think the Apex's, the Garner's, the Millbrook's, the Fuquay's all over the county were looking at Cary to see what was going to happen here when they bring those black kids to school. Are they going to have a race riot, or have a war, or are they going to burn down the school? What's going to happen? And then it went so smoothly.

That's another thing I feel good about when I talk about Cary. Cary was a leader. Cary always has been a leader in Wake County. They were a leader athletically. They had the first boarding school, the first public school, the first school to integrate. Those are things that a lot of people don't know. I lived two houses from the school all my life, and I used to read the plaque up there, "First public school in North Carolina." I always felt good telling people that I was from Cary because of the school, the athletic program, integration. Cary just did things before everybody else did them, and they did it the right way and it worked, so I felt good about Cary. And I'm pleased about that part of history and the role that my dad played in desegregation. It was not an easy thing to step forward back in the fifties and the sixties and say, "This is wrong and something needs to be done," and then do it. Because white Cary, white North Carolina, white United States was not ready for integration.

I caught some of the same flack. I was teaching in Cary when they were getting ready to close Berry O'Kelly High School in Raleigh, so I went to my principal and said, "You know, those kids have got to go to school somewhere. I'd like to go talk to them and see if they would like to come to Cary." I went over and met with a lot of the athletes, and they had the choice of going anywhere they wanted to go. Ultimately most of them chose to go to Ligon, which was another predominantly black school. But the word got out that I was visiting Berry O'Kelly and that I was at some of the basketball games, and I was trying to get some of the basketball players to come to Cary. I got some of the same hostile phone calls and letters and conversations that my dad had before me. Cary was just not ready for integration. We looked at them as human beings and not at their skin color, and it felt like that was the thing to do.

Paul Cooper Jr.: Daddy, Paul Cooper Sr., was principal at Cary High School from 1948 through 1967. He started out in the old building on Academy Street when there were all grades, first through twelfth. They moved to the new high school on Walnut Street in 1960. Daddy was principal all during the time they were desegregating the school until he retired in 1967. Throughout that time, I was on the west coast and about to get married, so there wasn't much communication between us. We talked over the phone, and there were letters sent back and forth, but there was no email yet, so I didn't hear a lot about Cary. Daddy wasn't one to talk a lot and tell me what was going on. I heard most of what I learned from Mother. But there didn't appear to be any problems in integrating the schools from what I heard.

Mr. Adams was chairman of the school board. I remember Mother telling me, he and Daddy wanted a head start on planning the desegregation of the schools in Cary. They could see it coming and thought it would be best if they did it their way instead of waiting for it to be mandated, and thrust on them overnight when there was no plan for it.

There was an advisory team from the town of Cary, and they came up with a plan. There weren't many blacks in the school district at the time. Most of them were across the line in Raleigh. They developed a plan to slowly integrate the school, a few at a time. It was mainly Mr. Adams and my dad that were pushing to do this on their own terms.

I know some of the white guys that were in my class were dissatisfied and went and talked to Mr. Adams about it at his drugstore. But they weren't far-sighted enough to see it was coming no matter what they thought, and the best way to handle it was to do it at that time under their own plan. They didn't threaten him or anything. I think there may have been a couple of meetings with the public, and once it was explained to them, then they came on board somehow. I don't know that they were ever satisfied, but I think they saw in the long run that it turned out to be the best for Cary. And that was the whole idea, to take care of the high school and Cary, and not let it get out of hand.

Billy Rogers: When I was in high school, my uncle, Henry Adams, was on the school board. He and Mr. Cooper were so close. The things that he could do for the Cary schools were phenomenal. They really tried to keep him quiet.

They held Wake County school board meetings at our restaurant. That was before it was consolidated with the Raleigh city school board. Henry Adams was powerful, and he was an outstanding politician who got things done. So when they had Wake County school board meetings, they had them right here in Roger's Restaurant in Cary. Henry Adams liked Barbara's pies. These people had to drive from Wendell and Fuquay, from all over the county, but Henry Adams had to walk across the street. That always was impressive to me. Henry Adams could call these people, and they would drive twenty-five miles, and all he had to do was walk across the street. They didn't meet in Raleigh somewhere, given the size of Raleigh.

I think that he was always so instrumental in keeping Cary ahead. In those times the local school board members had a lot of strength to be able to have the influence that Henry Adams had. He was a behind-the-scenes type person. He could get right up to you and talk to you eyeball to eyeball. He was a strong-arm type fellow, very convincing and plenty smart.

Sonny Keisler: Dad, Clyde Keisler, was always active on the local school board. In the late sixties and early seventies, he served on the Wake County school board. He worked with Henry Adams' group to develop the integration plan for Cary, and his part in that effort grew to almost full-time. They had the legal responsibility to plan that out and bring it to pass. It was a fairly difficult period of time. People don't like to change, so when you have to change, it always takes a lot of energy.

I don't think there were a lot of group problems. This was not the Deep South. Our black population was not as large as say, where they were the majority in the city. I don't think it was as problematic in this area as in some areas. This area has always been somewhat progressive. I recall him making a lot of comments about how he took a lot of time, energy, and a lot of patience to try to usher that in. There were some hard feelings from people in town, I believe. Whether they were racially motivated or not, they just didn't want to change. That was probably it as much as anything, because they saw it as the beginning of the breakup of the community's system. It was one of the first steps to integration of the community, followed by a lot of other events that pretty much have eliminated Cary as a community. I don't think there were any life-threatening situations. It was just a matter of going through the process, and dealing with folks that didn't like to change. They had to let them know that this is the way it had to be.

Phyllis Cain: My dad, Clancy Cain, was on the Cary Advisory Council. I vaguely remember that. I think he was influential in developing the plan to desegregate the schools in Cary, but I'm not sure. And also he served several years as the president of the PTA in Cary where I was in elementary school prior to desegregation.

Clyde Evans Jr.: Back to this slavery business, what were our forefathers thinking about at that time, using a person as a horse or a mule, a source of income? Or making a person work for what he could eat, and build a shanty and sleep on the ground. People have been cruel in their times, haven't they?

My father was part of the group to help put together a plan for integrating the schools. It was a small area here. Daddy and other blacks would get together and decide what they were going to do, how we were going to cope with this and that. Daddy was the head of the black school board at one time, but they would elect a new leader from time to time. Daddy was not an educator, he believed in the land. Some people believed in education, but Daddy didn't believe in education too much. We all finished high school but never went to college. Black people who worked with Daddy or worked for Daddy sent their children to college, but he didn't, but he left and estate worth more than a million dollars. There weren't that many people here to integrate.

Civil Rights didn't bother us too much. There were things we had to go to the grocery store to buy, like coffee and sugar and salt and so forth. The rest of it, we made or grew ourselves. We had everything we needed. You could work for whites and intermingle with them, but you didn't sit down and eat or sleep in their quarters. We worked for nobody. My father wouldn't allow us to work for white or black, we worked for him only. That was his philosophy. He had it in for nobody, he loved everybody.

Linda Evans: During the time that Cary was putting a plan together to integrate the Cary school system, Granddaddy, Clyde Evans Sr., was on the Board of Education, but I think he might have been a token representative. He did not necessarily have a lot of impact on decisions that were made. I wasn't here when all that happened, we were living in Raleigh. So we experienced integration in Raleigh more so than we did here in Cary.

Carl Mills: Since we had developed our own integration program in the county, the H.E.W. constantly sent us surprises. They were sending people to examine us and see if we were following all we said we were going to do. We just had committees within the county within each attendance area who met and decided how integration would take place. In Cary, it was done on a volunteer basis. We would send a statement in as to what we were going to do, and the H.E.W. always wanted to send somebody to inspect us and see if we were doing what we said we were going to do. Then we would meet occasionally with the city superintendent and he would have the biggest laugh. He would say, "I'm not going through all this turmoil of integrating. All I do is go to the judge, the judge tells me what to do and I do it, and I go home and get a good night's sleep." But what we put together met with the mandates of the laws that were being enforced at that time. The group in Cary was very cooperative, mainly because there weren't many black families in that attendance area. In Cary desegregation went beautifully.

Gwen Matthews: In 1962, my father was very active in the NAACP. Integration was just getting started, and there were a few schools in the state and a few in Raleigh that were being integrated. In 1963, Cary was more rural than it is now. It took a year's preparation to develop the desegregation plan for Cary. They chose six of us black students to be the first to go into Cary High. They were trying to get one black student in each grade.

My cousin and I had always been together in school and we were in the same grade. They selected both of us to go to Cary High, and decided there would be two black students in the eleventh grade. There was one in the ninth grade, one in the tenth grade, two in the eleventh and two in the twelfth grade. I knew all of them because we were at the same high school together. Francis White and Lucille Evans were the two seniors. Brenda and I were in the eleventh grade. Phyliss McIver was in the tenth grade, and Esther Mayo was the freshman. Gregory Crowe came a year after us. They decided to only send girls that first year.

I was not given the choice. My daddy told me, "You're going to Cary High next year. This is what you are going to do, and where you will be going to school next year."

I protested, "Oh, but Daddy...," to no avail. I didn't take part in the decision-making process at all within my family. I did what I was told. It was not cruel, he did not come across as being cruel. His message was more, "This is something you must do. I believe you can do this, Gwen, but it's not up for discussion. I know you're leaving friends, I know you're leaving fun, and I know you're leaving everything else, but you're going to leave it."

I cried, and I went to Mother and said, "Please make Daddy change his mind."

She said, "No, I can't do that."

I had great friends at Berry O'Kelly, and great teachers that I had to leave. Throughout those two years, we did stay in touch, but when you leave one environment and go to another, it becomes difficult to bridge the gap, because our worlds were just so different. I could not replace those lost years at Berry O'Kelly.

Lucille Evans Cotton: The year was 1963, and I had just finished my junior year at Berry O'Kelly High School. Sometime during the summer, my mama came to me and said, "You're going to be going to Cary High next year."

You don't question your mama. All she said was, "You will be going to Cary High." She named some students who had also been selected, and she also named my cousin Mitchell. But then they decided he would not be going because he was the only boy, and they only wanted to send girls that first year. So the final selection was just six girls. I knew the girls because we all went to the same school. There was one freshman, one sophomore, two juniors and two seniors. I was going to be a senior and Francis White was also going to be a senior.

So this was the year of integration. Up until then, there were no blacks going to Cary High, but the principal at Cary, Mr. Cooper, decided there were going to be new Negroes in his school. Word of his decision got back to some of the PTA members at Berry O'Kelly High School, and they had a meeting. They went to the official school board and agreed to contribute to the integration of Cary High. Then they chose some students to be the first ones to go.

How I was ever chosen I will never know, but our parents put in applications and the qualified students passed. The reason I didn't understand why I was chosen was because, although I was not a dummy, I was not a genius either. I was not brainy, and the other people that were chosen, I thought were smarter than me. But evidently they weren't so much smarter than me, and evidently I was just as smart as the ones at Cary High already.

I had the opportunity to ask Mr. White how we came about to be chosen. He told me that twenty black families put in applications for their children to attend Cary High, and the ones that were best qualified were chosen. So I asked him, "Mr. White, I know I'm not a dummy, but I'm not a genius either. Why was I chosen? I know a lot of other people that could have been chosen."

He said, "At the time, Mr. Moore, (who was the principal at Berry O'Kelly,) said Lucille Cotton can handle herself. He said, 'She isn't the type of person that gets in a situation, and she can overcome it. She does not let anything get her down.'" And I wondered, how did he know this? It was true, but I didn't know the principal knew me that well.

So I said, "I don't believe you."

He said, "You can believe me, because all of you were monitored. And we will keep our eyes on you while you were at Cary High. If you get into any trouble, there will be somebody there that can help you out. The whole time all of you will be watched." So I made it.

<u>Bertha Pleasants Daniel</u>: When they started integration, my daughter Anne was graduating from high school. Our housekeeper's niece was the first black student to walk across the stage on graduation night. Little did I ever dream that my housekeeper's little black niece would be graduating in the class with my white Annie. But that change had come about.

When my children were in high school, they started integration in Cary. It went very well. I think the children were hand-picked by the NAACP, and they were the select students, apparently. I never heard of any problems early on at all. There were not a lot of them, but they were nice children and they were well behaved. Children had a little more respect for their elders than they do now. There were so few that it was like a token thing, and it worked out very well.

I don't remember that my children had any feelings of resentment at all. I don't remember that they ever had a special friend that was black. But I was working and they were in school. I know their friends that came here were always white. I think they pretty much stuck together, whites together and blacks together. But it was certainly not a disruptive thing in Cary, early on. I don't know who was responsible for handling it, but apparently it was handled well.

But by the same token, I never remember any controversies between the black and white in Cary at all. When the town was segregated, it was an accepted thing. We had black families living all up and down Cornwall Road. Our house was down there, but there were blacks that lived over on this side, and they were nice. We called them "aunt" and "uncle." It was a respectful way to speak to them. My daddy did a lot of fox hunting and he had a lot of fox hounds. They were just as scared to come to our house as they could be because they were afraid of those dogs. They were really our friends. I never had any feelings of animosity toward any of them. I don't remember hearing about it.

There was another community of blacks over on the other side of Highway 54. I never knew many of those people, although that's where my housekeeper lived, and her family and her husband's family lived there too. They were light-colored blacks, and that set them a little apart, even back then. They had that community and we had ours over here.

When I was growing up there was a black school between Shirley Drive and Cary Elementary School, and a black church too. The school burned down and they built a new black school across Highway 54, called Kingswood. It started out as an all black school, but down the road it was integrated too.

People's conception of tyranny in the South against the blacks, I was never aware of any of that. I've seen it in the movies, unbelievably so, but I never saw any signs of it growing up. We were associated with them, but most of them around here were respectful of white people. They were of a little different class, and they seemed to accept it and recognize it, and we accepted it and expected it, so to speak. It was just a way of life. And of course, they were the ones that came in and did your laundry and helped with the housework, helped when babies were born and that kind of thing. They were available. Now of course they're not available anymore, and that's good for them and we do all right too. So I guess it's all well and good.

INTERIM SOLUTIONS – ONE-GRADE SCHOOLS:

According to the Civil Rights Act that was passed in 1964, the Wake County school board was required to submit a report to the H.E.W. on an annual basis stating what progress had been made with desegregating the schools. The first two reports were accepted by the H.E.W., but the report of August, 1966 did not measure up to the standards they set. The Wake County School Board was told that their efforts were inadequate, and they should consider transferring from 100 to 300 black students to all-white schools, or vice versa.

This could cause predicted chaos. So Henry Adams announced that the Cary Advisory Council was developing a plan that could satisfy the requirements of the H.E.W. The plan was to convert the two-year-old all-black West Cary High School to a ninth-grade-only school for all races. The Wake County School Board enthusiastically approved the plan which more than satisfied the H.E.W. for the entire county, not just for Cary. Everyone believed the problem was solved.

However, a group of parents who disapproved of the ninth-grade school plan banded together and filed a lawsuit against the plan. They argued that the new school was a merger of two schools, and such a merger would require a public hearing. The suit went all the way to the North Carolina Supreme Court, where it finally failed. Before the suit was decided, the school opened in the fall of 1967 as West Cary Junior High, a ninth-grade only school. Under the freedom of choice option, only four students requested a transfer to another school. J. Estes Byers remained as principal when the conversion was enacted, making him the first black principal of an integrated school in Wake County.

Following the success of West Cary Junior High, in 1969 Kingswood Elementary was converted to a desegregated, all-sixth grade school. Joseph Walters was named principal, and became the second black principal in an integrated school in Wake County.

Charlie Adams: The committee working on the integration plan decided that after they did this minimal beginning and a smaller transition, that the goal would be to work towards a separate campus that would be an integrated one-grade school. My dad's thinking was, this would be less of a volatile situation than having a four-year high school program, and all of a sudden, boom, everybody's dropped in there. They thought that if they could have this one school over at West Cary for just the ninth grade and all the black ninth-graders and all the white ninth-graders went there instead of all going to Cary High, then that would give them one year to get to know each other in a less volatile situation.

I think it really worked out well because number one, they got to know each other. They got to play ball together, they got to study together, they got to be in activities together, and it wasn't where the small number of blacks got lost into a big white high school. I think it was a very wise decision to do a one-grade experiment. It worked well as a precursor to all the students of both races coming into one high school. That made the next three grades much easier, because you and I have been together, we've played on the same team, we've studied in the same library, we've ridden on the same bus, but the blacks didn't feel as threatened because they weren't outnumbered so badly by all the whites. It was more of an equitable ratio. I had not heard of any school district setting up a one-grade only school.

There were a number of white parents who were very upset when West Cary was first converted to a ninth-grade-only school, and they actually initiated a lawsuit. I can remember a petition and a lawsuit, and I knew some of those white parents. They were petitioning the General Assembly and the Town Council because they did not want West Cary to be a one-grade school. But I think when the game plan was explained, most people said, "Well, you know, we don't want to necessarily integrate, but if we're going to have to, this is a pretty sensible way of trying to do it." I think sanity prevailed, and most of them were able to look at the big picture and say, "Here's where we hope to be someday. This single school is a step in getting us there." So I think more people bought into it than those that were unhappy about the black high school being shut down and turned into a single grade school. It was the small-minded looking at a lesser versus a big picture, and then realizing that down the road the wisdom made sense.

Of course, I was prejudiced because I believed very strongly in what my dad was doing, and I was certainly on that side. And at times it felt like we were really the minority working with the minorities, but as it turned out, I'm not so sure we were. I think there were a lot of good people in Cary who sat back and accepted my dad's leadership and said, "You know, if Henry Adams believes in this and he's leading it, then it must be okay." And you don't hear from the good people who are pretty satisfied or will accept it. It's the ones whose comfort zone is being messed with, and that's what this group was experiencing.

Paul Cooper Jr.: There was a plan to convert a black high school to an all ninth grade school for all white and black students that would be going to Cary High School the next year. They made that conversion, and it gave the blacks and the whites a chance to get to know each other, and play ball together, and study together, or do whatever they wanted to do, before they came to Cary High School, all in one big group. I'm sure there may have been incidents, but there wasn't anything big that I know of. I didn't hear my dad talk about any problems on campus of that ninth grade school.

Carl Mills: It so happens that when the decision was made and the Advisory Council recommended to the Board of Education to integrate, it made sense to put all the ninth graders into one school at West Cary.

Out of three hundred and some ninth graders, thirty were black students, which was somewhat of a token situation. There was a certain element of people in that area who were opposed to setting up that school. They took the case to court and protested integration. Just as soon as the case was presented to the judge, he immediately called a time out to confer with the two attorneys, and as soon as they returned to their seats, he said, "Case dismissed."

Part of the situation was that we had a black principal at West Cary, and he was very careful. He would come over and meet with the eighth grade kids in the auditorium during orientation, and that was the first formal look they had of him. He had a terrific personality. Then he would have several Sundays when the parents were invited to come in and visit. So if the kids didn't know him, it was their own fault. No surprises.

Deborah Matthews Wright: In 1968, for the eighth grade I went to Cary Elementary School that was then in the red brick building right in the middle of town. By that time integration was fully implemented, so there were many more black children in the school by then. In 1969, I went to West Cary for just the ninth grade. That school is on Evans Road, and now it is a middle school. And for grades ten through twelve, I went to Cary High School.

Carl Mills: When I first went into the county office as assistant superintendent in 1965, there were H.E.W. people who would come in from Washington to check on our plan for integration. I don't know why but they would always send four or five blacks to examine our program. The first time they came in to meet with Mr. Fussell, he called the assistants in and told them about the visitors that had arrived to see our system. They thought they were going to see 840 laws of Wake County in just an hour or two. We didn't get through half of it in a day's time. I had to be the smart-aleck. When they said they wanted to see what we were doing, I said, "You want to see what Boston has?"

"Oh no sir, we don't want to compare you to Boston." I said that because I knew Cary had more black principals than the city of Boston had. During those inspections, we found that Garner made a note of a black physics teacher with all white kids and the H.E.W. group wanted to know why. So we suggested we talk to the instructor and see what he had to say about it. He said he preferred to have students that wanted to learn physics, and the black students just were not interested in the subject. Another stop we made was to a school on the edge of Fuquay and Apex.

Again, the H.E.W. group had an awful lot to say. They asked why there was only one white kid in this third grade class. So we took a look at the third grade class across the hall and found there were only two white kids in there. I said, "This is a crime." But that's what our program said we had to do. Those three kids ought to be in the same class, but it would be in violation of the rules.

They just smiled and said, "Let's go on to the next thing." They found in one case a white bricklayer instructor in Wake Forest who had only black students in his class. That instructor told them that they had not forced the white students to take that class, and the black students seemed to go for the trades. They wanted to learn to lay brick. They even inspected our buses, counted the blacks and whites on each bus. We just had the best time with the H.E.W.

CHAPTER 9

CARY HIGH SCHOOL
THE FIRST DAYS AS A
DESEGREGATED SCHOOL

Clyde Evans Jr.: Cary had some fine people. During the transfer from segregation to desegregation, Cary had no problems at all. There were no marches, no unusual activities, and there was no upheaval. Cary just made the necessary changes.

Gwen Matthews: As I prepared for my first day at a white high school, my father and I had a discussion about how to act and what to do, what not to do, how to respond, how not to respond, and certainly not to retaliate. I was told to just go about attending classes and doing the kinds of things I should do as a student, and not get myself embroiled in any situation.

The first week was extremely difficult. My cousin Brenda and I were on the same bus because we lived on the same road. At that time, our road was called Rhamkatte Road because it was named after the Rhamkatte community. It went all the way to Holly Springs Road. The road is now called Tryon Road. She lived maybe three miles up the road from me, and so we rode the same bus.

When we got to Cary High and stepped off the bus, there was a crowd of people standing in from the school, blocking our way. They were all chanting, "Two, four, six, eight, we don't want to integrate." I don't think I'd ever seen so many red, angry faces in my life. As we tried to enter the school, nobody ever touched us physically, but they blocked our entry. They tried to spit on us, but none of it hit us. I would rather say we were "spit at," but not "spit on." And we were called lots of names, such as "nigger," "coon," and "bitches." Stepping off the bus and having to face that angry crowd was not fun, but my father was determined that I was going to go through with this. Because my parents and Brenda's parents were members of the NAACP, it was crucial for us to go all the way through and graduate from this white school. So we faced that crowd.

Stepping off that bus and facing all that anger has had a tremendous impact on me personally. Those were the angriest faces I can ever remember seeing in my life. It's interesting to think there were males and females, young and old in the crowd of people who were standing outside chanting at us. There were some students, but the majority of those people were parents. That experience has affected my relationships with white men, even though white women were there too. My memory of stepping off the bus is of seeing this sea of angry faces, of what appeared to be a lot of people (it could have been twenty, but at the time it looked like two hundred to me). Stepping off the bus I saw women and teenagers, and behind them lots of tall white men whose faces were so red, and they are the ones I remember, not so much the women and the teenagers. It took me many years to be able to trust white men, and be able to talk as freely and easily with them as I can with white women. I can sit and laugh and talk and joke with them without any problems. I just don't know that I trust them as much.

Lucille Evans Cotton: In high school, I never took college preparatory courses. I always took commercial courses because I wasn't planning on going to college. I wanted to be a secretary or an operator, and I could take business courses for that. The courses that I took were not hard, so I didn't have any problems with school.

As a senior, I had all the units that I needed except about two, so I could take anything I wanted, as long as I had English and one other course. So the subjects that I took that year at Cary High were bookkeeping, shorthand, typing, English, and home economics. I had already had home economics twice before, but I took it again so in case I failed something, I would have three more subjects to fall back on and I would still graduate.

HOW BLACK STUDENTS WERE TREATED AT SCHOOL:

Gwen Matthews: We never had any true friends at Cary High, but two young ladies did become friendly toward me. One was named Adonna and the other was Legare. I was befriended by those two and another young man who was in my math class. He was very friendly in a very sympathetic kind of way, and he would talk to me in class. Adonna and Legare also would talk to me in class, and that helped me get through my classes. They made such an impression on me that I asked my mother if I could name my new baby sister after one of them, and she said yes. So my youngest sister is named Adonna.

All six of us were the only black students in all our classes throughout the day. Our teachers did not call on us, even if we raised our hand. I cannot speak for my cousin Brenda. She is no longer living now. Students would not sit beside us, or they would move their desks so there would be lots of space around us so they would not be sitting close to us. I could tell, though, that some students would have preferred not to be that way, but peer pressure is so very strong. It would have been great if more students had tried to befriend us. Why those three individuals talked to me, I have no idea. I don't know whether they just didn't care what the others thought, or if they felt being friendly was the right thing to do. Maybe they just thought they would at least speak to me and see if I needed any help. But I did have those three people in my classes who were friendly enough to where I could get through the class.

The black students who came after us had a little easier time. But for those first years, it was not a good experience for any of us. It was very difficult when we were not called on, when no one really talked to us, when nobody wanted to share a locker, and nobody would sit beside us. People on the bus didn't want to sit beside us. We would get on the bus, and if the bus was filled we had to stand up. Everybody was scrunching so that we wouldn't touch them.

The turmoil was that very few people asked us any questions or wanted to know anything about us. I compare that to when I went to Meredith College and I was one of the first African-American students there also. Those white college students had lots of questions for me, such as, "Do you tan?" "Why is your hair like that?" They asked that because one day I could wear my hair in an Afro, and the next day I could wear it straight because we pressed it. But at Cary High no one wanted to know anything about us. A lot of that probably had to do with peer pressure. Those were very difficult years.

Lucille Evans Cotton: The students at Cary High acted like they had never seen black people before. They acted like if I got close to them, some of my blackness would come off on them. They would stand at a distance when I walked by. They were always whispering when I walked by, and it made me feel very uncomfortable and very unwanted.

So the six of us would always sit together in the cafeteria, but there was not another black student in any of my classes. Some of the students would speak to me when there were not many other people around, and in class they would sometimes speak to me. But when class ended, if we walked out of the classroom talking, the minute we got out of class and into the halls and there were other people around, then they would kind of skip ahead in front of me so that other people wouldn't know that they had been talking to me. And they were mean. They would call me names.

The school bus stopped right up the street from my house, and I was always the first one on the bus so I never had a problem with getting a seat. But the bus driver would always take off before I sat down to try to make me fall. So I started to sit on the front seat. That way, as soon as I got on the bus and he would take off, I would be on my seat.

But I would be picked up with all the elementary kids on that first bus, and the driver had to go to the elementary school first to drop them off. At the elementary school, I had to change to another bus to go to the high school. It just so happened that my second bus that went right to the high school was from Morrisville where another black girl lived. So when I got on that bus, she was already there. I always had a seat because nobody would sit beside her. That worked out well.

On my afternoon bus, if there were no seats except with me, instead of standing, the white students would never ask, "May I sit here?" They would say, "I want a seat," and sit down. So then when I started getting on the bus and there were no seats, or somebody had their books on the seat, I didn't ask them if I could sit down, I would just say, "I want a seat," and sit down. Because that's what they did, I started doing the same thing, and it worked.

But they were mean on the bus. They would throw spit balls at me. I had this little mean streak, and I'd say, "I don't have any spit balls, but I've got some rocks. So if somebody throws some spit balls up here, I'm going to throw some rocks back there." So spit balls stopped coming.

My daddy was a tall, black man. He was slew-footed, and I'm also slew-footed. When I was walking down the halls of the school, the kids would start walking slew-footed imitating me. So I would say, "If you think my feet are slew, you should see my daddy." And you know, they would just laugh and we went on.

One white girl would always talk to me in home economics. But in English class with the boys, they were always cutting up and giving me such a hard time, and that same girl became one of the fellows. She would not talk to me in English class. I sat in the second row from the front and they would sit in the rows directly behind me, and they would continually push the seats into my seat. I would turn around and they would stop and be looking somewhere else, but then they would start up pushing the seat again. Sometimes the teacher would say something and sometimes she wouldn't. So I would get up, go back there and take the seat out from between us, and then they couldn't push it into my seat anymore. There was another black girl in my English class, and they would hound her and push the seats into hers, and do everything mean, and she would just sit there and take it, and cry and sniffle. But I would move the seat away and then they couldn't push it into mine. But they were still mean and calling names.

In home economics, we had to bring some of our sewing things with us to class. This particular day, I had a pair of scissors in my pocketbook because I had just left home economics. The teacher in the room across the hall sent a note into my class asking the English teacher if she could borrow a pair of scissors, but she didn't have any scissors. Just by chance she asked our class, "Does anybody in the class have a pair of scissors?"

I said, "Yes, I have a pair." So I opened my pocketbook and brought out this great big pair of scissors. They didn't know that I had just come from home economics. They didn't know what those scissors was for. I never had any more problems in that classroom after that. They thought that I carried scissors in my pocketbook just for protection. They started coming around.

In my English class, they had an election for a student to take charge of the class when we first arrived. They thought they would be facetious so they nominated me. So I took over. I brought the class to order and asked for homework, and asked if they had any questions, and then I turned the class over to the teacher. This role was for only one week, and then somebody else was supposed to be nominated. They never nominated anybody else after I took over. I guess I was doing a good job, huh?

But there were a lot of instances where I hated to go to school because of all the name-calling and the bad treatment. When John F. Kennedy was assassinated, we were just getting out of school, and I was getting on the bus when we heard about it. I thought, "Oh, my goodness, we don't have a president. Boy, they're going to give me hell now." But everybody seemed to be of one accord on that particular day, so, I didn't have any trouble then.

Changing classes, the kids were always bumping into me or making cracks about me. Sitting in a classroom, I would look out the door and see two people peeping in with their heads together whispering and pointing at me.

I remember when the Beatles were first on the Ed Sullivan Show, and they were the first to have such long hair. One Monday shortly after they became popular, my curls from the weekend were falling out, but my hair still looked good, so I just combed it down. I didn't realize that it looked like the Beatles' hair. All that day when I was in class and looked out the door, two or three people would be standing there pointing at me, and then two or three more would come to the door and point. Later one of the other girls finally told me that I was wearing a Beatles hair style. It was all over school that Lucille had to be laughed out. I had no idea why they were pointing and laughing at me. But it must have looked good.

In the hallways there would be a parting of the ways to keep from touching me, as if they were thinking that some of my black would rub off on them. They would bump into me, or step on my heels, or try to knock my books out of my hand. They would say things real loud around me like, "I've got some Royal Crown on my hair," (a greasy product we used to put on our hair) just to tease me. But I was like a duck, I let it roll off my back because my mama told me I was just as good as they were. When they pushed me, I would push them back. When they would make nasty remarks at me, I would come back at them. When they gave me a little smart remark, one on one, I could flip it over and give it back without any physical contact. If there had been any physical contact, I think I could have held my own, but I was never in physical contact with any of them. Most of the people that gave me trouble all year, when we were one on one by ourselves, they were nice as could be, but if they were in a crowd, they wouldn't have anything to do with me.

At the end of the year when we had our yearbook signing, they wrote nice things in my yearbook. I guess the ones that gave me the most trouble never thought that I would ask them to sign my yearbook, but those are the ones that I really went out of my way to ask. And they wrote some of the nicest things, and I was really surprised.

GETTING THROUGH IT:

Gwen Matthews: All of us had very strong family support. Mother's family is from Philadelphia, so she was very Northern in her outlook, and she was very supportive. She said, "You do what you need to do to get through this, and if you have to come home and cry, you can cry." And I did. She was always very encouraging and comforting, but also one of those mothers who said, "Get that stiff upper lip," and, "You have been chosen to go through this because you can do it." She talked to me, and prayed for me, and cried with me. My cousin Brenda's mother did the same thing, and I would imagine everyone else's mother did too. Aunt Clyde, Brenda's mother, would come down and they would commiserate and talk about how we were going to handle this situation.

I think that if Brenda and I had not had each other, it would have been a much more difficult time for us. But we had each other, so that was something. Also we knew that we could go home, and home was a good place to go, because then we would get the comforting we needed and we would be allowed to cry. I don't know if Brenda cried as much as I did, but I did some crying, I really did. We had been honor roll students, and at Cary High it became very difficult to make good grades.

If it had not been for my parents, I would not have been able to get through those years. I think that was the case for each one of us who were the first six to go Cary High. If it had not been for our parents, if it had not been for the community, if it had not been for the church, I don't believe we would have been able to last all those years and get through it. Everyone surrounding us at home was very comforting toward us, and Brenda and I supported each other.

Lucille Evans Cotton: When I would come home upset sometimes or didn't want to go back to school, I remember my mama always telling me, "You are just as good as they are, and you can do anything that they can do. So you just hold your head up and go right on back to school." So that's what I did. And that kept me going, because lots of times I didn't want to go. But then I thought, "I want to make Mama proud of me, so I'm going to hold my head up and keep going."

EXTRA-CURRICULAR ACTIVITIES:

Gwen Matthews: I came from an environment where I was well known throughout the school, where I was very popular and well liked, and where I participated in most of the school activities. I stepped into an environment where all that stopped and I did literally nothing at Cary High. If I remember correctly, I did try out for something, but the experience was so devastating, I chose not to go back and try for anything else, and so I never did. I didn't go out for chorus, I didn't go out for track, I didn't go out for cheerleading, I didn't go for any of it because it was just too difficult to go through it. And so I did nothing extra, and Brenda did nothing extra either.

Lucille Evans Cotton: I went to the football games and the basketball games. I took my date and we were the only black people there. And the next day, I would tell one of the other girls on the bus to school, "You missed a good game last night."

She said, "You know you didn't go to that game."

I said, "Yes I did."

"I don't believe you." By the time we met for lunch, she believed me because it was all over the school that I had gone to the game last night. She told me, "That's all I've been hearing about all day. You were at the game last night."

I said, "Well, I told you."

Our class had a party and a dance at the Youth Center at the fairgrounds. They didn't expect me to show up, but I went to that party. I participated in everything they had to offer, and surprised everybody. Eventually they kind of warmed up to me, after they saw that they just couldn't tear me down.

Deborah Matthews Wright: Being eight years younger, I entered Cary High seven years after Gwen. The extra-curricular activities were still fairly closed, other than there were a few token black people who persevered to take part. There was a black cheerleader, and there were black athletes, and you may have a black person on the student counsel, something along those lines. But the other clubs basically were closed. I don't think it was a situation where they were actually closed to us, but that many black students just didn't try to join any of the clubs because they didn't feel welcome. And it was the same for me. I didn't try either. I wasn't very active.

SPORTS:

Charlie Adams: By 1971, my dad had died. I was working for the North Carolina High School Athletic Association, and we had all the schools in the state. By then, the black schools were being absorbed by the white schools. The black organization, the North Carolina High School Athletic Conference, was our counterpart in Rocky Mount. We merged with them in about 1972 and took in all the black schools in North Carolina. We caught hell for that too, and that was the right thing to do. We knew probably the best way to integrate the schools was through athletics.

I do not think the schools could have integrated without athletics. If you could go back and talk to any superintendent, principal, athletic director or coach for about a five-year block during desegregation, they would say that athletics was the thing that brought the two races together and kept the school open. It worked because the kids didn't care if you were black or white, they only cared about whether you could you play. They became teammates, and they were down in the trenches together, and they learned to appreciate and respect each other. And it carried over into the school. I really believe it would have been a blood bath for North Carolina had we not had athletics, because that was the filtering point that made it all happen, not just in North Carolina but in the South, in the country.

In the beginning they didn't know each other, and so they were stand-offish and taking a look and trying to size each other up. And then, once they realized they could play and they were good people, it brought them together. The only thing that I remember a lot of was where parents got upset because Sam came here from a black school and took Johnny's position. Of course, it worked both ways too. But I think the blacks enjoyed finally having the opportunity to be able to compete and see who was good. They fit in very nicely. And the whites were probably a little more stand-offish, but soon found out that these kids could play, and by and large they're pretty good friends and neighbors.

Sadly enough, here we are in the twenty-first century and they still segregate themselves. You can go into a school and the black kids will eat over here and the white kids will eat over there. On the bus, the black kids will sit over here and the white kids over there. But in athletics, it has put them more together.

At that time, the Cary team was called the White Imps, not because we were white. But like the Duke Blue Devils, it was just a color. It could have been the Cary Purple Imps.

Billy Rogers: Cary High School's ball team was called the White Imps in the fifties. The name "White Imps" came about because the University of North Carolina's team was called the White Phantoms, and the Duke Blue Devils were the Imps back then. There was some controversy over what to name the Cary High School team, so they took the Duke and Carolina names and put together, and that's where White Imp came from. Later after desegregation, that name was taken the wrong way. It had nothing at all to do with the fact that we were an all-white school back then. So the name had to be changed just to the Cary Imps to avoid offending anyone. But there was no derogatory reason why it was chosen in the first place, and anybody that knew the history of why we were the White Imps knew it was not a racial slur.

Guy Mendenhall: Cary had very few minorities until they started busing them in from some of the urban areas during desegregation. Those black students had been assigned to Cary High School because of the numbers of minorities that were required at each high school. That became a challenge for the coaches because when football practice started, they had to send a bus out to pick up the black football players. When school started, they rode the county-provided yellow school buses to school, but before school started at the end of summer, whenever sports started practicing, like cross-country, football, and girls' volleyball, they had no way to get to the school, so the school was required on its own to find a way to get them to school and to get them back home. The other problem was, once school started, after they got through with their practice, the school bus had already carried the kids that were not playing athletics back to their homes. So then the school system did assign a bus to come back for the kids who were playing athletics to take them home, but it was up to the coaches to get them on the bus before it left. During basketball season, you had J.B. basketball and varsity basketball. They practice one right after the other, and it would get pretty late for the last team practices. So sometimes the coach would have to get one of the vans to take the kids home, because that special bus had already left to take the first group of athletes home. So a lot of extra time was required of the coaches to drive kids home, particularly after a basketball game. At nighttime when it would get to be 10:30 and my kids had no way to get home, I would get the van and drive them home. Of course, they do not do that now. I don't know how it's done. There were some very good black athletes that came to Cary High.

I feel sure there was some tension between the races. As time passed there were some isolated incidents with some groups, but nothing really big happened that I know about. I was not there when desegregation first started so I really don't know for sure. But I have heard other coaches talk about how athletics helped more than anything else to ease any tensions with the teams and the groups, and with getting them all together. I remember one of the coaches telling me how, when they were having some trouble between the groups out where the buses used to park, the principal called for the coaches to come help. They were a big help in breaking up anything that started.

There are some black kids who have been state champions in wrestling. There have been students who have gotten scholarships to play football. Each year there are some students who get athletic scholarships from Cary High School.

WHY THEY ENDURED IT:

<u>Gwen Matthews</u>: We knew we were setting a precedent. We were cautioned by many men from the NAACP as well as from my father and the community, not to do anything that would make it difficult for those who came behind us. That was an awful lot of pressure to put on us. We were all of fifteen, sixteen years old at the time, and we had left our friends to do this overwhelming task.

The main thrust of their argument to us to get through Cary High was that we must do this for the others who would come behind us; all others, not just our siblings. I do not know about the others, but that was the pressure they put on me. That's why it was so crucial for us to not do anything or say anything that would make anyone lash out at us in a way that it would have caused a real mess at Cary High. Another argument was that we needed to help break down some of the stereotypes. We were chosen because of the kinds of things we had gotten involved in at school. We were chosen because we were scholastically very, very good, and we were chosen because our personalities were such that they thought we could control our reactions without ranting and raving, or getting physical. We were chosen according to very strict criteria because they believed we could succeed with the trailblazing, and we could succeed for everybody behind us, and we could succeed at getting rid of the stereotypes, and we were the ones who could make it easier for those others who would come to Cary High or East Cary Elementary or West Cary Elementary after us.

CHAPTER 10

THE TEACHERS AT CARY HIGH SCHOOL

Charlie Adams: When I was teaching and coaching at Cary High, I remember the principal, Paul Cooper, coming to me one day and saying, "Your dad wants to integrate Wake County, and he feels that to do it right, he has to integrate his own school in Cary first. I'm totally supportive of him. We would like to put one of the first black students in your class."

I said, "Great. I would welcome that student." So in 1963 I had one of the first black students in my class, the first one in Cary and the first in Wake County. We had no problems whatsoever. Things went well. It was never the problem everybody thought it was going to be. And each year it just got better.

Carl Mills: In 1965, a black male student arrived at Cary Elementary and Junior High School to be admitted. He was not expected. As principal, on a non-paid basis, I was at the school all summer enrolling students. Even so, I could still expect half the auditorium to be filled with new kids on the first day of school. This black youngster, Douglas Pennington, came in without his parents, and I thought, this is going to be interesting. At that moment I had something like two hundred new students in the auditorium to put into classes, so I turned him over to a teacher that I knew could handle the situation. It was noon by the time I got back to see what happened with him. When I found him, he had all the other kids entertained. He was telling jokes and he had these Caucasian kids just eating out of his hand.

We had the first Junior Beta Club in the state, the second one in the South. Junior Beta Club is a take-off on the National Honor Society. Within the year, there was no question about him being selected. This young man was terrific. So you see, we integrated at the least expense to anybody, and we gained so much by having a black youngster in our student body.

About that time I was transferring into the school's central office so I was not there the next year when more black students arrived. But we just did not have many black families in the Cary attendance area. The principal almost had the freedom to enroll any student in his district, but this plan was implemented by the guidance of the Advisory Council.

Ruth Fox: I was the first principal at Briarcliff Elementary School when it opened in 1967. I was so fortunate at Briarcliff during integration. They had closed Holly Springs School, which had been an all-black school, and all those students came to Briarcliff which made it very convenient to have all of them come together rather than from here, yonder and everywhere. I was principal of Briarcliff from 1967 to 1973. We had black teachers too. I was never accustomed to black teachers at Cary Elementary when I taught there. The black teachers were very loyal. Of course, our custodian and maid were black, and some of the cafeteria workers were black. We had always had excellent food service at Briarcliff.

Gwen Matthews: I found the teachers at Berry O'Kelly High School to be very nurturing and encouraging. When I got to Cary High, I no longer had that nurturing support. The teachers at Cary were much more distant. Faculty members at Berry O'Kelly did not become our friends, but they were very encouraging people. If we did not have our homework, for example, they might call my mother and tell her. At Cary, the teachers did not take that personal interest. They would not even ask us for it if we hadn't turned it in. It felt as if they didn't even expect me to have my homework. I almost always had it to turn in, but there were times I did not have it because I simply didn't understand it, and trying to get the help or answers to my questions was very, very difficult. I could ask the questions, but I would not get the response. The teachers ignored us, so I did not have the opportunity to get the answers. And that is where those three individuals who befriended me became crucial because they could get answers for me.

Clearly some of the instructors did not like us and did not want blacks in the school. That was obvious, they made that clear. But there were others that may have wanted to help, but simply did not know whether they should or could, fearing how they would be viewed by their peers. I could tell that there were some who would have wanted to help me, but the environment was not conducive to that. I did not feel that I could approach any of my teachers after class to ask for help or clarify questions I had.

Also, I do think the teachers were harder on us. There was one teacher who was not one of my teachers, but I felt very comfortable around her, possibly because her husband was a minister. I had him as a professor when I went to Meredith College as my religion teacher. She did not go out of her way for me, but she certainly made sure that we were comfortable if we were ever around her. So I specifically remember her, because she was very kind toward us and we appreciated that. I'm sure it had to be difficult for her. I don't know what her peers thought of her, or maybe they expected her to do it because she was a minister's wife. But she was very kind.

The following year Gregory Crowe joined us. We had always been friends. I knew him and I knew his sister, Sandra. Greg's personality was very friendly and he was very bright, so I believe that he may have had a little easier time because of his intelligence.

At Berry O'Kelly, my cousin Brenda and I were always on the honor roll and always had excellent grades. But at Cary High, we were almost shut down when struggling to get through our classes, because we would not be called on. We would have to become aggressive to give an answer when we wanted to let people know that we had an answer. I think for Gregory, as a male, it was a little different. He was not a very big young man and did not carry himself in a threatening way. He was able to respond in different ways than we could as females. Women's liberation was not quite as evident as it is now, so we responded a little differently.

Lucille Evans Cotton: I had the same teacher for three subjects. She taught typing, accounting and shorthand, so I was in her class for three different periods. Then I had the home economics teacher and the English teacher who was also my homeroom teacher, so I was in one teacher's class three times a day, another teacher's class twice a day, and another teacher's class only once a day.

The teachers were, for the most part, okay. My home economics teacher, though, didn't seem to like anything that I did in her class, and it came so easy for me because I had already had it for two years. Everything that she taught I already knew. So my mind wondered, and when she saw that it was wondering, she would call on me. But I could answer her because I already knew what she was teaching, and she didn't like that very much. There was a big mirror in the center of the room and

I was always looking in the mirror, checking my hair. She caught me looking in the mirror one day, so she got up, went to the mirror and turned it over so I couldn't see it.

One day she gave us a test about all the ways to help a sick person in bed. One of the things she did not tell us was that you could use a chair turned upside down and propped behind the pillows as a backrest. I knew that from Berry O'Kelly, but that was not a choice on the test. Even though she didn't teach us that, I wrote it on the test paper anyway. Then after the test was over, she said, "Oh, I forgot to mention one of the other things that you can use for a bed rest." She had to either do that or mark my paper wrong, but she did give it to me and told the class about it. Even so, I don't think she liked me very well.

Now my English teacher and my homeroom teacher was my favorite teacher. We got along very well. If I didn't have my homework for whatever reason, she would tell me I could turn it in tomorrow. Or if she had to have it that day, she told me I could bring it by her house that night. So a couple of times, I went by her house in the afternoon and brought her my homework, so it was turned in on time. We had a book report due every two or three weeks, and I hated book reports because I had to do all the reading. I guess that's why I love to read so much now. One particular time I did not have my book report on the due date. I worked on it over the next few weeks along with the next one coming due, and when the first one was two weeks overdue, the teacher asked for it, but I had my two book reports done and ready to turn in. So I never had a problem in her class. And that class was the only class where I got an A.

Deborah Matthews Wright: I started Cary High School seven years after Gwen had started there. By that time, there were black teachers in the school, and the white teachers were more open to the black students. So from an academic perspective, things went well, the teachers were fine.

But the guidance counselors tended to primarily ignore the black students. Either we weren't guided at all, or we were steered toward a trade rather than to college. We were not encouraged to go to college. We were not readily given information about college, we had to seek it out for ourselves. I do remember receiving the information, but it was never given to me. I remember seeing other white students with it. The information had just been given to them, so I ended up going to the guidance counselor's office to ask for it. I think because my grades were pretty decent, I was given more information about college than some of the other black students who asked for it.

Marie Seeger: I knew Ella Williams-Vinson when I was growing up, even though we went to separate schools. She ended up teaching my daughter in the third grade, and had a very profound effect on her. From the time my daughter was two years old, she always said she wanted to teach school. She said, "When I teach school, I will remember the good teachers that I had and I will do things like they did. And I'll remember the bad things that the others did, and I will make sure I don't do those things." She picked out the role models, and Ella Williams-Vinson was one of those. My daughter taught school for many long years.

In the third grade at Briarcliff, our daughter had one black boy in her class. I think it went fine for him.

They had more than one third grade class, and both of the third grade teachers taught different subjects. One taught the language literature courses and the other one taught social studies and math. Both of those teachers were black. Ella Williams-Vinson was one of those teachers.

Carolyn Rogers: After graduating from Berry O'Kelly High School, I went to Barber-Scotia College in Concord, North Carolina. I majored in English and minored in French. I have always thought of Scotia as a finishing school because they taught us how to walk, how to talk, how to set tables, how to interact with people, and how to carry ourselves in a certain way. I hear people say now that I have this certain aura about me, which all came from Scotia's training. When the girls went to town, we had to wear gloves, carry our little pocketbooks, and wear our little pumps. The store owners would say, "You must be Scotia women." Of course we stood out as Scotia women when we went uptown wearing gloves, carrying our pocketbook and wearing our pumps. I appreciate the training I got at Scotia. Because Scotia was an all-girls' school, I was sheltered. It seems that Daddy was always around making sure that his little girl was protected.

When I graduated from Scotia, I took a teaching job in Cheraw, South Carolina at Robert Smalls Elementary School. Mr. Smalls, the man for whom the school was named, was one of the first black naval officers. At that small school, I found my niche as a teacher. I had some wonderful, challenging seventh grade students. My first year of teaching taught me a lot. I thought I knew everything and I didn't know anything, as I found out.

I had one challenging class of students who were low achievers, and I didn't have any materials to work with. I went to the principal's office one day really depressed because I didn't think I was getting anywhere with the kids. He gave me a comic book on Robert Smalls. I started using that comic book as a textbook, and my kids just came alive. So I went from the comic book to comic strips from the newspaper, and my kids learned so much. They were still getting reading and spelling and grammar. They got everything they would have gotten from a regular textbook. It turned out to be one of the most joyous years of my teaching career.

I got married my second year in South Carolina, and my husband and I decided that I would come back to Raleigh at the end of the school year. For awhile I continued to live in South Carolina while my husband lived in Raleigh. After I returned home, I went sent to Cary Elementary School for an interview with Mr. E.B. Comer, who was the principal. During the interview, he said something quite odd, I thought. He asked, "What would you do if someone called you ugly names or someone made some derogatory statements to you? How would you handle that?" He looked me directly in the eyes and asked, "What would you do and how would you act if someone called you a 'nigger?'" It took me aback. I had been insulated from all of that ugly talk. Robert Smalls was an all-black school and I lived in an all-black neighborhood. I went to college at an all-black school. I went to an all-black high school and an all-black elementary school, so I had been in this all-black environment insulated from the outside world, except for when I was living on the farm as a child. When we lived on a farm, we lived in a house on the owner's land because we were tenant farmers. We established a relationship with them that was a cordial relationship. So I had been insulated from all derogatory remarks.

My dad and mom could not make that claim, because they experienced it all. I'm sure they made a pact between themselves declaring, "Our kids will never ever face what we had to face. They will never hear what we heard. They will never be treated the way we were treated." My parents were a team and they insulated and protected their children from the ugliest of segregation.

So when Mr. Comer asked me how would I respond or how would I react and what would I do, I said, "I don't really know what I would do. But I'm not going to let people reduce me to their level. I know what the "n" word means, and anyone who called me one I would consider to be ignorant."

Mr. Comer said, "That's exactly what I want you to do. That's exactly what impresses me about you. Good. So can you begin work immediately?" I started Cary Elementary that fall of 1969.

I had a wonderful experience there. I was one of three black teachers on staff. LaVerne Hairston was a P.E. teacher and Arthur Vines was the shop teacher at that time. Then they hired me, another black lady to teach English. It was just at the beginning of integration, so I was on the rough edges of it.

There was one teacher across the hall from me, an older farm lady who taught English too. One day, she came across the hall to my classroom and said, "I want to ask you a question. I want to know why you want to be in my school?"

I said, "Your school?"

"Yes, why do you want to be in my school? We don't want you here, you know that."

I said, "Well, I was hired to do a job, and I'm going to do that job the best I know how."

As the year progressed, she and I became the best of friends. She invited me to her home. She invited me to her daughter's home. She used to cook chicken and dumpling and bring it to me because that was one of my favorite dishes. We became very good friends. Even when our school moved to East Cary Junior High, she stayed in contact with me. Even when she retired, she would still call me in the afternoons and say, "How are you doing, Carolyn? I was just thinking about you." And sometimes we would go back to that conversation when she asked me why I was in her school, and she said, "That was just my ignorance showing, but you taught me differently." She was able to talk with me about that day. Being an older person, she was brought up in that world where the blacks stayed in their place and the whites stayed in their place, and never the twain shall meet. For her to be able to see that this is not the way it should be was a milestone. When she realized that we should all be together, and that she was able to actually sit down and talk about it made a big difference in her life and in mine. She was a very talented teacher and we learned a lot from each other.

I had only one student who had a problem with my complexion. I parked my car on Academy Street near the First Baptist Church. I went to my car one afternoon and the windshield had been bashed in. They discovered that it was one of my students who obviously had a problem with me. He had taken a bat to my car. He named his bat the "nigger bat." That was his way of getting back at me. I know that they suspended him, but after that I don't know what happened to him. He never came back into my classroom. Obviously the problem was too deep. I never saw any signs or warnings at all that he had a problem with me. He was always low-key and never got excited about learning. My expectation of all of my students was that they would be excited about learning, because there is so much to learn.

My students would challenge each other. I had two black students in one class and one of them was very, very smart. He always challenged the smartest white girl in the class. The two of them were so competitive. When they got their tests back, they would get in a little huddle to see which of the two got the higher score on the test. And then it just caught fire and the whole class became very competitive. The students and I challenged each other. They kept me on my toes. That was an exciting year for me.

During this time, corporal punishment was in place. All teachers had a paddle that was kept in the desk. I remember this big boy who lived across the street from the school who stood at least 5'7" tall, and I'm a little five-footer. I hated paddling with a passion, but I had to paddle him, because he had done something wrong that merited a paddling. He looked down on me and said, "Mrs. Rogers, you gotta do what you gotta do, so just go on and do it and get it over with."

I was thinking to myself, "Oh my God, this boy's bigger than I am, and I'm going to paddle him."

I will never forget how he looked down at me and said, "You gotta do what you gotta do."

I said, "I don't like doing this. I hate doing this."

He said, "Well, if you don't do it, you're going to lose your class." He understood. I think I gave him two licks and that was it. I was not good at paddling. I would rather talk with the student and chastise the student than to paddle them. I was so glad when corporal punishment was outlawed. I don't remember what year that was. I don't know where he is today either.

Cary Elementary School had the junior high in the main building with the elementary classes in the Dry building. Then the whole junior high moved over to East Cary on Maynard Road. I worked there for over twenty-five years. I taught language arts for eighth grade and English for ninth grade, in all ability classes, and it was wonderful. I had some challenging students again, but not any who had a dislike for what I looked like on the outside. If I had any students who disliked me, it was because I was a strict teacher, not because I was a black teacher.

However, the parents were different. I had one parent who came into my classroom and quizzed me as if I were still in college. I later found out he was a professor at State who wore a pair of old overalls when he came to talk to me, so he was definitely in disguise. You never would have thought he was an English professor at State.

Then I had another parent who came to see me who said that her child could not understand the way I talked. Being a black person, you're not supposed to be able to talk, let alone teach English. So this Italian lady said to me, "My daughter cannot understand you and we need to talk about that." Because her accent was so thick, I could not understand her. I was constantly saying, "Excuse me. Excuse me." She finally got the message and went away. We talked about it later, and she decided that her daughter must have been making some things up because she could understand me perfectly.

When I taught at East Cary, I was the only black English teacher on staff for many years. There weren't that many black teachers on staff, so to be the only black English teacher on staff, you stick out. I would always have the most parents of any teacher during open house. I would have standing room only in my classroom. Naturally, they were coming to see if I could talk, and if I knew what I was doing, and if I deserved to be there. I knew that because it was very obvious. We would have to bring in chairs from the other teachers' rooms so all my parents could be seated.

Most parents were not overtly ugly to me because of my complexion. They tried to make it as low key as possible. They would claim things like, "Oh, you didn't grade this paper correctly." Or, "My daughter didn't understand what you were talking about." Or, "My son said you told him this, and that is wrong." They would double-check everything I did, and write little comments on the papers to correct my corrections because obviously I did not know what I was doing. But I knew what I was doing and I knew I was right. And sooner or later most parents would come back to apologize.

I had one parent who set out in August to give me a hard time, and she did all year. At the end of the year when the kids bring teachers presents or flowers, she sent me a bumper sticker that stated, "War Zone." Oddly enough, her daughter graduated from college and became an English teacher.

I had an illustrious career. I have strong faith in God, and I would always pray before I went to school, because I knew it was going to take that for me to get through what I needed to get through that day. My faith has sustained me, and I had a terrific career. I was nominated as Teacher of the Year at East Cary, and became one of the fifteen finalists for the county. That in itself told me that everything I had gone through, and everything that I did was worth it.

Then after I left East Cary, I went to Davis Drive Middle School as an assistant principal when Dr. David Coley was the principal. He was a dynamic administrator and teacher. Dr. Coley is now the principal at Cary High School. If you followed and implemented Dr. Coley's teachings, there is no way you could fail. Mr. Luther Cherry who is now the area superintendent was my last principal at East Cary. He was a dynamic leader. He was knowledgeable, compassionate and professional. He would always say, (and I took that into my leadership position,) "Try it. If it doesn't work, then try something else. If you fail, you fail because you tried it and it didn't work. But just think that if you had not tried it, you would have been more of a failure. So you get out there and try it. Try it." Success often is shrouded in failure.

I would say to him, "Mr. Cherry, I have this idea."

"Well, let's try it. If it doesn't work, then we'll know that it didn't work and we'll amend it and go on." He was tremendous. I have been so blessed by having great leaders, each with a different leadership style. Mr. Comer at Cary Elementary was one. Maude Reese was my assistant principal at Cary Elementary and later became the principal of Cary Elementary for years. They too were dynamic leaders. Harry Stanfield was my principal at East Cary also. I always said, "This man is in charge of his school." He ran that school. He ran a tight ship. But when Mr. Cherry came on board at East Cary, he taught us how to run a school and still be a compassionate individual, and how to treat people, and how to have expectations of professionalism. That's why I'm so blessed. I've had a variety of leaders. Each one gave me something very positive that I used in my own life, both professional and personal.

I went to Davis Drive as the assistant principal and I was there five years before I retired. Now I'm playing. I do some consultant work from time to time.

I believe in being an effective teacher, because what is important is the students. We need to give them a good, solid foundation. We must never forget who we are, and treat kids accordingly. We should always let them know that they are important and that they can learn. We all learn differently, and we all learn at different rates. It doesn't mean that because I learn this way and you learn that way, that I'm an inferior student. It simply means that I learn differently than you, and the teacher should teach me the way I learn. That's what I expect teachers to do, and I always told our teachers that. Kids are here to learn. You're here to teach, and to help students be able to think for themselves. So you teach students the way they learn, not the way you teach. This statement is important to me.

Integration is something that still raises questions to this day. The positives far outweigh the negatives. And now that black students attend day care and kindergarten with white students, it is no big deal. But then it was a big deal. When you have one black student in a class of thirty white students, that child is all alone. There is no one who looks like him in that class. When you have three black teachers on staff, that black child is probably not going to encounter any of those three black teachers all day long. So that child is in a sea all by him or herself. There are so many other things going through that student's mind, until it is virtually impossible to learn. You're not in a comfortable environment or one that is conducive for learning. Black students' test scores reflected that. But how are those test scores interpreted by other people? As black kids are inferior learners? Not true.

If you put yourself in the same environment, as a white student in a class of thirty black students, are you going to learn? Are you comfortable? No, it's impossible. But now the kids are growing up together. For example, my younger sister who was born in Cary started kindergarten with white students, so that is all she knows. If she is the only black person in a group of whites, it doesn't bother her at all because she's so comfortable in that situation. My career took me in that direction where I would be the only black person in most gatherings, so I had to learn to be comfortable in that situation. Believe me, that is work, especially when the environment is not welcoming.

One thing that I tell teachers now is, don't look at a black or Hispanic student and automatically decide that that student's learning ability is inferior. You need to be careful that you don't make that an automatic assumption.

CHAPTER 11

DESEGREGRATING OTHER SCHOOLS

Deborah Matthews Wright: In 1965, there was a law passed which supposedly gave everyone the freedom to choose the school their children would attend. My parents asked me if I wanted to attend all-white Swift Creek Elementary School, so my going there was my decision. I'm not certain that I understood the ramifications of agreeing to go, but at the age of ten I did choose to go to Swift Creek Elementary School, which is just outside of Cary. As I entered the fifth grade, I was one of four black students to integrate Swift Creek Elementary School for the very first time.

That was quite an experience, as you can imagine. My first experience with integration was at the age of ten. I was not yet in high school, like my sister Gwen. It began for me at a much earlier age.

My first day was awful. It was absolutely, positively awful. Even though my parents gave me an opportunity to choose, I don't think they understood what it would really mean in terms of the day-to-day interaction and just the process of going to school. I think from their perspective, they saw this as an opportunity for me because I would be closer to home, since Swift Creek was closer to my home and I would not have to ride a bus as long. They also recognized the distinction between the quality of education in the black schools and the white schools, so from their perspective, my attending a white school would be advantageous. It would be beneficial for me to begin to go to a white school at an even earlier age than Gwen did, because it would have been supposedly a better quality of education. So when I was given the choice, I said, "Oh well, yes, I'll go."

Getting to school that first day, being one of four black students, we had to stand the entire way to school on the bus. We were never given an opportunity to sit down, even though there were plenty of two-person seats on the bus. One white child would sit in an aisle-side seat to keep us from sitting down, so we stood for the entire time from when we were picked up until we arrived at school. The bus driver did nothing because that was just the way it was. And of course, during the ride to school we were teased and ridiculed the entire time.

In school, it was the same scenario, being teased for being different. Not having been around black children, the white students saw that there were obvious physical differences. We were just like them, we had the same likes and dislikes as any other child, but the white children took it upon themselves to mimic us and ridicule us, and make fun of the differences between us and them. This was a daily occurrence. It was just life.

The four of us were not in the same class. I was in the fifth grade. A cousin of mine was in the first grade, and a friend of mine was in the sixth grade, and there was a young boy who was in the second or third grade. For the first two or three years I was all alone as the only black child in my class, so it was a lonely situation. But the next year, or maybe two years afterward, there were one or two people who began to befriend me, more or less. When that began to happen, it was somewhat comforting. But the first year was pretty traumatic. For those one or two children who did begin to talk or share or even just have a conversation with me, eventually they would begin to be teased for it. So it was an up and down kind of situation with seesaw relations in school. I had no real relationships or friendships in school, just acquaintances and people who took the time to share with me or to talk with me.

The first year, the teacher did not treat me too differently outwardly, but she did not do a whole lot to try to keep the other children from teasing me, or to keep them from saying things to me, even when she heard them. The thing that I remember most about her was her feeling toward my ability. I remember, after the first reporting period, she sent a note home to my mother. The note basically told her to please talk to me, because I was obviously copying from another child's paper. Her note strongly implied that I could not be performing or doing satisfactory work because I was black. She had never caught me cheating or copying from or even looking on anyone else's paper, but she sent the note home because it had to be happening. My mother was livid. Like many mothers I'm sure, mine was like a mother hen. There were a lot of things that were outside of her control, but this was an untruth because she knew our ability, and she knew that I had not been cheating. She was very upset, and she went to the school. I don't know whether she talked with the teacher by herself or with the principal too, but she did confront the situation. Afterward, we never received another note like that. I continued to excel and she gave me my grades. I think my mother wondered for awhile whether or not she would be willing to be fair to me if she had this doubt or concern in her mind that I wasn't doing my work. But my teacher gave me the grades that I deserved. She wasn't necessarily unfriendly or ever mean to me, but she didn't go out of her way to try to make life any better for me either.

The first year, academically, was a good year for me. I went on to the sixth grade and had a very kind teacher that year. Things went pretty well for the next two years. The school went to grade seven, so I was at Swift Creek for three years. By the seventh grade, there were a few other black students. We were so spread out, however, that there was still only one black child in a class.

Linda Evans: I was in the seventh grade when I went to a mixed school for the first time. I went to Hugh Morrison Middle School in Raleigh when it was being desegregated, and that was quite a transition at that time. There weren't many other black students in the school. They put a few of the black students into the predominantly white school. It was never the other way around. We didn't see very many white students coming into the black schools. Desegregation was only about the black kids going into the white schools.

We were not ready for it, and they weren't either, because we came from different cultures. When I went into my seventh grade classroom, I was the only black student, or the only student with some color. A lot of the white kids didn't know what I was, but being different, I got called names. Later, I did manage to befriend some of the students and began developing a relationship with them. It was just that I was not approached the same way, and that really affects your self-esteem. I remember thinking, how can I be less than they are? I went to school. I have parents. We have a house. How can you look down on me like this? And we didn't feel inferior. We felt like we were human beings. We knew how to be neighborly. We knew how to share. That's the way we grew up.

I only attended Hugh Morrison for half a year, because desegregation of that school took place mid-year. So it was only part of a year in middle school where I was thrown into a class of all-white students.

At the end of that year, I went into Carnage High School in Raleigh, and that school was predominantly black. Now, as I reflect back on that half year experience, I often wonder why things were so different there. In our black schools, we were very disciplined. If we did wrong in school, we got our butt whipped. They would spank us at school, and when we got home, we would get another spanking. We did not disrespect our teachers, and we did not act out. When I was exposed to the white schools, I couldn't believe some of the things that were going on. I remember thinking, "And yet I'm supposedly inferior, and I'm watching these white kids do this?" We have more respect for our teachers. I literally saw one teacher have a nervous breakdown in the classroom because the students were driving her crazy. I wondered how they could let that happen. In our black schools, we would never have done anything like that, never. We would never disrespect a teacher. They were calling her names. There were two guys in her class that were particularly terrible to her, and she just went berserk right there in the classroom. I remember walking down the halls, changing classes, and I saw guys and girls in corners, just carrying on. I couldn't believe it.

Then I went to Carnage High, and I felt a whole lot more comfortable there. I moved back into the environment that I had grown up in, with respect toward our teachers and everything else.

I changed high schools and went to Ligon High School, which was also a predominantly black school at that time. I graduated from Ligon in 1970. I don't think there were any white students there yet. In 1971, Ligon was changed to a desegregated middle school. In this case, they actually started bringing white students into a black school. In Raleigh, Boughton and Enloe High Schools desegregated first. Since Ligon was a black school to start with, it was probably one of the last ones to desegregate, because they typically did not bring white students into black schools. I remember a couple of my friends went to Broughton and it was already desegregated. But on weekends, we gravitated back to our basic friendships. We got together for parties and spending time together.

Gwen Matthews: I know that there were times when people were very angry and very upset. Berry O'Kelly was the only black high school in that part of the county. Although there were other black high schools around the county, Ligon was downtown, and it was a school full of pride. Lots of well known black families, parents and their children had attended Ligon, so it was a landmark. When it was time to change Ligon to what is now a desegregated middle school, there were some very, very angry words said. But there was not the kind of violence that had taken place in some of the really Southern areas, because they said, "Why don't you let Ligon remain the landmark that it has always been? Desegregate it if you will, but let this school continue to serve the black community." Obviously that did not take place. Within the city of Raleigh, changing

Ligon High to a junior high was one of the more difficult times I remember within the black community. There was no physical violence because they had lots of discussion about it, with lots of write-ups in the newspapers and town meetings, trying to get everyone to agree to the best way to make the conversion. In the end, of course, the city won, and now Ligon is one of the magnet middle schools in the inner city. They began to bring white students into a former black school and neighborhood, so it could have been very explosive. I remember it just being a verbal dispute and there was no physical violence whatsoever.

When I was at Berry O'Kelly, my English teacher and the principal both said to me, "Why don't you think about going to (all white) Meredith College after high school?" They thought I was a good enough student to be accepted. I looked at them and laughed. This was before I went to Cary High. So it's very interesting that I eventually ended up at Meredith, and completed my undergraduate degree there.

Meredith was a different type of environment from Cary High. The people there were very different, just because of their wealth. There were those who did not like me and did not think Meredith should allow blacks in. But overall, Meredith was much more fun than Cary High. I thoroughly enjoyed my time at Meredith. I majored in English and was very active, so my years there were fun. My sister Deborah graduated from Meredith also. I realize now that I influenced my siblings, but I particularly influenced Deborah since she also attended Cary High and later also graduated from Meredith College. My other siblings have told me I influenced them too.

I think my experiences at Cary High made me the person that I am. I think it made me much more able to laugh at some of the things that took place at Meredith. For instance, at Meredith one day a young lady walked up to me and said, "I've never been this close to anybody black except my maid."

I laughed and said, "Well, I am not your maid." Then she laughed, and afterwards we became friends. So going through Meredith was quite a bit easier than Cary High had been, and much more fun.

Guy Mendenhall: In 1961, Broughton was the only high school in the city limits of Raleigh that admitted three minority students. But when I taught at Enloe High School, it was the first truly desegregated school in the Raleigh city school system. Enloe High School was built in 1962 as a desegregated school. The next year, Cary High School was desegregated in the Wake County school system. Ligon High School was an all-black school before they made it a desegregated middle school in 1971. So they started moving the minority students around. In Cary, a lot of black students went to Boughton.

Deborah Matthews Wright: After high school, I wasn't quite sure where I wanted to go. I tossed around Wake Forest University and thought about Carolina, and I thought about Meredith, especially after Gwen went there. I could live at home the four years I was there, and the small college atmosphere, all girls' school appealed to me. So I applied to Meredith and to Peace College. I was given an academic scholarship from Peace, but chose not to go there. I didn't actually apply for financial aid from Meredith until the second year, but ended up going to Meredith. I'm glad that I went there.

I can't say it was a real positive experience, but looking back on it, I would say it was an overall good experience because it was a good opportunity for me. It lacked a lot of the other things that I think people enjoy when they go to college; such as the interaction, the special friendships, the relationships, the extracurricular activity and involvement, and those types of things. But from an academic perspective, I know that they prepared me well. The campus was relatively receptive to my being there. I was one of twelve black students, and there were about twelve hundred on campus, so only one percent of the students were black at the time.

I think Gwen had graduated three or four years before I went to Meredith. I majored in psychology with a minor in sociology. I wanted to work with people, which is the standard kind of statement you make when you're young, but I did also want to go into some phase of counseling, so I majored in psychology. While I was there, I was president of the non-resident student association and involved in Psychi, which is an honor psychology club. So I was more involved there than I had been in high school.

At Meredith the interactions were pleasant. The climate there was a lot different from high school. I just accepted the fact that the girls at Meredith probably had not been exposed to a lot to people of other races. Many of them came from middle class, white backgrounds and from private high schools, so they never really had a lot of interaction with people of color. They were pleasant and weren't necessarily unfriendly, but I think their attitude toward me stemmed from not having had any experiences with blacks at all. There again, I was the one black person in the class.

Interestingly, I had a similar experience at Meredith as I did with my first teacher at Swift Creek. I had a social statistics class. I had heard all sorts of things about this class and I became fearful of it, so I went to see the professor, and shared with him that I didn't know how I would do in the class. He said, "Oh there, there. You'll be okay. You'll make at least a C." That really bothered me and angered me very much. I took his comment to mean that I would make no better than a C and would at least pass. I wondered if he said that to anybody else. Was his assumption that a C would be okay, and that was all that I should even strive for? So I took it very personally. I was determined that I would make better than a C, and I did.

The psychology department was a very good department. The professors were extremely friendly and open and supportive of me, so that was a positive experience. I think that Gwen helped pave the way for me. I don't think I got any preferential treatment, but Gwen having been there before me helped me to develop relationships. The school was a tough school, and I know that they did a good job of preparing me overall.

Sallie Jones: I taught in Parmele, North Carolina for five years, which is in the eastern part of the state between Bethel and Robersonville. They burned that school down, and it was arson. They think that someone in the neighborhood had done it, because it was named after the founder and the school board had problems with him. He was constantly protesting against the way they were running things, and the way they were treating the students. When it burned down, they moved the school to Robersonville.

Then I started teaching at Goldsboro High School, where I stayed for seven years. I left there in 1962 and went to teach French at Horris Mann High School in Gary, Indiana. I stayed there until I retired and came back home to Cary.

When I started working at Horris Mann, there were nine people in the language department. They offered French, Russian, German, Latin and Spanish. This was a high school. Gary had a wonderful program. Indiana University sent thirty students from the various high schools in the state to spend seven weeks in France or those countries that spoke the language they were studying. Indiana also had a program for teachers, so I got to go to France with their summer programs a few times. I also went to France on my own. A friend and I decided that we were going to go every place that French was spoken, so we could experience the difference accents.

In Indiana, the schools were segregated. Gary was an interesting city. There were seven high schools, possibly to keep the races separated.

The school I went to hired me because they had been ordered by the federal government to integrate if they wanted to continue receiving federal funds. I was one of the first teachers that they hired to integrate the faculty. At the time that I went there, they had a staff of 165, and only six of us were black. And at the same time, they were bringing in their first black students.

The supervisor and the principal assigned me the advanced courses, which touched off reactions of resentment among the teachers in the language department who had been there. But that worked out.

Two parents complained about me, and one actually took her child out of the classroom because she didn't want her child to be in the room with me. But other than that, it went pretty well. We didn't have any problems mixing in the black students because there were so few of them. The way they went about it was, they went to all the predominantly black high schools and picked their top students. Then there was resentment among the black schools that they chose their top students to bring them into the white schools. They began their program by bringing in thirty black students to start with, and it grew from there. The reason they chose the top black students was, because there was the tendency to underestimate black students' intelligence, they wanted to show the white students that they could perform on the same level. Once they had established that, then they would open the door for the rest to follow.

Carolyn Sampson: I was living in New York, and at a party one of the guests told me that she had gone to SUNY, (State University of New York,) on a grant and didn't have to pay any tuition. She told me who to contact and I made an appointment to see him. When I got there, I told him why I was there, and he began to tell me how I was not qualified for this grant. I listened to him, and when he was done, I said, "Are you finished?"

He said, "Yes, I am."

I said, "I really didn't come here for you to tell me how I do not qualify. I came down here for you to tell me how I could." He stopped talking to me in the negative, and began to tell me how to position myself to be eligible to receive the EOC grant money. I did get accepted into the program. You were not supposed to have an income, so he told me to quit my job, which I did, but I knew I couldn't make it financially. I was a single mother at the time. Then he worked thing out so my books and things were taken care of, and also that I could get a job. He allowed me to put all these pieces together so that I could hold on and make it. So I worked at La Salle School as a tutor, and I did complete college.

CHAPTER 12

THE SECOND YEAR AND BEYOND

Gwen Matthews: There are eight years between me and my sister, Deborah. By the time Deborah and our oldest brother Alton were ready for high school, all three of us went to Cary High. My youngest brother, Gary and my youngest sister, Adonna, went to Athens High. Seven years passed between my graduation and Deborah's arrival at Cary High, and by then it was a totally different world.

By that time, for the parents of the students that came into the school with Deborah, the primary issue was quality of education, not who the other students were that were coming into the school. Because people were moving to North Carolina from other parts of the country to work at IBM and all those other companies in Research Triangle Park, a very different group of people began to come into the Cary community. Their requests for things were much different from those of people who had been in Cary all their lives. So by the time Deborah arrived, it was easier. The students were different, the camaraderie was different and it was easier to get involved.

Seven years made a great deal of difference. There were always pockets of people who didn't like her or didn't want her, but she had white friends. I never experienced that the two years I was at Cary High on the level she did. Her level of friendship included going to their houses and their coming to ours. The acquaintances I made never came to my house and they never invited me to theirs, so it was different by the time she came there. One of her good friends happened to be white. My brother Alton had lots of white friends as well as black friends. They went out and did all kinds of things together. My brother is twelve years younger than I am, so that makes a difference. He had a wonderful time at Cary High.

Deborah Matthews Wright: Gwen had some experiences at Cary High School where the teachers would not call on her, and would not answer her questions. They basically ignored her and were not open to even having her come up to them after class to ask questions. By the time I got to Cary High School, things were much better. I didn't ask a lot of questions, I have to admit. I think that probably came from a feeling that I had to prove myself, and any indication that I didn't know something or that I had a question would be a reflection on my level of intelligence. Gwen was very gregarious and outgoing and talkative. I was much more reserved, and tried to figure out a lot of things on my own, so I didn't ask a lot of questions. I kept up fairly well. It probably took me a little bit longer, but I struggled through it. When I did raise my hand, I didn't feel ignored or mistreated.

By the time I got to Cary High School, white students were used to having us around, but we still kept ourselves segregated. There was not a lot of interaction or socializing together. Even by the time I got to high school, I still had feelings of loneliness and being apart and being separated. There was still only one black student in a class, and we sometimes did not have lunch with any other black students. Usually I ate lunch alone, and I didn't have much interaction with white students. By the time I was in high school, there wasn't a lot of teasing or ridicule and calling names or racial slurs as there had been when I was younger, but there was the separation of the races. Black students typically socialized with each other and sat close to each other in class, and white students did the same. I think there was much more tolerance, and there was some interaction. I don't want to give you the impression there was none. There was a higher level of tolerance by that time.

I started tenth grade in 1970, and there was a little bit more tolerance by then. The races were used to being around each other a lot more. And from the tenth grade through the twelfth grade, there was one particular white girl who befriended me. I was eating lunch alone in the cafeteria one day, and she came over and asked if she could sit with me. It took me by surprise. I thought, "You want to sit down here at the table with me?" And we became best friends, all the way through high school, to the point of spending time at each other's houses and doing a lot of things together. I think that in her own right she was a trailblazer. I remember seeing a puzzled look that her friends gave her, but she always included me. It was almost as if she didn't see any color. I must have been just one of all of her friends, and whenever she did anything, I was included. I could feel the distance of her other white friends. She never seemed to feel any difference toward me or feel any slight toward me at all, which was a good feeling. No other lasting or strong friendships occurred in high school, but that one good friend made the high school experience at least more tolerable and a little bit more pleasant.

Lucille Evans Cotton: At the first ten-year anniversary, I got letters to come to the reunion. I never went though because, I guess you could say I felt inferior. I was sure that all of the others had good office jobs or something, and I just didn't feel comfortable. When the twenty-year reunion rolled around, I didn't go. When the forty-year reunion comes, I probably still won't go. They write to me every so often, and want to know how I'm doing. But they gave me such hell then, I just didn't want anything else to do with them.

AFTER HIGH SCHOOL – WHAT THEY DID NEXT:

Gwen Matthews: After high school, I went to St. Augustine's College in Raleigh for one year. When I left Cary High I thought, "I don't intend to see another white person in school as long as I live." So I went to St. Augustine's, made friends and partied the whole year. Needless to say, I did not do well that year. I was making up for missed fun.

My father then said, "We're not paying for this, so get a job." So I went out and I worked for six years as a keypunch operator at Wachovia Bank. I think they're called data entry people now. When I realized that I could not do that for the rest of my life, I knew it was time to think about going back to school.

So I began to take courses. I took a course at N.C. State, and another one at Meredith. When I applied to N.C. State, the Admissions Officer looked over my transcripts from St. Augustine's. I had one A in English, which is my major. He said, "You have this A, and obviously these other grades don't count."

I said, "Yes sir, I know."

He said, "Now you know that A in English from St. Augustine's is equal to a C here at N.C. State."

I said, "Oh, okay," and I did not go back. That was so humiliating. It was embarrassing. Was it a slap at the school? Was it a slap at me? Was it a slap at the teacher? Was it a slap at all three? I honestly didn't know what he meant by that. All I knew was my feelings had been hurt. So I chose to go to Meredith.

[In 1971, Gwen was the first black woman to graduate from Meredith College. Then in 2006, the African-American Alumnae Chapter established the Gwendolyn Matthews Class of 1971 Scholarship to honor her accomplishments and recognize her as a trailblazer for the college.] After I graduated from Meredith, I taught at Broughton High School for three years, and then decided to go back and get my masters from Teachers College at Columbia University because I wanted to teach on the collegiate level. I came back and taught at N.C. State for three years. I left N.C. State and taught at Hampton Institute, which is now Hampton University in Virginia.

Then I came back to Raleigh because my mother became ill and died. My youngest sister was twelve or thirteen at the time. Deborah was living at home already and I moved back in, so we lived there and raised Adonna. I took odd jobs because I did not know what I wanted to do next. I had always kept up with data entry so I would do data entry jobs.

One day Deborah was reading the paper and said, "Gwen, Wake Technical Community College has a position open for an English teacher." So I said, "Oh okay, I'll apply." In the black community, Wake Tech did not have a very good reputation toward blacks. But I thought, "Oh well, I can apply," and I was hired. I have been here ever since then. I started out in the English department. There was only one English teacher then. There is a developmental education program there, but at that time it was called Academic Enrichment. I transferred over to that department and loved it. I loved teaching the developmental students. I ended up being the department head for fifteen and a half years, and the department grew from four teachers to eleven full-time and nine part-time while I was its head. Then I moved into the Academic Advising Center, and I loved advising students and talking to them about where they wanted to go, what kind of plans did they have, and what did they want to be when they grew up.

As an advisor, one of the things I'm very conscious of is not saying anything that would damage a student's feelings, ego, pride, or self-esteem. I really do make sure that I don't say anything that will offend them in any way, because what was said to me at N.C. State was so discouraging. I have since taken courses at N.C. State and done well. But because of what was said to me, I decided to go to Meredith instead of N.C. State. For one thing, I thought I would never be accepted there. Then later they hired me, so I must have been good enough.

Deborah Matthews Wright: I finished my psychology degree and then went to work as a college counselor at St. Augustine's College in Raleigh. While working full-time, I also pursued a masters' degree in counseling from N.C. State University. After working at St. Augustine's for three or four years, I got a job at N.C. State in personnel. When I finished my masters' degree in 1983, I started a career in human resources at N.C. State. I have been at N.C. State in human resources ever since, and I've progressed over the years. Now I am the assistant director of human resources. I'm working with people and I have the opportunity to use a lot of my counseling skills. I have also become a certified mediator, which has come in very handy in dealing with employee relations.

I also have a ministry, where I utilize my counseling background outside of my actual paid job. I am a licensed minister, and I counsel women who are in various situations, and have various issues going on in their lives. My ministry is called Sister to Sister. I'm also married to a minister, and being by his side provides both of us the opportunity to work with people.

Linda Evans: After high school, I first went to Wake Tech for one semester. Then I decided to go further in college, so I applied to N.C. Central University in Durham. After I was accepted, I went there for a second semester and lived on campus. It wasn't far from home, being right there in Durham, but I got homesick, so I started driving back and forth. I eventually eased on back home.

Then I met a young man, we got married and I had my first son. After awhile we split up. I moved back to Raleigh where my sister and I moved into an apartment together. I started working at CP&L, (Carolina Power and Light,) in 1974 and I stayed there for eighteen years. I did fairly well there. I started out as a draftsman and I progressed and was promoted. I met my second husband at CP&L. After eighteen years, I really wanted to do something different, so I decided to go back to school to finish my degree. I graduated from St. Augustine College last year. My major is in organizational management because that was the program that they were offering, but I'm really an artist, and I want to pursue my talent in art.

Years ago, I started doing some cake decorating and I do a lot of illustrating on my cakes. After twenty-three years, people still call me to decorate cakes. Maybe one day I'll have a business in cake decorating. I also work at a little retail lighting store where I do a lot of lamp restoration and glass painting. They're always calling me to do the artwork there. Since I've gotten my degree, I think that I may want to check into some teaching.

Carolyn Rogers: While I was in college, I came home for the summers to work at Rogers Restaurant. I worked in the kitchen washing dishes, and occasionally they would let me work out in the dining hall to wait tables. I would get a 25¢ tip, and that was a lot of money. I don't know if I got less than the white waitresses. I wasn't inquisitive. You just didn't ask those kinds of questions. If they needed me to go in the dining hall to pour tea, then that's what I did. But I never heard anybody say anything derogatory to me, even when I was out in the dining hall.

Sallie Jones: After I graduated from Berry O'Kelly High School, I had a scholarship to go to a small college near Salisbury named Barber-Scotia. It was an all-girls' school. I entered Barber-Scotia in the fall of 1940, never having been away from home. I got homesick. Having skipped grades before high school, the other students in my college classes were all older than me. They had all these rules you had to obey. You couldn't do this, or you couldn't do that. I didn't want to be there, I felt out of place. They were very nice to me there, it was just that I couldn't adjust. The president came all the way to Cary and told my mother that he didn't think I was going to make it. Actually, they didn't want me on their hands. So he told my mother he was going to send me home.

I still knew I wanted to go to college, but then it was too late to enroll in other classes that fall. My sister went to St. Augustine's and I had been there to visit her on campus. I decided that was where I wanted to go to college, so in January I enrolled at St. Augustine's. I didn't feel displaced there, and I graduated in 1946.

George Bailey: During the time I was being raised, the Civil Rights movement started and the identity of people started changing. Throughout my life, I never thought I was Indian, I always thought I was black. But if you were to slice me up into pieces to determine what percentage I had of this blood or that blood, you would find that black would be the smallest of my percentages. The reality is that I was raised in a black environment where I knew I was beautiful. So my confidence level came from that environment as the movement started, and the schools that I went to were segregated schools which just compounded my identity as black. I knew there was nothing I couldn't do.

When I finished A&T College in Greensboro, I joined the Peace Corps. That is something that black folk don't do. I was one of three black individuals in the Peace Corps Ethiopia out of 150 volunteers. Oddly enough, those same three people finished up their two-year contract with the United States government, which is a 100% completion rate of their contracts. However, out of the other individuals who were white, only 70, (less than 50%) finished their contracts. It came down to their association with people and their ability to adapt. Being black puts you in the situation where you have to adapt to other cultures that have been dictated to you, or other environments that you are being constantly thrust into. As I look back at it, I realize that the reason I survived my two-year contract was very simple. I did not go to Africa thinking that I was an American. I did not go to Africa thinking I was a black American. I went to Africa to help. I did not try to adjust the African country to my American attitude. I let the African country adjust me. When I had to wait in a building to get somebody to sign a piece of paper, I brought a book and I patiently sat there for three hours. Other Peace Corps volunteers got so upset because they couldn't get something done. It bothered them. It put a lot of stress on them. It didn't bother me because this is the way it's done there. I didn't go in there trying to change Ethiopia to make it a little America, and I was successful in completing my two-year contract.

Throughout my life, I have always planned what I wanted to do many years in advance. I knew what I wanted my college major to be four years before I got to college. I set my goals. I knew that when I left the Peace Corps I was going to return to Africa within four years. I was back in four years. I knew when I left the Peace Corps what I wanted to do next as soon as I hit the ground in America. I started a company and was back in business. I have never worked for anybody, I always worked for myself. In the Peace Corps I was independent. I've never really had a boss in almost everything I've ever done. All of the Baileys, my whole family is to a degree like that. We've been in business or around business all our lives.

I think the generation after Clyde Evans Sr. is a multi-faceted generation that has no limits. Getting an education to us means, "you can carry it as far as you want to go." We have nothing stopping us in the areas where we were involved.

Even today, there are only a few black students in advanced classes here in North Carolina. My children grew up being the only one in the class. This is just a way of life. There will be a limited number that are excelling in education, and blacks are the smallest of the population, so we're going to have a smaller number in the advanced classes.

I never grew up with anybody white. Even though we lived basically in a black community, my kids grew up having white friends. Their association and their structure of involvement were very wide. Their involvement was with the full culture rather than with the segregated culture. So their whole attitude toward everything is different from mine. My attitude is always one of caution.

I don't want to speak for my twin daughters. I know there were things in their life that confronted them that had implications of segregation or racism. But they are children of an educated family, so they didn't necessarily have to call us to confront any situations that they knew how to confront themselves. They didn't have a problem with challenging any teacher if they thought their grade was not appropriate.

Herbert Bailey: After I finished college, I taught in junior high and senior high in Washington D.C. for half a year and in New York for one year. I hated teaching. Even though it was during the time of integration, the school in Washington D.C. was 95% black. During the time I was there, the school had 54 teachers to begin the year in September. By the following January, 27 of the teachers had quit because the school was so rough. The kids were rough, mostly from poverty. Probably 60% to 70% of the kids only had one parent. It was a brand new school the day that I walked in, and by January every window on the first two floors had been replaced, and one teacher had been sent to the hospital. So I thought, this is not for me. I was a country boy who knew nothing about fighting or about drugs. Also, I was only making $7,000 a year and I could not make a living teaching out of state, so I came back home.

I had grown up to be a pipeline contractor. I really like to brag that you can't get a drink of water in Raleigh, Apex, Cary, Holly Springs, Roseville, Garner, Burlington, or Wake Forest without that water coming through pipe that I've installed. I've laid a lot of pipe in a lot of the towns. But actually, I worked on the pipes at the potable water plants that furnish the water for the whole town, so all the water has to go through my primary pipe first. I like the pipe business. I'm primarily a ditch digger. My goal in life is to always put in one foot more than I did the last time I put in the most. Success is measured by change. If you can't change, you are not succeeding.

Phyllis Cain: I attended North Carolina Central University in Durham and got a degree in sociology. Then I became a social worker. My first job was at Central Children's Home in Oxford, North Carolina where I was their first social worker. I worked there for about seven years. For about three years, I also worked in Franklin County as a social worker. I've been working at Human Services of Wake County in Raleigh since 1988. I've done other jobs in between, but I always came back to social work.

CHAPTER 13

LESSONS LEARNED

By 1970, Cary's schools had been desegregated by local school board initiation rather than by a court order. This is an achievement in which all those involved should be extremely proud.

Gwen Matthews: What did I learn from the experience of being the first black student at Cary High? I learned that I could do anything, that I could get through anything. That experience even taught me that I could get through my mother's death. I was out of state when she died, and I was very sad about that, but I knew I could get through it.

Very few people at Wake Tech knew about my experiences at Cary High. I choose not to talk about it, not because I'm embarrassed or because it's too painful. It is just a part of my life. One of the sociology teachers at Wake Tech found out quite by accident and asked me to speak to her class, and I did.

I also learned that not every white person is a bad person. I have friends who went through other circumstances, such as those at Ligon High School, and they are just angry people because Ligon is no longer a high school, and all kinds of other negative feelings that they have from the days of Civil Rights. I believe I came through without as much anger because of my parents, not that their parents taught them anything different from mine. I believe that because of my mother's faith and strong beliefs, and because she prayed for me a lot, and prayed with me a lot, that she taught me I could get through this trial with God's help. And knowing that she would let me come home and cry in her arms, and her willingness to say, "It's going to be all right," gave me strength. My mother told me, "Gwen, not all white people are like those that were in front of the school that first day, and you have to remember that." She repeated those things at least three times a week which helped me to be less angry and less bitter. I think otherwise the experience was so difficult that I could have become a Black Panther. I could have felt what an unfair situation I had been forced to go through, and how dare people spit at me, and what do you mean, you don't like me because of the color of my skin? I still don't understand that. I simply don't understand that. But I'm not bitter about the experience, and I think it has made me a more understanding person, regardless of what minority you are. I can be more compassionate toward anyone who is in a situation that is very difficult and they are struggling trying to go through it, and to find answers, and asking for help, and wanting someone to empathize with them. I think it has made me that way so that I'm able to help those others.

Until recently, I was in an education environment, and I had students going through all kinds of things. I think going through that experience really has made me a compassionate person. It was so mind-boggling at times hearing what I would be called and nobody, no adult would chastise the student, until I came away thinking, "Did I just hear what I just heard, and then did that teacher just let him get away with it?" Those times were tougher than almost anything you could imagine. So I'm glad I went through it.

I think that my experiences with desegregating schools have opened many doors. For those African-Americans who took part in desegregation, it has been a good experience because we have gained knowledge about people and the world that we may not have had any other way. We have improved our standard of living, so I think it has been good for us generationally. There are things that we have gone through that we are able to share with those who come behind us, for them to have a better understanding of some of the things that are taking place now that they may not have understood, or would not be able to understand if we had not gone through them ourselves. I think it has been good for us on two fronts; individually, and certainly as a race. It has been good for us to share with those who have come behind us what the sixties and the seventies were like, and what it was like under segregation, and what it was like under integration. And it is good for them to hear the kinds of things we've learned about people, and about ourselves, and about the world in general. It has been good for our standard of living that we may have had to work much, much harder for and much longer for had integration not taken place.

If there is a downside, I think African-Americans have lost the sense of extended family that we used to have. I don't see in generations behind us the kind of extended families that I had in my little community where we all knew each other. Even if you were not part of the family but you needed some food, we gave you food. Grandmothers were feeding children in the community without there being any questions asked or any expectations for anything in return. The community was caring for its children and watching out for each other. That sense of community has been lost. When integration came, we were able to go into so many different communities, and we don't have that same sense of community with grandmothers and aunts and uncles and cousins right there together. So I think that sense of family, for us as a people, has been lost.

When I told my story to the sociology class, the questions that the students had were incredible. They said they did not personally know anyone who was the first to do anything of that nature. More of them were surprised that I'm not bitter. They said things like, "I'm surprised that you don't hate us." They wanted to know about the school. They asked how the students reacted toward me, how did I react to them, and why didn't I become an active militant. Another teacher also asked me to speak to an African-American history class that was made up of African-Americans primarily. There were only two white students there. And again they asked, "Why aren't you angry?" Once I got older, I realized that being that angry eats away at you and you become a very bitter person, a very negative person.

Deborah Matthews Wright: I think my experiences as one of the first black students in a white school have allowed me to be able to develop relationships with people who are different from me, and to try to understand people from other perspectives, not just my own. I think that was a lot of the problem then. Each person, each race was looking at the situation from their own individual perspective. The white community was looking at it from their perspective, and we were looking at it from our perspective. Since we have become a society that is multi-cultural and is integrated, we have had to learn to live with each other and to have relationships to enable us to work together to raise our children in integrated communities. That transition has been much easier for me than it probably would have been had the Civil Rights movement never taken place.

I worked at St. Augustine's College, which is a predominantly black school. One of the struggles I foresaw for the African-American students was going out into the working world without having had much interaction with the predominantly white society. Because there isn't any doubt that the predominant society is the white race. So not having had that interaction and that perspective and that experience can put African-

Americans at a disadvantage. And I saw that when I was working at St. Augustine College. My transition into a multi-cultural society, and being able to develop relationships in the working world, and doing things with people who were different from me has been much easier because of my experiences.

There is five years between me and my next younger sibling, six years between the next one, and ten years between me and the youngest. Adonna, the youngest, is thirty-five and Gwen's fifty-two, so there is quite a spread. It was a lot different for the younger ones in my own family. Integration was full-blown by the time Adonna was going through school and its acceptance was much better. Society was dealing with a different generation of students, and so they were more open to interacting with each other. My brothers, the two siblings next to me, were engaged in inter-racial dating, so it was completely different. My brothers and my youngest sister were very involved in a lot of activities. I was able to watch them throughout those years because I was in college and still living at home. Their friends were different from us. They were a variety of people, not just racially but socially and economically, so their friendships were multi-cultural. So the relationships and interactions my younger siblings had were quite different from mine, and I know they were very different from Gwen's, in a positive way.

(This interview is taking place in 2000,) and my daughter Brianna is only five. She is in pre-school, and it is really interesting to hear her dealing with the whole issue of race. We are working through what it means to be African-American, and what it means to be white, what it means to be Chinese, and Latino. She has lots of questions about race and color. I try to talk with her about the differences in people, and help her identify people, and share with her that although they may look different, they are just like us underneath. This friend likes ice cream too, just like you do. There is a Latino girl in her class, so we talk a lot about her. Whenever we see Spanish things or Mexican things, I tell Brianna that this is the kind of background her friend has.

Where will I take her? How will I raise her? How will my experiences impact my parenting of Brianna? I basically want her to be open and receptive to people of color and people of different backgrounds. I would like for her to be as multi-cultural as possible. However, there is such a fine line because I do feel that my experiences had an impact on my self-esteem in terms of my abilities, always feeling as if I had to prove myself. I never doubted that I had the abilities, but what I doubted was whether or not the majority would accept the fact that I was capable, and that I am intelligent, and that I can accomplish things. And the types of experiences that I had do have an impact on one's self-esteem, on one's self-concept. You just can't go through something like that and not have your self-esteem affected. So there's a fine line. I want her to be open and to experience different things, but I also want her to be comfortable with who she is. I want her to be comfortable with being African-American, and with her own background in her own culture.

What I have tried to do is give her a solid background about being African-American first, and then we're building on that, because I think that it is very important, being comfortable with who she is. Then a good, positive self concept is important to accepting other people, because I think that not accepting other people comes from your own sense of insecurity, of not knowing or not understanding who you are, and who you are in relation to other people. When you feel good about yourself and who you are, and when you feel good about your own race and how you look, and the fact that your hair is curly although theirs is straight, and you have brown eyes and somebody has blue eyes, I think you're going to be open to accepting other people for who they are also. You can be open to the difference and by the same token not be intimidated by it, because you can be open to other people but still be intimidated by that difference also. So I don't want her to be intimidated. I want her to have good, positive self-esteem and realize that she's okay and so is everyone else, regardless of who they are.

I don't anticipate the kinds of challenges for her that I had. I think that her challenges will be more subtle. Integration has done a lot for society as a whole, but we all would be fooling ourselves to say that prejudice and discrimination are gone and that it no longer exists. It's just not as overt as it used to be. I still experience discrimination at work, but it is more subtle. So I think her challenge will be to be more astute about racism and discrimination, because it's going to be a lot more subtle.

It's much easier now. I would put "easier" into quotations because for me it was out there. People let me know how they felt, I knew how they felt, they didn't like me; they didn't want me there. But in the years to come there will be an undercurrent of prejudice and discrimination that the people of color will have to be more aware of than we have been in the past. And the challenges eventually may become more obvious as society becomes more multi-cultural, because as we know, the number of people of color is going to increase, and so the current white majority will no longer be the majority. That may be a little unsettling for white community, and by the same token, it may affect the society in a strange way. But relationships are ones to cherish. I think that Brianna's challenge will be to be more aware of the subtleties of discrimination.

Lucille Evans Cotton: On a whole, it was an experience that I would not trade anything for, because now when I can see all the hate on TV between black and white, I know exactly what they're going through. I can feel their pain. I can feel their anger. If you don't experience it for yourself, you can never know how they felt. But I know how they felt, so I learned from it. I wouldn't want to put my kids through it, but I wouldn't trade it for anything either.

The night that I graduated, when I walked across that stage and they gave me that diploma, I just waved that paper over my head and said, "Thank you, Mama." I got it. And I was so happy.

SJ and Leonia Farrar - Leonia: I wish Civil Rights could have come before our day, but we survived and we learned a lot. We learned the hard way so we really appreciate what we learned. Today the children have everything. This is a different world, with computers and everything now. We had the teaching and the training and the love. We had love. We had family together in those days. With our aunts and our grandparents, it was just a village of love. We don't have that anymore.

So that's why I say those were the good old days. All that hard work was good but we were treated so badly. We needed to work but we were treated like we were nothing. I hate that because we were somebody. (**SJ**): Those days were not good to me. (**Leonia**): That's because your childhood was much harder than mine. Your father died and mine didn't die, and that's what makes the difference. If we were poor, I didn't know it because we never woke up hungry. We had food. Daddy kept food on the table for all of his nineteen children. He would sell some tobacco, then go buy a hundred-pound sack of pinto beans or cabbage and we never went hungry. Mine was a big family. We played and fought hard together, but we loved each other.

(**SJ**): We agreed to be interviewed because we would hope that it would inspire others. There was a Durham radio station, WDNC, who sent one of their newscasters down to interview us, and it was on TV and radio several times. I did that so that it would inspire other young blacks who might think, "I can't make it." Since then, I have had many people who saw that interview say to me, if you made it, I can too. You have to get up and do something for yourself. That's my theory. I don't have time for a lazy person. If you get up, study hard, work hard and plan, you'll make it. But if you sit and wait for somebody else to do it for you, you're going to be sitting there a long time.

Carolyn Rogers: Times have really changed for the better. I think the more different cultures live in neighborhoods with each other, the easier things get because you grow up not knowing anything different. My little sister knows nothing else but a mixed culture lifestyle. Of course she had an easier time because my parents were doing much better when she came along than when I was born. When I was young, our parents were farmers. My little sister didn't grow up in the lifestyle that I knew.

In the beginning, the few black students in the schools pretty much stayed to themselves. You may have one or two white students becoming friends with a black student, but outside of class you didn't see much interaction. So the black kids would find each other and go back to their comfort zone, and the white kids would go on about their business, same as always. As a teacher, over time I saw more interaction between the students, no matter what the culture was. Little kids don't see color and will play together. But when they're taught to see color, it makes a big difference, and you can tell that has happened. Kids are very forgiving. They're very honest, and they're very loving to each other. But when the adults' racist teachings creep in, then their little fights are about something else, such as when one says, "My mom says you I'm not supposed to play with you because you're black."

I dealt with some of those fights by saying, "Well, that's no reason to not play with each other. You shouldn't play with each other because you're not a nice person, not because you're black."

Sometimes we had to negotiate with students and say, "Why is it that you're having a problem with this child?"

And when the child said, "Because my mom says this child is black," then you use it as a teachable moment.

We might say, "Because this child is black, what does that mean, really? And because you're white, what does that mean? If I cut you, are you going to bleed white? Is that child going to bleed black?"

"Well no, I don't think so."

"Well, then there's nothing different about you beneath the skin color. You're all the same." When kids come to that conclusion themselves, it's fantastic.

Leroy and Betty Farrar – Leroy: I have had an enjoyable life. Altogether I wouldn't say I've had a terrible life. (**Betty**): No, it hasn't been bad. We've always had something to eat. It may not have been what we wanted, but it was something to fill our stomachs. (**Leroy**): My brother SJ had problems with his landlords, but I never did.

George Bailey: It's interesting to think about desegregation and the problems that we as family have had, and what people in general have had. I do read a lot, about how racism has existed throughout the history of the United States. I have found James Mitchener's books to be fascinating. His book *The Source* is about the Jewish experience in Israel and Palestine, and his books *Hawaii* and *Chesapeake* are about racism within the United States. All of these books portray racism in various forms as America was being conquered, and the progression of European invasion throughout the United States.

The experiences that America is currently going through are not black versus white. They are truly about the American experience. The world is a very complicated place. America can't afford to be color-sensitive because we're all of color. What we represent truly is part of the history of America. And that history is white, it is black, it is Indian. I am all three, even though I grew up on the black platform, and I have always associated myself with that power movement. That is not necessarily true of our younger people. And that was not necessarily true of our older people, because there was no movement.

Herbert Bailey: Cary is a wonderful town. I have observed that without change, a society will fall apart. And when you start regulating change, the regulations impede change. If a society doesn't grow, if there is no change, I think it actually starts to diminish.

It is true that all of the rich folks have to die too. All those who have imposed their will on you, their time is written down. You can try to run from it, but death is always one step behind you. So you cannot continue to treat your fellow man without fairness, because death is chasing you all the time. You have to be fair. And I think in Cary sometimes there hasn't been fairness. I have seen my father go into a store and give people money to buy equipment, and then have to go and drink at the second water fountain. I have seen the people that worked for that company go to the second water fountain. I have seen that, and it is just not right.

I think there is always going to be prejudice. No matter how good a person is, how fair, how honest, or how strong their integrity, there is always going to be disparity. People will pick on the fat guy, people will pick on the skinny guy, and people will pick on the guy that loses his hair. There is always going to be some form of prejudice.

I don't understand segregation because I've only ever seen but one side of it. I figure there is probably going to be segregation forever. It gets down to the minute things. We have to live on the same planet, and we have the same God. One thing that makes people the same is money. If you have $10.00 and I have $10.00 when we are standing in front of a store counter, your ten is as good as my ten. There have been a whole lot of successful black people, and I believe that anyone can be successful. But people are people, and there is always going to be differences. We have to live and deal with that fact the best we can, making sure that we treat our fellow man honorably, with respect and with fairness, because we are all God's creatures.

At one time Cary was a very rural place. Evans Road has long since been filled in, paved over, and shaped into a budding metropolis, one that my grandfather possibly never imagined.

Clyde Evans Jr.: Daddy told me a few things. He was a very honest man. He said that in his day, a contract was sealed by shaking hands. Now you've got to sign a paper this long to have a contract. Daddy said one time, "Son, do you know what a devoted brother is? If my brother is going to be hung, and he has business to attend to before the hanging, would I go and put my head in that noose until he tends to his business, and when he comes back he will put his head back in the noose and turn me loose. I would do that." That's loyalty. There's no such thing as that anymore. Like father and son, or mother and daughter, there used to be a bond between the two. But there is no such thing like that now, is there. Fathers shoot their sons, daughters kill her mother. It's so sad.

TRAILBLAZERS:

Deborah Matthews Wright: I think that you could truly consider Gwen to be a trailblazer. I think she underestimates the contribution that she's made. Because of her gutsiness and courage, she provided an opportunity for people to be exposed to black people in a positive way. Gwen's personality and the way Gwen is and who she is adds a lot to how she paved the way. Our experiences were very different, because Gwen was somewhat of a forefront person where I always stayed in the background. I was more reserved than Gwen was, at Meredith in particular. Gwen was in plays, she did things, and she was very active so she was very well known at Meredith. Everyone knew Gwen Matthews, not because she was black but because of who she was. And I think that she presented African-Americans in a way that helped others see us in a real positive way. She provided the opportunity for people to experience her personality, her friendliness, her laughter and her ability to interact with people well. I think the way she became a trailblazer was in how she provided an opportunity to put people at ease with African-Americans from the very beginning. She has that way about her. She did things a lot differently than the way that I did them. She jumped right in there, she grabbed the bull by the horns, she worked with what she had, and she did what she needed to do.

The prime example is how she was assertive when she had a question, and how she went to the teacher to ask the question; whereas I was more reserved and sat back and tried to figure it out for myself. I think there's a lot to be said about that. Her approach helped to dispel some of the myths that people had about blacks by showing that we are interested in learning, we do want to know, we are curious, we do have interests, and we have the same likes, dislikes, and values that white people have. She was probably more forthright with that than I was, and took the opportunity to share more of herself. I think that's important about a trailblazer. You have to be willing to share yourself with others so that they can begin to know you and experience you, and know about you. If you aren't willing to do that, if you can't do that or you don't do it for whatever reason, then you may not be as effective as someone like Gwen who was very willing to share of herself, to be out there, to be in a play, to put on a funny costume, and to laugh with people. Doing all those things will help people see you as a real person and not just a black person.

I think the impact she had on my life comes primarily with knowing that it could be done, that it was not impossible. Integration was something that we had to deal with, but the success of integration, at that time, was yet to be seen. I think that that's the key with Gwen.

We went through integration because at first, supposedly, we had the choice and then eventually because we were bused. But for many people, it just happened. But at that time, what was the fruit of that occurrence? How effective was integration? What was happening? That was yet to be seen. For me, growing up and seeing Gwen be successful, going through that process of the teasing and the ridicule and having courage, and then after leaving Cary, to go into another situation where she was a minority, that took a lot of courage. And out of that courage came a success story. What it did for me was show me that something good can come out of these efforts. There was a lot of pain, but also a lot of success and good, positive things could come out of it.

The strength that my mother showed us makes her a trailblazer. She taught me to love and not to hate, regardless of the situation. That was probably somewhat unusual because it was much harder to teach. It would have been easy to say "Well, they hit you, you hit them back," or, "They said something nasty to you, then you say something nasty to them." I think that would have been the easier thing to teach your child. But she didn't teach that and she didn't encourage that. She encouraged us not to be doormats, but she encouraged us to understand that a lot of things the children were doing were things that their parents had taught them. And she tried to help us to separate the children's actions from the children in terms of, they were doing things they probably had been told they should do, or they were behaving in ways that they were probably told they should behave, but they were children just like me. What she tried to help me understand was what I wanted them to understand, that they were no different from me. Different skin color, some had different experiences, but we were still all children underneath. We liked the same things. They played with dolls, they played with balls, they teased each other, even at home in their families. They beat up their brothers and sisters. Basically we were all still children. She encouraged us to continue to love regardless, and to see the light at the end of the tunnel, and to understand the benefit in all this for us as individuals.

My father was a trailblazer in that he had relationships with people in the white community, and that was probably rare. It was rare for a black man to have positive and good relationships with white people at that particular time. He had that way about him, and maybe that's where Gwen got it from, where he interacted well with white people. That was a hard thing to do at that particular time, and he did it well. How? Why? There was the ability on his part to help us to understand that there was a need to work together and to develop some sense of relationship with the white race, regardless of what was happening. He was active in the NAACP, and they were helping to promote a better community and a better society. It was important for us to see his role and contribution to that effort also. It wasn't only about getting equal rights for blacks, it was also about seeing what we could do as races coming together and understanding each other. And I think that was a big issue for the NAACP, trying to bring about some sense to what was happening, and bring about a positive effort in terms of unity and cooperation between races.

When we were young, he worked in situations where he was primarily the only African-American. When I was fourteen or fifteen, he went to work for a small, private, family company. He was hired by the family and they took him under their wing, which became a very positive experience for our whole family, because that was really the first close interaction we had had with any white people. In that small company, he was the only black employee. He shared a lot of things with them, and we saw him help them understand black people. Over time, we all began to consider them friends. They weren't just Al's children, they all came to our weddings. Even after my father retired, these people were part of our family. So it was more about relationship building. What they added to this whole issue of trailblazing is the importance of relationships, regardless of what color you are, and how those relationships can impact your life as a whole.

Gwen talked about how members of the NAACP actually coached her on how to be tolerant of the taunts, and not to provoke any kind of hostilities, but I didn't have any contact with them. I felt their influence through my father, through his guidance, and just by his sitting me down and talking to me and sharing things, but I had no actual coaching from them as an organization. It was communicated through him.

Leroy Farrar: There is a bank here in Cary that has been a really good friend to this family. Along the line, I've had to borrow a little money at times and they have been so great about it. I had no problems getting whatever I needed from them.

One of our neighbors is Joe Bailey. He put the plumbing in this house, our first home. His children are now working in his company. When our house burned down, Joe had a house up the street beyond the church. He came and told us to move into that house and stay there until we had rebuilt our home. When we moved in, he would not charge us a dime. The house had a tank full of heating oil. We stayed there for four months and used that oil, but he never would let me give him any money. At least he could have let me pay for the oil that we used, but he refused. That will go with me to my grave, because people don't usually do that. That was the Lord making a way.

I had planted a garden on a piece of land near Highway 54 at the end of Evans Road. I have a little tractor that I drove back and forth to plant a garden. We had a good time planting a garden there, but the deer came and ate our garden up. One day I told Joe about the deer and said that I would rather have a garden in my back yard so I could take care of it more easily and keep the deer out. A few days later, he brought his heavy equipment down and cleared off a place in back for our garden. He just came and did that for us. He had the equipment that he brought down and said, "I'm going to fix you a garden here." He started pushing down trees and plowing it up. So I planted a garden out there and I just love it. I enjoy it. Joe has been a true friend. Now we give our neighbors corn and string beans, cucumbers and such. We share out of the garden. I have about a quarter of an acre planted back there now and I grow a lot there. I guess I'm still farming. I have my little cub tractor and I go out there and have a ball.

Clyde Evans Jr.: My father was the greatest man in this territory, black or white. He was a very brilliant man. My father was a great land lover. He acquired many acres of land when prices weren't too high. Daddy wanted to build a town for people who were not fortunate enough to have any land to build on. He began selling lots on this side of Evans Road from Highway 54 all the way down the street. And he donated land for a church on Evans Road.

Charlie Adams: A school in Cary was named for my father, Henry Adams. He fought that because he did not want a school named after him. He did not believe any building should be named after a living person. But there was a move in Cary when they decided to build a school, to name it Henry Adams Elementary School. He said, "Absolutely not." And then the Wake County Board tried to pass a bill saying that it would be named for him, and he refused to let them do it, he outvoted that bill. He really never wanted credit for anything he did. He was one of these guys who liked to work behind the scenes. He liked to work in the back of the drugstore or after the store had closed, or in the den, or in the kitchen. He never wanted recognition. He really didn't want people to know that he was taking $300 out of his own pocket to give to a kid to send him to camp, or raising $500 out of his drugstore to help light the playing field. He was just a behind-the-scenes player and did not like center stage. He really got adamantly angry when they began even talking about naming a school after him, and refused to allow them to do it. So they didn't. And then when he died, they did it.

Today, he would think that school is the best school in Cary and one of the best in Wake County. He wouldn't care whether it was named after him or not. That would be totally meaningless to him. He would not ask the question, why did you name it after me or who did you name it for, but he would ask, do the kids have enough paper? Do they have their computers? Do they have any good teachers? Are they getting the core curriculum? He would be very concerned with the academics and the background and the abilities of the teachers, and how well they were competing, and how well they can write. That's all he would have cared about.

My dad died in '68 or '69. It was the opening night of football season. I was going to go to Goldsboro that night and catch the game. Dad had the appliance store then, and I went down to the store to ask Dad if he wanted to ride with me. He said he wasn't feeling well, and he went home to rest. So I decided I'd run up to Academy Street and check on him. When I got there I found him on the floor. I think he'd had a heart attack. So I picked him up and put him in the car, and started to Rex Hospital. I know he had a heart attack right behind Meredith College. I got him to the hospital, but he died that night. He had an aneurysm and they couldn't find it because it was bleeding on the back side. So he never knew what happened to Cary. He never saw the growth or the progress. He would be so incredibly proud. He wore Cary on his sleeve.

I'm proud for him. When I went out to speak at the dedication of the school named for him, I was proud. I know what he did and I know why he did it. He did it for all the right reasons. And he wasn't a showy man. People still joke about how, if he showed any emotion the most he would do would be to stick up a finger or have a slight smile. He was not a demonstrative person and he wasn't a heavy hitter, but behind the scenes he could get anything in the world done because people respected him, and they liked him, and they believed in him. But he would not want the fanfare, and he would not want to be on display. He would divert the attention to somebody else. He would find a way to put it on a child or a teacher. I went out there the day of the dedication and I was very proud for him. And I felt good and my family feels good, and I think my mom was proud. I don't know whether he would be proud or not. He would think they should have named the school for somebody else.

My mom was still alive and she was still teaching, under Carl Mills. She was seventy-one when she quit teaching, because they kept bringing her back. Each year after a certain age, the principal had to make a request to the county to bring a teacher back. I think Carl brought her back six or seven years. He would say, "Mrs. Adams, will you teach one more year?"

She finally started losing her eyesight, so she told Carl, "Carl, I can't teach anymore."

He said, "You're not going to do this to me. You're going to teach as long as I'm principal."

And she said, "I can't see anymore." She hemorrhaged behind the retina and had macular degeneration and went completely blind the last twenty years of her life. But she loved kids.

She taught third, fourth, fifth, and sixth grades for thirty years. I can remember some of the people who worked for my dad and worked for her, black folks who couldn't read, and she taught them to read at lunchtime. They would go out and sit on the porch. I used to go through there on my travels, and I would stop by. She would be on the back porch with someone having a reading lesson. This person would be fifty, sixty years old, and couldn't read a letter. My mother taught quite a few of them how to read. I would sit there and I'd listen just a minute to them struggling. She did this after she retired from teaching and after she had lost most of her eyesight.

Her role in integration was supporting Dad. She went to Western Carolina and N.C. State. And then when I was born, she didn't work until I graduated, except she did all the cooking for my dad's drugstore. She made the potato salad, pimento cheese, chili, and all of that. She was very involved in the Woman's Club, and Eastern Star, and the PTA. She was very, very civically minded. Both of them were. His focus was more on schools, hers was more on community. Then when I got out of school, she went back to teaching and taught until she was seventy-one years old. And her role during the time of integration was to be the good, supportive wife.

But my mom was very outspoken, very independent, and very much ahead of her time. I remember coming in one day from school and there was a note lying on the table that said, "I've gone to Florida for the week. You and your dad take care of the house." She was a very well read, very bright, very intelligent lady. And she was a very strict disciplinarian. She was not a housewife. She was out there and she was doing things in the Garden Club, and the Woman's Club, and Eastern Star and running the PTA. She had her own agenda. She was very supportive of what my dad was doing because she felt the same way he did about equal opportunities.

CHAPTER 14

BEYOND THE SIXTIES

BUSING:

In the 1971 case of *Swann v Charlotte-Mecklenburg County* (North Carolina,) the U.S. Supreme Court upheld the decision in support of cross-town busing to be used as a tool to implement desegregation. A federal court judge ruled that the Raleigh city school board must show a system-wide racial ratio. The school board introduced busing and redistricting to bring the percentage of African-Americans to the designated 30% in all schools.

At the same time, to "racially balance" the 43 schools in the Wake County school system, a plan was devised by the H.E.W. to combine the Cary, Apex and Holly Springs attendance areas into one. Students would be bused between the areas until each school reached the minimum requirement of 26% black student population. At the time, the ten schools in the Cary area had about a 10% black population. This compares to Apex which had a black population of 50% and Holly Springs with a 90% black population.

In reaction to this plan, 6,000 parents signed a petition in an attempt to stop the H.E.W. from enacting this plan. The Board rejected the plan, but then closed the Holly Springs School and bused its students to Cary. This brought the Cary enrollment closer to the requirements set by the H.E.W.

Before 1976, when there were two school systems, the Raleigh city school system was made up of mostly minority students. The Wake County school system in the suburbs and outlying communities was made up of mostly white students. All over the South, including in Wake County, once desegregation was mandated, white families moved their children out of the inner cities. This became known as 'white flight."

Once the *Swann* case was decided, white flight out of Raleigh accelerated as families moved so their children would be in the county school system. White flight caused the inner cities to lose much of their tax base, which meant less money for urban schools.

In the 1974 case *Milliken v Bradley*, the U.S. Supreme Court ruled that suburban children (mostly white) could not be bused to desegregate inner city schools. White flight continued to accelerate. Local business leaders, fearing a negative impact on the entire county's economy, proposed merging the two school systems. In 1973, the measure was put on the ballet as a non-binding referendum, but local residents rejected it 3-to-1. So the business leaders convinced the North Carolina General Assembly to force the merger. It was adopted in 1976, creating the Wake County Public School System (WCPSS.) Busing continued and test results were carefully analyzed.

Robert Heater: I served as county commissioner beginning in 1974, during the time they were merging the two school systems, city and county. Cary was in the county school district. We were opposed to it because we thought the county schools were better. If they merged them, they were going to start busing city students into the community schools. We thought community schools were better and so we opposed it very strongly. We had local school boards at that time, and there was a school board in Cary that controlled Cary schools. The majority of the commissioners voted for the merger, but not for the funding that would have supported it. It was very emotional.

Charlie Adams: In 1971, Holly Springs High School was closed down, and that began a busing program. I had been gone from Cary for five years, my dad was dead, and I wasn't involved in local politics. But I do remember when they shut Holly Springs down and began busing because I know how it affected us here. When we had the Wake County school system, the rule was that to go to a specific school, you had to live in that community, which meant to go to Cary High School, you had to live in Cary. Then Judge McMillan came out with court-ordered busing, which did away with that old rule. We could no longer say you were only eligible to attend the school where you lived. We had to change our rule to make you eligible to go to whatever school the Board of Education assigns you. And that initiated busing. This was being done at the state level at the same time that Holly Springs was being shut down and the students were bused over to Cary. At that time, busing was going on pretty much all over the state. There was huge opposition to busing, because you were taking kids out of their neighborhood school right across the street and sending them ten miles away. They would have to get up at 6:00 AM, and they would not get home until 5:00 PM. Nobody liked busing. It destroyed athletics for awhile because when the players were living here and they had to play ball over there, they had no way to get home after the game. And people didn't have any allegiance to this other school across town. So busing created probably as many problems as we've ever had in this state. I don't even know whether a jury would say it worked or it didn't work.

Carolyn Rogers: I was bused as a high school student. I had to get up early to get through my routine at home so I could catch my bus. I started out on the bus at the black elementary school, then change buses at another school, then get on the high school bus and ride thirty miles or thirty minutes to the all-black high school. By the time I got there, I was exhausted. To be able to then sit in a classroom, do you think I was going to be alert and ready to learn? You think about yourself, when you travel a long distance, what do you want to do? You just want to recline, relax. But students can't do that. They are riding all those buses to get to school, then sit in the classroom and be alert and ready to learn. We didn't have the breakfast program when I went to school. My mom cooked breakfast every morning. Today, some of the students don't get breakfast in the mornings at home. When you ride that distance, you need to be refueled, and that's why that breakfast program, in my opinion, is an important one. Once they're refueled, they're re-energized, alert and ready to learn.

I had one little boy in my first period when I was at East Cary who lived in a satellite area. When he got to school and came into my class, he would put his head down on the desk and go to sleep, and I mean a sound sleep, I could not wake him up. We were very concerned about that. I tried everything I knew to keep him awake. I used to call him my "Omega Psi Phi man," which is a black fraternity on the predominantly black campuses. I would do anything that I could do to make him alert and able to learn because he was very, very smart. I would call to him, "You've got to wake up now. You've got to be an Omega Psi Phi. When you're an Omega man, you 'represent.'" You've got to be alert, so come on, wake up."

I finally called his mother to find out what was going on and why he slept every morning. She said, "You're the second person to call me this morning, because the school my other children attend just called me to say the same thing. The problem here is the gunfire in the neighborhood at night that keeps them awake until the wee hours of the morning. About the time they finally are able to fall asleep, it's time to get up. They don't have time to eat breakfast because it's time to get on the bus and then ride to school."

I called the police chief at that point and said, "You don't know me from Adam's cat, but I have some kids... This is happening because there is gunfire in the neighborhood and it keeps them up every night until the wee hours of the morning. Do something."

The police chief knew that it was a drug infested area. He said, "I'll send somebody over there to clean it up because we cannot be losing our kids."

I said, "When I have a black male who shows that kind of intelligence, I have to do everything I can do to save this child, and I need your help to do that. He's my Omega Psi Phi man." I don't know if Chief Mitch was an Omega man or not. I said, "I've got to keep my Omega Psi Phi man on the ball, I've got to get him alert." Chief Mitch sent someone in there immediately, because the next three days that child did not go to sleep in class.

It makes a difference for those kids who are forced to go to school long distances away from home, unless you do it by choice. For those students who live in Cary and choose to go to the magnet schools in inner city, that's a choice they make, so it's not so difficult for them. Of course, they still have to make that long ride, but it's their choice. When I don't have a choice in the matter, it becomes drudgery.

I had one little girl at Davis Drive who had been acting out one day. She said, "I live in the projects, what do you expect?"

I asked, "What does that mean, you live in a project? You live in an apartment. If your apartment complex was in the Cary area, it would be called an apartment, an apartment complex, and not a project. So what is it that you're living up to?"

She said, "Oh, well I never thought about it like that."

I said, "'The projects' is just a term used by the federal government. It is a project for them to give you affordable housing. It is a project just like you do projects for me. That doesn't mean it should have an effect on your behavior unless it is a positive one. Don't let people tell you what you're home life is like. You think about it. Most of us blacks came from conditions that were not necessarily conducive, but we use that as our motivator to do better things, greater things. It's a project for me to go to school. It was a project for me to go back to college as an older woman to get my degree to be an administrator."

"Well, I never thought of it like that."

I said, "Well, let's change the thinking."

Students who live in the satellite areas would change when they came to school so that you never knew what their home life was like by the time they got to school. Some students do bring that home life to school with them. But we never knew some of these students were up all night, and some of these students were "the fathers" in their homes, and some of these girls were "the mothers" in their homes because the parents are out working. We never knew it. It was just a change they would undergo to become what they wanted to become at school.

If I was a student being bused from, let's say a downtown "project" in Raleigh and I passed all of those beautiful homes on my way to the Cary schools, would I get an attitude? I might. Or I might get an attitude if I'm sitting in class with this little Cary kid who has no idea what it's like at my home. The Cary student has no idea what it sounds like hearing gunshots all night, or seeing people standing on the street corner shooting up. He has no idea. Now I'm going to go in the classroom and compete with these kids? And then all the test scores are going to tell me that I'm not as smart. That's a hurdle. That's a big hill that I would have to just chip away at constantly to let people know, I do have a brain, I can learn. In my mind, I am screaming to my teachers. My living conditions don't necessarily have anything to do with who I become. I can aspire to be anything I want to be. All I have to do is have the work ethics. As a teacher, that's what I would tell my students, just have the work ethics. If you've got the work ethics and you have a dream, there is nothing that can stop you, nothing and nobody.

Jeanette Evans: The school bus came from Apex and Morrisville into Cary. We had to stand out there in the cold and wait for the bus, on the corner of Highway 54 and Harrison Avenue in front of the Grocery Boy Jr. The bus had many stops. It took me only about five minutes to get where I had to go to catch the bus. It did bother me when I had to pass by the white school to go stand out there in the cold to get my bus, and go about six or seven miles to my own school. We all had to do that, right in Cary. But those days are gone now.

Phyllis Cain: We were bused to West Cary High School from all over the place. There used to be a stop sign where the stop light is now on the corner of Chapel Hill Road and Nowell Road. This community is called Lincolnville, or the Asbury community. I went to school with students that lived in the Millbrook area, Morrisville, Method community, Bayleaf, Jefferies Grove, and Cary. All of us were bused to West Cary on

Evans Road. My bus ride was only maybe fifteen minutes long, because there were no traffic lights or stop signs between my house and the school like there are now.

When they talk about busing now, I laugh. We were bused all over the place, but I never heard of any problems. It was just a given at that time. There were no community schools like there are now, so we all had to be brought in to the same school. I had a friend when I went to North Carolina Central who was from Murfreesboro, a small town where everybody lived close to their school. She thought that was the funniest thing, how we were bused from all over the place, going to one school. But it was just normal for us.

Barbara Rogers: Our children were in the fifth and the ninth grade when the segregation of the schools came about in Cary. Our youngest child didn't talk about it much. It was harder for our older child because he was in the ninth grade. Henry Adams was very, very instrumental in getting the students bused to Cary rather than our students being bused away. I still am thankful for that because it was not such a transition for my children. And not that many black students came to Cary in the first years.

FAR FROM OVER:

In 1999, three court rulings changed desegregation in North Carolina. The three rulings, two by the U.S. Court of Appeals in *Tuttle v Arlington County Public Schools* and *Eisenberg v Montgomery County Public Schools*, and the third ruling by a federal district court sitting in Charlotte in *Capacchione v Charlotte-Mecklenburg Schools* together forbid all school boards from considering race or ethnicity for student assignments to public schools, even if it led to re-segregation in the schools. These rulings, in essence, overturned the *Swann* decision of 1971.

Following these three court rulings, WCPSS sought to find a solution not based on race that would support diversity while increasing academic achievement. The board examined numerous studies and considered many new ideas. The studies that were the most intriguing were those that showed how student achievement is highest in middle-class schools. These studies found that mixing low and middle or high-income students of all races was far more effective in elevating academic achievement than simply mixing black and white students together.

Based on those findings, in January 2000, the WCPSS adopted a new race-neutral plan where student assignments were determined by socio-economic status and academic performance. Student socio-economic status is measured from applications for the free or reduced-price lunch (FRL) program. The goal of the plan is for every school to have less than 40% of the student body on FRL, and less than 25% achieving an academic performance score below grade level. Only a few other school districts in the country have adopted a similar plan.

One way to achieve this goal has been through the expansion of the magnet school system that began in the 1980s to bolster desegregation. Gifted students are enticed to magnet schools in urban areas by offering strong college-prep courses and enhanced curriculums of science and the arts, for example. Thus, suburban students who choose to attend a magnet school will usually be bused away from their neighborhood. (Charter schools, in contrast to magnet schools, are often in the suburbs and are geared to primarily meet the needs of the local neighborhoods. Desegregation has not necessarily been a primary goal of charter schools.)

Another challenge for WCPSS has been dealing with record population growth. To adequately accommodate all the new students pouring into the county, a plan has been adopted that requires yearly student reassignment throughout the school district. This is not a popular plan.

In 2003, the WCPSS was the 27th largest school system in the United States. In that year, three years after implementing the new plan, WCPSS had an overall high school graduate rate of 75%, the highest of any large metropolitan county-wide district in the country. 23% of the students in the district qualified for the FRL program. In the 2005-6 school year, WCPSS students were 31% black and 9% Latino. The WCPSS and the few other communities in the United States who are also implementing a program based on socio-economic status are being closely analyzed by school districts all over the country.

In contrast to the WCPSS plan, the Charlotte-Mecklenburg school district took a different route. As North Carolina's second largest school district, prior to the three court rulings in 1999, Charlotte-Mecklenburg had one of the most successful desegregation plans in the country, which was based on busing. Following the court rulings, in 2002 they ended busing for diversity and adopted a "race neutral," school choice plan, giving parents their choice of schools for their children. The result was that most students chose the schools in their own neighborhood. Two years later, 87 of 150 schools were racially identifiable, and predominantly white middle and upper class schools were essentially closed to low income and minority students because they lived outside of those neighborhoods. Thus, in essence the Charlotte-Mecklenburg school district is in the process of re-segregation. In 2003, their overall high school graduation rate was only 57%, with 40% of the student body qualifying for FRL. In the 2005-6 school year, Charlotte students were 45% black and 12% Latino.

CARY – THEN AND NOW:

Gwen Matthews: In Cary, the blacks lived on the other side of the railroad tracks. That's how I knew Cary to be. All of my black friends were on the other side of the railroad tracks that run through downtown. To see Cary now and how it has grown and how far it has extended its boundaries is just phenomenal. I had a friend who used to live in black Cary proper. He was considered "old Cary" because his family had lived there, he was originally from Cary, he grew up there, and he always attended Cary schools. Today Cary is nothing like what it was when I started going to Cary High. It had a much more rural flavor to it when we were growing up. It was a very small town. Now that it is this large place, I'm not sure that I like it. It was so quaint when I was growing up, and I really liked Cary, the town itself. I don't remember much about Cary's racial situation, as much as I do about Raleigh.

Deborah Matthews Wright: We hear about the statistics of Cary being one of the fastest growing towns in the country. I have seen a tremendous change in the attitudes of people. I think that has to do with the fact that a lot of people who live in Cary today are not from Cary. When they moved there they brought a different perspective about the ways of the world and about how they are different from other people. That's a positive thing. Cary is still predominantly white, but I don't think that the African-Americans in Cary feel the way we used to feel. We no longer feel as if we aren't wanted, or that we shouldn't be there. In past years, I think that was the case. There was the feeling that we shouldn't be there because we were black. I think the community and the town as a whole has changed in that regard, which is very positive.

Sonny Keisler: It was a small community where everybody knew everybody. There were set rules, and if you followed the rules then everything was okay. But if you broke the rules, somebody would know it and remind you that you don't do that. Consequently there was a lot of emphasis placed on education. The Cary school was one of the best schools in the state at that time. School and church and family were the centerpieces in life. Mr. and Mrs. Dunham lived on Kildare Farm Road. He was an agriculture teacher and he had a lot of impact, not just from what he taught but from the person he was. He was a good role model for a lot of people. The impact of the churches and ministers back in those days was very significant.

During Civil Rights, we had the Vietnam War going on and that affected everybody to a certain extent. Cary was still a fairly small town, fairly conservative, a bedroom community to Raleigh. Most people worked in state government or the university and lived out here. So I don't think things changed a lot, other than the seeds for change were being planted. Research Triangle Park was just being built. The people who were responsible for the planning of Research Triangle Park and for promoting growth lived in Cary. It was a conservative town but progressive by some standards. So people just started sensing what was coming down the road, and you could tell that there were a lot of changes in the air. People were beginning to see the handwriting on the wall. But the wall didn't really get written on until the eighties and nineties, in a big way.

It was fairly rigid, but there was probably not much room to get into a lot of trouble. Some people can handle freedom responsibly, but a lot of people can't handle freedom, and therefore they go off the deep end one way or the other. In those days you didn't have much freedom to get into much trouble. These days you have a lot more freedom and a lot more trouble. I was not here during the days of desegregation, but being a conservative community and fairly affluent even for those days, I would guess there was no significant amount of drugs in Cary. That probably didn't occur until Cary as a community pretty much disappeared with the development of lots of subdivisions connected by streets. I came back to Cary in the mid-eighties.

The development of Research Triangle Park brought with it the advantage of a lot of new people moving in and creating a lot of new social initiatives and new environments. That's the good part of it. They broke down the old rigid structure and gave people a lot more opportunities and choices. So in that regard it was a good thing. The reverse approach is that it can become somewhat stifling. And if the community goes too far out, then it becomes "anywhere-ville." I think that's where Cary is now.

Charlie Adams: There were four classes of schools: 1A, 2A, 3A and 4A. The 1As were the really small schools. The entire time that I went to the Cary School, it was a Class 1A school and had not done a lot of changing. The face of the building was still pretty much the same. When I came back there to teach and coach, it was a 2A school. When I left there after four years, it was a 3A school. And when I checked several years later, it was about the tenth largest school in North Carolina.

SJ Farrar: Hardly any sharecropping is done in this part of North Carolina now. I was in the area where we were raised one day last week, and there was no tobacco in that area at all. The land is too expensive. Instead of growing tobacco or anything else on it, they sell the land.

Robert Heater: There are people that are low in the socio-economic group and those that are high. At the Masonic Lodge, everybody is considered equal. The Masons are not desegregated in the South, where they are known as "the ancient, free and accepted Masons." The word "free" was put in there for that reason. But the blacks have their own lodge that is much like ours. How similar, I don't know, but probably almost identical to ours. I think up North they have desegregated, because a lot of those lodges don't include the word "free."

Jeanette Evans: My oldest daughter went to Kingswood Elementary, and then segregation came in so she went to West Cary when it was a high school. From there, she went to Cary High. She didn't ever go to Berry O'Kelly because it had closed by that time. The schools were all desegregated. She graduated from high school in 1969.

My kids didn't really have a hard time, because kids are going to be kids. Once they get to school, I don't care whether you're blue, white, or green, they get together. I think it was bad at the time that I was growing up; might have been, might not have been.

Billy Rogers: In our motel, we have had all kinds of people stay with all kinds of different problems. In 2001, a black young man and white girl came to the door. They moved to Cary to get away from a segregation problem in South Carolina. He was working painting houses every day, and she went right out and got a job at Food Lion two days after they came to Cary. In a few weeks they had saved enough money that they were on their feet and able to rent an apartment. To me, it had not mattered what nationality they were, or what their problems were, as long as they were not a problem here.

When I was growing up in Cary, it was different. I told this young man, if being a mixed race couple was his only reason for moving to Cary, he would not have any problems here. I believe that now Cary is an

International community. I'll rent you a room, but I want you to be doing better in pretty short time. This is not where you want to live. Some of them do a lot better, but some of them stay for a long time.

A lady that was working with my daddy when we bought the motel from him in 1966 lived in the Green Level-Carpenter section. It was so far for her to come to work to downtown Cary. We were able to buy a little lot over on Johnson Street and put a small rental house on it. She still lives in that house. I told her when I built it in 1974 that it was her home. That little house was worth a lot more than what she pays me in rent. I'd love to sell it, but as long as she lives, I'll keep it for her to live in because she is close to me.

When I was growing up, we had a lady that came and helped my mother. We called her Aunt Alice, that's the only name I ever knew. Aunt Alice was part of our family. She sat with us and had lunch every day. She would come in and help mother with the ironing and whatever there was to do in the house. I remember Aunt Alice and I loved her.

I had a friend who went to the black school and we went to the white school, but he came to play baseball with Charlie (Adams) and me. He was one of our neighborhood baseball players, but he couldn't play on our school team and we didn't know why, and didn't question why. It was just the way it was. I realize now like everybody else, that desegregation should have been done, but it couldn't be done in one day because it had to evolve, and I think we are still in that process now. I don't know when, if ever, it will be complete because there is so much resentment now, more from the black side than the white side. Some blacks resent us so much and we can't say to them, "We didn't do it, it was our parents, and our grandparents who kept us separate."

Carl Mills: The interesting thing about Cary is the people. The people were always interested in doing new things or doing them in a different way. They helped quite a bit to initiate things to improve Cary. It is just the most exciting place to work. So whatever has happened to me as far as establishing the first Lion's Club here, or my career, or the recreation programs, or what-have-you, it has been something. Whenever a need arose, Cary people got involved in meeting it. I shouldn't get the credit for anything.

The feeling was that the Cary people were willing to finance the best academic program in the area, and the best athletic program in the area.

Leroy Farrar: When we moved here, there was one stoplight in Cary at the intersection of Academy and Chatham Streets. Evans Road dead-ended just below Dynasty. We knew everybody that drove down the road, and everybody in the neighborhood. It sure was quiet. There weren't many cars. If there was a good little rain, it was hard to even get out of the driveway because of the red mud. It was terrible.

But then they built the West Cary school, and they built the church, and of course then the people started building houses and moving in. Research Triangle Park with IBM was built and it just started booming. People came from everywhere and moved into Cary from all over. So the neighborhood changed in the last fifteen years. There were few houses down at one end when we arrived. The woods were so dense surrounding the neighborhood, it looked like you could get lost in there. Now at certain times of the day I can hardly get out of my drive because of the traffic.

Charlotte Phelps: We used to go walking in and around the black cemetery off of Kildare Farm Road, near the black church. That was an old, small church, as I remember. When we were Girl Scouts, we went over to the cemetery as part of a group one night. They told us ghost stories, and some of the Girl Scouts got so scared, they were ready to leave.

Sallie Jones: The Morgan family owned a farm on Reedy Creek Road with some farmland. There were some graves that my brother and I saw on that farmland. They were the graves of my grandmother's father and his family. By the time I moved back to Cary, they had built the houses on that land, and nobody knew anything about what happened to the graves. I tried to look it up, and asked questions to try and find out, but they didn't know anything about them.

I heard that they were planning to build Glenaire Retirement Center. When I found out where Glenaire was going to be, I knew the Cary Colored Cemetery was near that land, and my grandfather and all the other family graves were in danger. I did not want what happened to my grandmother's father to happen there. There was some talk about turning the cemetery into a park, or having the town take it over because it wasn't being kept up. That cemetery belongs to my church, and it wasn't being kept up because our church membership was small and they didn't have the money to care for it. When my mother was living, we would go over there in the summertime and rake leaves, clean, cut grass, and clear the graves. But other than doing that, little was done. There were complaints about it, and there were even a few articles in the Cary News. People wanted to know why the town didn't take it over. But I didn't want that to happen, so I set out to make sure it was preserved.

The Cary Colored Cemetery was by the old church next to the Cary Colored School that was burned down. We used to go to that church sometimes and have youth activities on a Saturday, making things for us to do. We would make a bonfire and roast hot dogs and things like that. There were graves there, and there were holes where some of them had sunk in. Somebody said they were the graves of slaves. Nobody seems to know much about the cemetery. But I knew the people in it weren't a part of the church, because the church had their cemetery on Cornwall Road as far back as 1868. They said that was where the little church was started, in what they used to call it a "grape harbor." I used to ask, what was a grape harbor? They said it was a little shelter made of tree limbs and leaves and things. They said that's where they held services until they built that little old church that was over there.

So I started work on the cemetery and tried to save it. This was my own personal project. I just didn't want to see my grandfather and those graves lost. We had it surveyed and got it protected, and I registered it with the state. I had it added to the map, because it wasn't even on a map. Cary didn't know where it was. We would ask downtown and they didn't know. Now it is on Cary's map and it is on Wake County's map. Now we have it protected. They can't sell it. It is registered with the State Archives. We have some of the names of people who are buried there, so anyone can look it up and find those names. The Archives have a list of cemeteries, so I registered it with them.

I had an archeologist go through and survey it. They did their prodding to let us know where there were graves, even where there is no marker. The archeologist told us we probably wouldn't find anything in the graves if we opened them up. I didn't want to see them mutilated. We have had a lot of vandalism, and stones were broken and some of the markers were moved or taken. That accounts for some graves not being identified. There are somewhere around 274 graves, and 141 of those are unidentified graves. The cemetery is on Cornwall Road behind Glenaire.

Carolyn Sampson: I am the president of the Martin Luther King Jr. Taskforce of Cary. Dreamfest is one of my initiatives. In 1995, when I got involved, it was the MLK committee for this area. It was created by two churches, Good Shepherd United Church of Christ, which is the white church, and at that time, the Cary United Church of Christ, which is the black church. They have since changed. They are no longer a member of the UCC. Now they are called the Cary First Christian Church. Those two churches started the MLK celebration for the town of Cary. 1995 was their very first year, or possibly their second year. I joined as a volunteer committee member. At that point, the two churches had a relationship that they had developed over the years where, every fifth Sunday, one or the other congregation would go to the other's church. So the blacks would come over and perform the worship service for Good Shepherd, and vice versa. A meal is always served afterward so that people can get to know one another. And they have also communicated and worked with each other in other kinds of ways.

I became the chairperson of the events of the program committee for the taskforce. I said to them, "You've done such a good job in developing this relationship between the black church and the white church, maybe you need to open yourselves up to grow this fellowship around the town of Cary." I was moving toward making this a community thing rather than a shared thing. They bought into that, and in 1996-1997 we moved toward activities that were expanded to include the community of Cary.

In 1998, Lyman Collins, Cary's cultural arts manager, came to our meeting and he said, "We've been watching you with the Martin Luther King committee, and you've planned some really great programs. Why don't we partner with one another to provide an MLK celebration for the Town of Cary." At that point we had established the Dreamfest concept, so they took the idea to the town council. Jesse Ward was on the council, and he was also a member of our committee. So they discussed it and went through their decision-making process, and in that year they agreed that the town would partner with the MLK Taskforce. 1999 was the first year of our partnership, and we've been working together ever since. And it has become known as the MLK Jr. Dreamfest, and taking on the number of the year.

That very first year, we had an eight-day celebration. It was quite something. Because it was a lot to handle, we decided that we would move the activities to a weekend. In these past few years, because of the entertainment and how we were trying to orchestrate it, we've had to stretch it out a little bit more. And the past two years, we added a celebration on Martin Luther King's actual birthday, which we hadn't been doing before. We moved to a luncheon this year, which was very good. This year is the eleventh year.

Every event had a dream theme: dream of history, or dream of expression which is for the art exhibit that is on display every year. These are all the parts of MLK. In that first year when we started, we had a dream. We called it "Dream of Inspiration," which was a musical celebration, and we start with a musical event. In the past three years, we combined what was once one song, an independent activity, in with the Marvelous Music series, and we now have what we call a One Song Review. We feature just one song as the pre-performance kickoff event for Dreamfest every year. For the one song event, an invitation goes out to the world asking musicians to bring one song to the occasion. And all I know about the people who respond and sign up is their name, their group name, how many are in that group, and what they are going to perform. I never heard them ahead of time. They had to be there by five o'clock if they were going to perform. Every year, the performances were excellent. To this day, we have never been disappointed. Now, I always had a cameo performance in the wings, so if it all fell apart there were professionals somewhere on the lot, who could tell them how to play it. But it didn't matter. The caliber, the material, the execution was excellent.

Nobody is excluded from the celebrations, they are all family-friendly. I like inter-generational events, so we want kids there as well. Your kids can sing, they can stand here with you and take part. I am not excluding them from anything.

Now, over all these years, it has been something else to get an audience. These are free things. They pay $18.00 to come to the Marvelous Music series. We have the same thing down the street for free, and very few people attended. The participants were there, and when we had large groups or choirs, their parents would come. But as far as the public attending, that didn't happen.

So, when we had an opportunity to mesh with the Marvelous Music series, I said, "Why not. Let's give it a try." So for all those people who had supported the events over the years, they receive the same invitation, and what I asked people to do was to come and join together as a community choir. I called it Vision United Singers. Let's perform this one piece. You learn your piece, either as a choir or as an individual. We have one mass rehearsal, and then we rehearse for call, because you are always about an hour out on call, and that's it. And then we perform our piece at the beginning as a pre-performance for the event. Fantastic, really.

We had forty-four performers this year as the Vision United Singers, and maybe seven Vision United dancers. The one song is the theme, and that's usually danced every year. The one song is something unifying. The song this year was *Miracles,* which talked about the things we need to do in the world. The message is, just let me do what I can for those who come within my reach, because that's the way miracles happen. The song for last year was *Make Us One*, and if we all sang one song, what a wonderful world it would be. That's the kind of message we have in our one song, so it has meaning. I believe that when we get the chance, we need to leave our captive audience with a message about what this whole thing is all about.

As soon as Dreamfest is over, we meet with the town and start working on next year's event. It takes a year to get it together. People probably don't understand the labor of love it takes, but we keep working on it, we keep perfecting, and we keep doing what we can do.

I have this saying, that we just cannot not work for peace, work for the realizations of people's dreams, continue the work of those individuals who died on the line for all of us, for equality. We just cannot not do those things. So I continue to do what I can do for this community. I sometimes revisit the fact that, in this area with Raleigh, Cary and Durham who orchestrate an MLK celebration of some sort, if I had to put the celebrations in order, it would be Raleigh 1, Cary 2, Durham 3, in terms of the amount of impact they have. Cary is ahead of Durham, in my opinion. And Raleigh has been doing this for almost thirty years.

We used to try to have a march here in Cary, and we might get to 125 people participating. But it occurred to me some years back to encourage our people to walk with the Raleigh folk. Let's join that effort. Ten o'clock is the hour to come together. This year hoards of people came out of nowhere in Raleigh. There were women pushing their babies in strollers, walking with purpose, not just lagging along. I'm telling you, we were just surrounded by folk. And it has grown. Last year there were 2,000 or more. This year, people were going to Washington D.C. for the Obama inauguration. I said, "Go, we will be here next year. Go to Washington." We were walking down the street from the capital toward the memorial auditorium, and six full buses went up the street, headed for the inauguration. There were camera crews and all the news people were out to cover the Raleigh march.

Marge Eckles is 96 years old. As I was walking, I looked over and there she was walking. And I thought, let me not open my mouth to make another complaint. I'd better step it up a gear. If Marge Eckles can walk, I can walk. I'm executing, executing. I'm doing my part.

In the afternoon, we do service projects. This year the Town of Cary and MLK concentrated on refurbishing trails at Bond Park. There were 23 volunteers from the Service for Peace, kids and their parents who showed up. Some of those kids were not any taller than three feet high. They enthusiastically embraced the work of shoveling mulch into the wheelbarrows and pushing them down the path. They weren't fooling around, they were really working. And that wasn't a clean job either, they would get a little dirty. They worked, and worked to get the job done. I was very happy, very pleased because I felt that they understood the importance of doing service. Martin Luther King had a saying, "Anybody can be great because anybody can serve." That was anybody serving in action, and they did it with cheerful hearts. When the work was called to a halt, they were sad. "Oh no, you mean that's all we had to do?" I thought, "Oh, wow."

Jeanette Evans: I managed Cary's Christian Community in Action thrift shop, the Dorcas Shop from day one. I was the manager there for fifteen years, and I'm still the day manager on Mondays. We all work together. Our original founder was a lady who had an idea to bring all the churches, black and white, together and open a shop for anyone that needed help. It doesn't make any difference what color you are. So we opened the first shop on Cedar Street, right beside the railroad tracks. We had a little building down there for about a year. We help folks who need food, or assistance with paying their bills. Different churches send canned food and any non-perishables to the shop. We may pay your light bill twice, and show you what to do.

We were the ones that started the Carying Place, an organization that assists people who are in danger of becoming homeless. After they started up, we have continued to help them, but not as much as we used to in the beginning. There are different people who are running it now. I still go there and help. We help folks get homes, and then we take dinner over to them and feed them. They love Cary First Church of Christ to come because they know they're going to have a good dinner.

Along with Good Shepherd Church, we work together. We all go over to their church every fifth Sunday. Then the next fifth Sunday they all come over to our church. We've been doing that for over twenty-five years or more, ever since they started, before they even had that church. That's the way it should be. We work together for Habitat for Humanity too, both churches go help there.

Sallie Jones: Here on the hill, where the parking lot is for Kingswood Elementary, there was a little church that faced the road on the very corner. They always said it was a holiness church, but there was nobody there to operate the church. People used to come through and hold services there. Sometimes they would be here for two or three days, or for a week at a time to hold services. Whenever those people would come, they said they evangelized, so we would go to the church for their services. I don't know what happened to that church. It disappeared.

I'm a member of Cary First Christian Church. Good Shepherd started in our church. When the Reverend Rawls came, they used our church for a number of their meetings and organizations, when they were just getting organized. Our church allowed them to use our facilities until Good Shepherd built their own church on Maynard Road. Every fifth Sunday our churches still meet together. The Good Shepherd Church is primarily a white church, and we are primarily black. We have some white members and they have a few black members.

ACKNOWLEDGEMENTS

This book would not exist without the voices of forty-three people who share their memories and stories with us. Several of those people are no longer with us, but their voices will live on in this book. For many of those who we meet in these pages, telling their story was risky and painful, but they were willing to tell it nevertheless. We can all be grateful to them that they did, for they have expanded our knowledge and understanding of those difficult times in American history when so many suffered and struggled for something better.

Research for this book was conducted at the Olivia Raney History Library in Raleigh, North Carolina which houses the extensive Elizabeth Reid Murray collection of historic facts about North Carolina. This staggering collection fills dozens of archival boxes that stand side by side on hundreds of feet of shelf space in the library's archives. I am so grateful to Elizabeth Reid Murray for her monumental lifetime achievement of tracking down and compiling all these facts into one place. I am also grateful to Karen Allen, the library director at Olivia Raney for all her help.

I would like to thank Tom Byrd who wrote the definitive history of Cary in his book, *Around and About Cary*. Many of Tom's research notes found their way into the Elizabeth Reid Murray collection as well, which were helpful in clarifying a few points.

I would also like to thank my sister, Linda Gaertner, for her encouragement, support and advice throughout this project. Last, I want to thank my mother, Joann Van Scoyoc, for believing in me. On her deathbed, she made me promise that I would finish and publish this book. Here it is, Mom.

www.ingramcontent.com/pod-product-compliance
Lightning Source LLC
Chambersburg PA
CBHW022126080426
42734CB00006B/253